Managing
Economic Development

Jeffrey S. Luke
Curtis Ventriss
B. J. Reed
Christine M. Reed

Managing
Economic Development

A Guide to State and Local
Leadership Strategies

Jossey-Bass Publishers

San Francisco   •   London   •   1988

MANAGING ECONOMIC DEVELOPMENT
A Guide to State and Local Leadership Strategies
by Jeffrey S. Luke, Curtis Ventriss, B. J. Reed,
and Christine M. Reed

Library of Congress Cataloging-in-Publication Data

Managing economic development.

(The Jossey-Bass public administration series)
(The Jossey-Bass management series)
Bibliography: p.
Includes index.
1. Industrial promotion—United States.
2. Industry and state—United States.   3. State
governments.   4. Local government—United States.
I. Luke, Jeffrey Scott.   II. Series.   III. Series:
Jossey-Bass management series.
HC110.I53M36   1988   338.973   87-46347
ISBN 1-55542-092-3 (alk. paper)

Manufactured in the United States of America

The paper in this book meets the guidelines for
permanence and durability of the Committee on
Production Guidelines for Book Longevity of the
Council on Library Resources.

JACKET DESIGN BY WILLI BAUM

FIRST EDITION

Code 8818

A joint publication in
The Jossey-Bass
Public Administration Series
and
The Jossey-Bass Management Series

Contents

Preface

State and local economic development has become a key issue for public managers and policymakers, and by most accounts will remain a critical area for public policy into the 1990s. The causes, to a large degree, are changing economic realities, including a major employment shift from a goods-producing sector to a services-producing sector, uneven development within metropolitan areas as well as between different regions of the country, growing interdependency of state and local economies with the global economy, and corporate divestment. In addition, federal disengagement from state and local economic development is forcing public executives at those levels to be more responsible for job creation. Complicating the policy-making process are three critical insights which have emerged from development efforts in the 1980s:

1. Communities cannot rely on federal initiatives and must take an active responsibility for developing and testing appropriate economic development strategies.
2. There is no single best way for communities to stimulate economic growth. They must develop individually tailored strategies that are custom-designed to the strengths and capacities of their local and regional economies.
3. Custom-designed strategies must be developed collaboratively among key government and business leaders, not unilaterally by any individual public chief executive.

As a result of these trends, some public managers and policymakers are beginning to forge new economic development strategies, while others have adopted a "wait-and-see" attitude. These reactions are understandable, given the difficulties in stimulating economic development and, more important, the paucity of reliable evaluation data on what really works in today's rapidly changing economy. Thus, state and community leaders are confronted with difficult choices illustrated by the following questions: What is the appropriate government role in stimulating economic development? What kind of public leadership is needed to achieve economic development goals? How can private investment be stimulated? Where should scarce public resources be invested? What economic strategies will foster long-term economic growth?

This book is our response to the needs of state and local leaders who are grappling with these difficult and salient policy questions. We do not attempt to provide policy recommendations for economic development; rather we recommend a strategic process through which policies can be developed and implemented. The process we present in this book is predicated upon three crucial assumptions: First, different economic development strategies that are formulated at the state and local levels should be custom-designed according to the unique strengths and weaknesses of the regional economy. Simply put, no one strategy or policy for development is appropriate for all state or local economies. Second, successful economic development emerges from a collaborative effort, not singular leadership. Collective action that is mobilized by public leadership is essential in achieving economic development goals. Finally, effective economic development requires explicitly a *learning process approach* rather than a blueprint plan. In other words, as new strategies are implemented, ongoing evaluation must occur to determine their efficacy so that new knowledge can be incorporated into the planning process. These three assumptions have guided us in providing technical assistance to state and local government agencies since 1982. Out of those efforts has emerged the process model presented in this book.

Our early experiences providing factual information to communities regarding local economic shifts, labor trends, and incorporation rates often failed to generate effective development strategies. Several attitudinal, perceptual, and institutional barriers prevented full and accurate utilization of the information. As a result, we first developed an economic development technical assistance process based on Lewin's action research model. The increasingly popular strategic planning model provided a second framework from which to provide development assistance. What precipitated over several years of field work is a unique synthesis of the action research and strategic planning models, a learning process approach that is externally focused (like strategic planning) and that inherently assumes that human attitudes, perceptions, and behavior are keys to effective organizational and policy change (as in action research).

Our approach to managing economic development strategically aims at influencing the process—not the outcome—of economic development. Our theory of strategic economic development is not policy- or goal-oriented, but process-oriented. It does not prescribe or seek specific policies for stimulating economic development. Rather, it specifies a process for identifying and testing economic development strategies that are custom-designed for a particular community or state. As the economy shifts over several years, each community must reassess its economic strengths and weaknesses and pursue strategies of development that conform to these new realities.

Who Should Read This Book?

This book is designed to help policymakers translate available ideas into pragmatic strategies. We have written it for those generally interested in the field of economic development, but in particular for those state and local government managers and public executives who must cope with the complexities inherent in economic development. We have made a deliberate attempt to link theory and practice, as is evident from our extensive reporting in this book on the current literature and what it means in the world of practice. The value of this book is that no other work, descriptive or empirical, has yet taken such a comprehensive look at economic development. Consequently, we believe that *Managing Economic*

Development will become a valuable resource for professionals who deal with development issues.

Overview of the Contents

Chapter One reviews the influential economic changes that are now confronting public managers as they formulate economic development policies. These economic changes include the shift from a goods-producing economy to a service economy, the changing role of the federal government, the internationalization of state and local economies, and regional economic disparities. These trends imply that new economic development policies must be forged and made congruent with the long-term strategic strengths of state and local economies.

The question "Why is it so difficult to stimulate economic development?" is addressed in Chapter Two. Here we make an analogy to the stages of death and dying to explain why some communities and states suffering economic distress deny the reality of the changes taking place. The chapter also explores institutional barriers to effective strategic planning for economic development, especially barriers in the public sector and obstacles within traditional economic development policies.

Chapter Three describes in detail the strategic planning process in economic development. The chapter proceeds step-by-step through the organizing of a strategic plan to development and implementation of the action plan. Examples from communities and states around the country provide illustrations of how the process is actually conducted.

In Chapter Four, we focus on the various organizational approaches to planning for and implementing economic development at the state and local levels. In particular, the chapter reviews the optional structures that can be considered in both state and local governments and the numerous forms of private for-profit and nonprofit organizations that are commonly used in economic development.

Enterprise development, the formation and expansion of business enterprises, is discussed in Chapter Five. New and young businesses generate the bulk of new jobs in the postindustrial economy, and this trend is likely to continue owing to federal deregulation, downsizing of larger corporations, and increased service employment. The general process of new venture creation is discussed in this chapter, and factors for targeting small businesses are identified.

Attraction and retention strategies in state and local development are discussed in Chapter Six. Particular attention is given to the attraction of both industrial and service industries as well as the attraction of the relatively new high-technology industries. The chapter concludes with a detailed discussion of retention activities that states and communities can undertake to ensure that their economic base is not seriously eroded and suggests an early warning program that can help anticipate potential problems before businesses decide to leave.

Chapter Seven analyzes the recent involvement of state and local governments in international economic affairs. As a result of foreign competition, states and communities are developing new strategies for export promotion and foreign investment. This chapter outlines a series of policy questions that should be addressed before state and local governments become involved in formulating "foreign economic policies." Moreover, a strategic framework is suggested for the development of export promotion or foreign investment strategy specific to the state or local economy.

The potential roles and activities that institutions of higher education can now pursue in state and local economic development are highlighted in Chapter Eight. Colleges and universities can be important resources for public managers in three areas: adult training and education (human development), scientific research and technological development, and economic analyses and policy development. Although there is resistance within many universities to joining with industry, there are several areas in which collaborative action can foster economic growth.

Chapter Nine provides an overarching approach to understanding how local economic development efforts can be undertaken. The chapter provides three strategic frameworks for local development as well as a discussion of financial and nonfinancial resources that can be used to help implement various local strategies and actions.

Chapter Ten examines how states can formulate economic development strategies that acknowledge the strategic importance of capital resources, human resources, infrastructural resources, and natural resources. These strategic goals—as suited to the states' and communities' particular needs—imply a rethinking of the development process in four broad categories: (1) interdependent policy strategies (relationship of economic development policies to broader social policies); (2) innovative and inventive efforts (custom-designed policies focused on long-term investments in the state's economic well-being); (3) integrated strategies (strategies involving local, state, and federal involvement); and (4) an investment strategy (strategies focused on the economic capacity for longer-term economic growth).

In Chapter Eleven we analyze the skills needed by public managers to stimulate action in the interdependent policy arena of economic development. New collaborative approaches are now needed because the policy-making responsibility for economic development is dispersed and shared by a multiplicity of elected and appointed officials, and because no one government agency or individual manager can effectively act unilaterally in economic development. As a result, the public manager's role is that of a catalyst—neither passive nor charismatic—and new skills in catalytic leadership are required to manage economic development strategically. This chapter outlines the interpersonal, conceptual, and technical skills required for such catalytic leadership.

Acknowledgments

Many individuals and agencies have contributed to this publication. We are first indebted to several national associations that have been actively funding research in this area, and that have provided much grist for our mill: the Council of State Policy and Planning Agencies, the Council for Urban Economic Development, the National Association of State Development Agencies, the National League of Cities, the National Governors Association, and the Committee for Economic Development. Considerable support was provided by the Nebraska Department of Economic Development, in particular Robert Blair, for the development and initial field testing of the economic development strategic planning model. Earlier drafts were improved through the candid reviews of Tom Chumura, Randall Ebert, Michael Hibbard, and Edwin Mills. Word processing was skillfully coordinated by Bobbette Elliott at the Bureau of Governmental Research and Service, with the assistance of Marlene Koines and Doreen Jones. Graduate assistance was provided by Jane Press Barlowe, Brenda Couture, and Thomas Holland. We are especially indebted to two professors who died while we were working on this book: John Dyckman, professor of public policy and geography at Johns Hopkins University, and Neely Gardner, professor of public administration at the University of Southern California. Both most generously provided encouragement and valuable insights.

Finally, we are grateful to those around us who graciously put up with our behavior while we were writing this book: Iris Teitelbaum-Ventriss; Peggy, Kavi, Mona, and Tori Luke; Charlie Reed, and Brenda Reed, who was born on the day this book was completed.

March 1988

Jeffrey S. Luke
Eugene, Oregon

Curtis Ventriss
Burlington, Vermont

B. J. Reed
Omaha, Nebraska

Christine M. Reed
Omaha, Nebraska

The Authors

Jeffrey S. Luke is director of the Bureau of Governmental Research and Service and associate professor of public affairs in the Department of Planning, Public Policy, and Management at the University of Oregon. He received his B.A. (1972), M.P.A. (1974), and Ph.D. (1982) degrees, all in public administration, from the University of Southern California.

Luke's main research interests are in organizational development, economic development, and public management. He is the coauthor of *Management Training Strategies in Third World Countries* (1987, with J. Kerrigan) and coeditor of *Nebraska Policy Choices* (1986). In 1986, he was a trainer at the World Bank's Economic Development Institute. His previous public management experience in the city of Scottsdale, Arizona, and the county of Monterey, California, and as consultant to a wide variety of state and local governments, has provided the basis for much of his research.

Curtis Ventriss is associate professor of public administration and director of the Master of Public Administration Program at the University of Vermont. He received his B.A. and B.S. degrees (1973) in political science and environmental science from California State University, San Jose, and his M.P.A. (1976) and Ph.D. (1980) degrees in public administration from the University of Southern California.

Ventriss's main research interests have been in organizational theory, economic development, public health, public policy, and citizen participation. He has been vice-chair of the Economy and Efficiency Commission (Los Angeles County), a policy adviser to the California Economic Development Task Force on the Pacific Rim, and a member of the Advisory Policy Committee for the Speaker of the Delegates (Maryland). In 1986, he received the Laverne Burchfield Award from the American Society of Public Administration for the best review article published in that organization's journal. He serves on the Board of Editors of *Public Administration Review* and was associate editor from 1985 to 1987. Ventriss was program adviser of the Planning and Policy Management Program and academic director of the International Fellowship Program, Center for Metropolitan Planning and Research, Johns Hopkins University, from 1981 to 1985. Among his publications are the book *Public Health in a Retrenchment Era* (1986, with H. Muller) and numerous articles that have appeared in major journals of public administration.

B. J. Reed is associate professor of public administration and chair of the Department of Public Administration at the University of Nebraska at Omaha. He received his B.A. (1971) and M.S. (1972) degrees from Fort Hays State University, Kansas, and his Ph.D. degree (1977) from the University of Missouri at Columbia, all in political science.

Reed's main research activities have been in economic development, intergovernmental relations, and local government management. His experience as the development director of Mexico, Missouri, and as the director of community and economic development technical assistance at the National League of Cities helped provide a basis for much of the research he has conducted in these areas. Reed has recently completed the book *From Nation to States* (1986, with E. T. Jennings and A. Pattakos) and is the author of numerous articles on city management, local economic development activities, and intergovernmental relations.

Christine M. Reed is assistant professor of public administration and associate director of the Center for Applied Urban

Research at the University of Nebraska at Omaha. She received her B.A. degree (1971) in government from Connecticut College and her M.A. (1974) and Ph.D. (1983) degrees in political science from Brown University, Rhode Island.

Reed's main research activities have been in housing policy and economic development. She is coauthor, with B. J. Reed, of a chapter on changing intergovernmental relations in housing policy in *Housing and Urban Development: A Fifty-Year Perspective* (1986) and an article on local economic development for the *Journal of the American Planning Association* (1987, with B. J. Reed and J. Luke). Her previous experience at the National Community Development Association and the U.S. Department of Housing and Urban Development has formed the basis for her research interests.

Managing
Economic Development

Part One

Realizing the Potential of Economic Development

Since the 1981–1982 recession, state and local governments have been exploring various strategies to stimulate economic growth and diversification. Plant closures, the collapse of rural banks, and expanding international competition, for example, have stimulated many state and community leaders to pursue a wide variety of strategies and projects, while others have adopted a wait-and-see approach.

These reactions are understandable. On the one hand, the complex shifts in the American economy can drive public and private executives to try almost anything that might work—or, on the other hand, can encourage them to wait or do nothing new. The economy is changing from a national to a global network and is moving from a manufacturing-employment base to a services-employment base. The remaining manufacturing production is shifting from labor-intensive to technology-intensive processes. Because the impacts of these broad economic changes are not evenly distributed, some regions are experiencing significant economic growth while others are suffering from serious fiscal stress. What works in one community or state may not work in other regions. Old industrial development strategies are not productive anymore, either, yet there are insufficient data on what does work in today's economy.

Chapter One considers state and local leadership in light of economic changes and the federal government's diminished pres-

1

ence in regional development efforts. In a movement that began during the Carter administration and was amplified during the Reagan administration, the national government has withdrawn most of its state and local funding and policy guidance for local development. Cities, counties, and states are on their own to a much greater extent than they have been for decades and are thus forced to take active roles in stimulating growth and diversification in a complex, interdependent global economy.

State and local leadership is now the crucial component in the promotion of long-term economic growth. Custom-designed strategies, based on local economic strengths and weaknesses, must be pursued. The public, private, and nonprofit sectors must all become involved, however, if the full potential of state and local development strategies is to be realized. Chapter Two analyzes the significant barriers that often thwart such strategic economic development efforts. Economic diversification and development is a slow and often painful process of change for many states and communities. The public sector leadership face such challenges as institutional obstacles, attitudinal problems of denial and blame, and constricted perspectives—which can combine to stymie efforts for state and local development.

1

Providing Leadership
at the State and Local Levels

Since the late 1970s, the issue of economic development has
commanded more than ever the serious attention of public
managers and state and local officials. While state and local
economic efforts have a long history in the United States, it was
during the 1981–1982 recession that economic development became
the major public policy objective for cities, counties, and states
throughout the country. The reason for this concern is not hard to
understand. In California, generally considered to have a diversified
and stable economy, more than 1,200 plants closed between 1980
and 1983, displacing more than 105,000 workers. Other plants have
closed around the country, many of them obsolete and victims of
foreign competition. In 1982, for example, Ohio had fifty-eight
plant closings that idled 18,000 workers, Alabama experienced
eleven closings with a loss of 5,400 jobs, and Texas has twelve
closings in which 5,480 employees were laid off (Advisory Commission on Intergovernmental Relations, 1985).

As the effects of the recession faded, state and local governments continued and even expanded their efforts to stimulate
economic development. The importance of economic development
is due, to a large extent, to major structural shifts in the American
economy, first reflected in urban communities where older manufacturing industries are concentrated. Plant closings, business
failures, and corporate disinvestment, however, are not simply
phenomena of the industrial Northeast. Rather, they are evidence
of widespread economic shifts affecting the South and West as well

3

as the Northeast and Midwest, including urban and rural economies (Bluestone and Harrison, 1982).

The economic decline facing much of nonmetropolitan America is as significant as that facing cities, and the absence of economic recovery in rural areas in increasingly evident. A rural county in Minnesota provides a poignant example: since 1979, in Fulda County, Minnesota, land values have declined more than 50 percent, the population has declined dramatically, a local bank has closed, and the number of property tax delinquencies has doubled. The economic hardships in Fulda County are not unique and reflect several urgent economic realities facing rural America. These are the failure of rural banks; dramatic increases in home foreclosures; 30–60 percent reductions in the market value of rural properties; a 200 percent increase in property tax delinquencies; declining city and county tax revenues; and the elimination of some public services and a decline in the quality of the remaining services (U.S. Extension Service, 1987).

Rural financial institutions provide clear evidence of continuing economic dislocation and the need for rural economic development. In 1985, there were 124 bank failures nationwide, more than in any year since the Great Depression, and two-thirds of these failures were in rural areas. Worse yet, bank failures during 1986 surpassed even the post-Depression record of 1935.

These economic changes have been accompanied by an intergovernmental shift in authority and responsibility for local economic development. In the late 1970s, federal involvement in local economic development dropped significantly. After decades of federal decision making, financing, and policy guidance in local economic development, many state and community leaders had grown dependent on the federal government. In the 1980s, they have been left to fend for themselves in an uncertain and complex arena of economic development.

The federal government's changing role is reflected in the precipitous decline in total federal aid to state and local governments. In 1980, grants to state and local governments stood at 15.5 percent of total federal spending, or $91.5 billion. Federal aid has dropped steadily since 1980 to 10 percent of total federal spending, or $70.6 billion (in 1980 dollars) in 1987. Moreover, the elimination of revenue-sharing funds for local governments (revenue sharing to the states was discontinued during the Carter administration) will especially hurt small municipalities in the Farm Belt and other rural areas as well as older declining cities with large underclass groups. While there are sentiments in the Congress in favor of increasing federal aid to states and localities, it is generally agreed that national policymakers are under political pressure to reduce the enormous federal budget deficit before such aid can be realistically increased. It is for this reason that state governments are now under the "intergovernmental spotlight" (Stenberg, 1985).

What is particularly vexing for state and local governments at this time of federal aid reduction is that different regions of the United States have been growing apart since 1979. The economic disparity is especially great between California and fifteen states along the Atlantic Coast on one side and states heavily dependent on energy, farming, and smokestack industries on the other. According to a 1987 study conducted by the United States Commerce Department's Bureau of Economic Analysis, the Southwest, the Rocky Mountain states, and the Southeast had per capita incomes well below the national average of $14,641. The Great Lakes region also had a per capita income below the national average. In other words, those regions that depend on high-tech industries, services, and defense have prospered while those that depend on agriculture and traditional industries have declined. New England, for example, which has enjoyed growth in high-tech industries and services, has the highest per capita income of all ($17,166). Despite this growth, however, there is genuine concern among policymakers that both high-tech industry and the service economy are vulnerable to foreign competition. As the farmers and mineral industries discovered when they lost customers to foreign competitors, the United States no longer dominates the world markets. The federal government's role in stabilizing this situation and the policies it will eventually enact remain issues of serious debate.

In light of these circumstances, it is not surprising that some state and local governments have decided to launch bold programs to aggressively address local and state economic issues. These programs include creative reinvestment financing packages for businesses; government-supported venture capital programs; probusiness campaigns and legislative reforms; publicly financed and operated small business incubators; university technology-transfer programs; publicly funded export trade companies; enterprise zones; public-private joint equity partnerships; and public education reforms. As state and local officials now recognize, the primary responsibility for economic development now rests firmly on their shoulders; they cannot adopt a wait-and-see attitude. Many policymakers, however, are feeling overwhelmed by the complexities of corporate disinvestment, accelerating technological change, structural shifts in the national economy, and an expanding global marketplace.

The traditional strategy of recruiting manufacturing plants by promoting the advantages of low-cost labor, cheap land, and governmental subsidies no longer works as well as it once may have. Most economic growth and job creation are occurring in new small- and medium-sized firms and in such new sectors as advanced manufacturing, information, services, and, to a lesser extent, high technology. However, because there is no economic theory that can help state and local government officials design economic development "blueprints," urban and rural policymakers have often pursued outdated strategies or politically driven policies that emphasize short-term goals. New economic trends, however, are forcing state and local governments to develop more strategic and long-term interventions into their economies and to formulate economic development efforts tailored to their region. This chapter will examine why states and communities must continue to expand their efforts in economic development and why strategic economic development is crucial to the formulation of their programs.

Changing Economic Environment

As we approach the twenty-first century, it is clear that the nation as a whole as well as its states and communities are undergoing a major economic transformation that rivals the earlier industrial revolution in terms of painful changes and new development opportunities. The "great recession" of 1981–1982 sparked many state and local leaders to reexamine their historical economic development policies and stimulated a renewed interest in economic growth. The recession and the accompanying financial stress at both the state and local levels significantly increased competition among states and communities to attract jobs. This was combined with several significant transformations in the structure of the national economy: from the production of goods to the production of services, from a national to a global system of trade, and from labor-intensive to technology-intensive manufacturing.

The Shift from a Goods-Producing to a Services-Producing Employment Base. The bulk of the new jobs created in the last decade were in the services-producing sector. From 1981 to 1984, 3.3 million jobs were created in this sector, expanding its employment by 6.6 percent; during the same period, 850,000 jobs were lost in the goods-producing sector. This is not merely a result of the 1981–1982 recession; in fact, manufacturing employment has not increased much since the Korean War. Manufacturing has maintained a relatively constant share of the gross national product (GNP), accounting for 21.4 percent in 1950 and 21.7 percent in 1986.

Service jobs have grown largely as a result of international competition, technological changes, and increased demand for services (Shelp, 1987). Of the 111 million people employed in 1987, the vast majority, approximately 82 million, worked in the service sector; 26 million were in goods-producing jobs, and 3 million were in agriculture. The goods-producing sector includes manufacturing, mining, and construction; the services-producing sector includes a wider array of classifications. In general terms, the service sector runs on information and trade, while the goods-producing sectors runs on raw materials. The growth of new service jobs is uneven, however, and is not uniform throughout the service sector. The retailing, consumer, and distribution portion of the service sector employs the bulk of new workers; however, the other service-sector areas are now growing faster nationally. Retailing and consumer services have steadily decreased from 33 percent of the service sector in 1959 to about 25 percent in 1983. On the other hand, those areas dealing with health and education, business and professional services, and entertainment are experiencing rapid growth. Health and education services, for example, have increased from 15 percent of the service sector in 1972 to almost 20 percent in 1983 (Birch, 1987a). Most estimates indicate that by 1995 the United States economy will have added about 15 million new jobs, and that 90 percent of these will be in the services-producing sector.

In spite of this shift toward services, the overall strength and productivity of manufacturing are actually increasing. Productivity gains in the manufacturing sector rose from 2.1 percent in 1981 and 1982 to 4.3 percent in 1986. Industrial output, measured by the industrial production index, has grown from a little over 100 in 1982 to almost 130 in 1985, and it is projected to be close to 140 by 1987. This growth has been due to cost-cutting, corporate restructuring strategies, and the use of advanced production technologies and is not a result of employment growth. Thus, while the number of manufacturing jobs has decreased, the manufacturing sector is still important. Therefore, effective state and local economic development strategies cannot rely solely on services-producing jobs for growth. America's services also depend on the vitality of its manufacturing base. "A substantial core of service employment is tightly tied to manufacturing. It is a complement, not a substitute or successor, to manufacturing. Lose manufacturing and we will lose—not develop—high wage service jobs . . . [for] some 25 percent of GNP consists of services purchased by American manufacturers. Lose manufacturing and we would lose not just millions of direct production jobs but also a good hunk of those service jobs" (Cohen and Zysman, 1987b, p. 2). According to one study, nearly 90 percent of the income generated from services consists of investment income from manufacturing firms (Reich, 1983). Simply put, the services sector cannot survive without manufacturing, owing to the direct relationship between the service and manufacturing sectors.

What is often overlooked is that the service economy is interdependent with the different sectors—agricultural, service, and manufacturing—and all are important, even though employment tends to be concentrated in the service sector (Shelp, 1987). In short, the service sector alone cannot revitalize the economy, particularly in view of the fact that total productivity in the services-producing sector has been rather low. The American Productivity Center in Houston has calculated that productivity in the service sector increased only 0.1 percent from 1979 to 1983, well below that of the goods-producing sector. While professional and business services outperformed goods-producing industries during this period, productivity dropped in finance, transportation, and utilities. Thus the crucial issue is not whether the service-sector economy is dominating the declining manufacturing sector, but rather the recognition that each sector depends on the viability of the other. It is worth noting that General Motors' largest supplier is not another manufacturer, but Blue Cross/Blue Shield ("Now, R&D . . . ," 1986). This restructuring of the economy has created new dilemmas for state and local economic development efforts while at the same time providing new challenges for stimulating job creation and long-term economic wealth.

The Shift from a National to a Global Economy. A second major economic trend is the shift from a national economy to an interdependent system of worldwide production, trade, and financing. In the past, the national economy shifted from local to regional and from regional to national markets. A global economy has now emerged. Nearly 80 percent of all new manufacturing jobs in the United States are related to exports. More important, overseas producers have rapidly increased their penetration of traditionally American consumer markets. As a result, the United States' share of world manufacturing exports has dropped from 25 percent in 1960 to 17 percent today (Shelp, 1985). The globalization of the economy is further illustrated by the growth of trade from 8 percent of the GNP in the 1970s to almost 15 percent in 1986. Not surprisingly, it is estimated that 70 percent of U.S. companies are now affected by international trade. A good example of the new economic web is a silicon microchip—designed in California, fabricated in Scotland, assembled and tested in the Far East, and returned to the United States for sale (Wishard, 1987). The result is that state and local policymakers must now look beyond national boundaries and view their state and local economies in relation to an international economy. Currently, forty-five states have created international offices to deal with state exports and foreign investment, twenty-nine of which have foreign offices in more than one country. The emergence of what some have called "state foreign economic policies" (see Chapter Seven) is an example of how state governments have become active in the international economy.

The Shift from Labor-Intensive to Technology-Intensive Manufacturing. Adaptation to new technologies such as robotics and computer-integrated flexible manufacturing systems poses major challenges for maintaining jobs in communities and states. These systems are replacing assembly-line and semiskilled manufacturing jobs with fewer, more highly skilled technical jobs. Miniaturization and other advanced technologies are changing the manufacturing production process of the steel industry (for example, with mini–steel mills), electric power generation (for example, with smaller-scale power plants that improve efficiency through cogeneration), and most other industries. The wood products industry in the Pacific Northwest provides an excellent example of how advanced technology eliminates semiskilled jobs. Laser-guided, computer-controlled milling operations allow smaller logs to be more accurately cut and milled at faster rates with fewer mill operators. These technological innovations have allowed the larger mills to be less labor-intensive while maintaining or even increasing actual production, resulting in the closure of less modern plants, particularly in small, isolated, single-industry towns (Hibbard, 1985). These technological changes result in the "uncoupling" of the production of goods from the employment of workers (Drucker, 1986). The increased use of sophisticated technology is reducing employment while maintaining manufacturing productivity. Throughout the United States, and in each of the industrial sectors (such as agriculture, timber, and automobiles), manufacturing output, as a percentage of the gross national product, has remained roughly the same since 1950, while at the same time employing fewer people. In other words, fewer and fewer jobs are needed to produce more and more goods.

Emerging Fiscal Difficulties

As the economy shifts toward the service sector and away from the manufacturing base, state and local governments may face increasing difficulties in raising adequate revenues. In a services-producing economy, the traditional taxes on property, sales, and income produce smaller amounts of revenue than when goods-producing industries dominated local and state economies (Academy for State and Local Government, 1986). The economic attributes of the service sector create fiscal difficulties when the tax revenues from the service sector do not offset losses in the manufacturing sector, even if there is no net job loss in the community. As the U.S. economy has become more dependent on services, the tax structures in many states have lagged behind.

Presently, twenty-one states have no tax on services (except those taxes on transient accommodations, utilities, and theater), and four states tax only certain services (Ross, 1987). Recently, Florida attempted to shift its tax base toward services by extending a 5 percent sales tax on goods to all businesses and consumer services. Other states with broad service levies are Hawaii, New Mexico, and South Dakota. However, one of the difficulties in service levies is that often a fiscal gain will occur only once, and this gain will most likely decrease steadily to only about a 0.2 percent annual increase in the tax base (Mikesell, 1986). Furthermore, an unanticipated consequence of taxing a broad range of services is a tax incentive for vertical integration of businesses (Mikesell, 1986). In other words, there will be an incentive for larger companies to buy out their suppliers.

Another crucial issue is that the ten service-sector occupations that will supply the most jobs (for example, cashiers, nurses, janitors, sales workers, nursing aides, and waiters) pay as little as 60 percent less than goods-producing jobs. According to the Academy for State and Local Government (1986), this will lower potential income tax generation. While many advocates for a service economy contend that higher-paying jobs in the service sector are growing, they neglect to point out that this growth is occurring from a relatively narrow employment base and is not projected to produce most of the new jobs in the future ("Now, R&D . . . ," 1986). Furthermore, a substantial share of service-oriented enterprises escape property taxation and corporate profit taxes because of their status as "nonprofit" or public agencies. Consequently, the revenue base for state and local government may shrink as the economy becomes dominated by services-producing enterprises.

While government revenues are being squeezed, state and local government's responsibilities continue to increase. Citizens' demands for public services expand while tax revenues diminish. Many urban and rural areas find themselves caught in a spiral decline when structural changes in the economy increase the demand for certain government services at the same time that the industrial tax base is being eroded. Structural changes in agriculture and other natural resource industries, combined with severe adjustments in the industrial sector of the American economy, have caused economic hardship and personal stress in metropolitan and nonmetropolitan areas alike. Rural areas, for example, are experiencing the traumas of declining population, unemployment and underemployment, business losses, and reduced governmental revenues. As many states and communities are beginning to understand, increases in per capita income and employment opportunities become very difficult to sustain as a region's population declines or gets older. Economic theory indicates that when population is constant, economic development and growth can occur only when there are continuing capital investment and innovation (Vincent, 1985).

As a result of these economic realities, the formation of successful state and local economic development strategies becomes critical to sustain the U.S. economy, particularly as it confronts an expanding set of foreign competitors. Equally important, economic development strategies forged at the state and local levels should be directed not only toward the maintenance of basic public services, but toward a decent quality of life. While federal policies in the 1980s have focused on national economic growth—primarily by emphasizing reduced taxes on corporations, decreased governmental regulation of industry, and less macrointervention in the economy—there has been no substantial decline in poverty (Advisory Commission on Intergovernmental Relations, 1985). As a result, many states and communities are still facing increasing demands to finance and provide public services, especially for four groups: displaced or laid-off workers who need retraining in a new field or profession or small business assistance to start their own enterprises; minorities, especially minority youths, who need appropriate training to gain access to jobs on a nondiscriminatory basis; underemployed men and women who need basic training, literacy training, or placement services; and homeless men and women and single parents in large metropolitan areas who need basic employment services.

The impacts of these broad economic changes are not evenly distributed, and they result in regional disparities in economic growth and serious fiscal stress for many government jurisdictions. Some regions benefit greatly owing to the historical diversity of their own economies, while others suffer. The variety of problems and potentials require tailor-made solutions or strategies to be developed at the state and community levels, in which government agencies go beyond their traditional supportive role into a more active partnership.

Changing Locus of Decision Making

The recent political shifts that have changed the locus of decision making and reordered the federal system are also forcing states and communities to take a more active role in development. The Reagan administration returned authority and responsibility for local economic development to the state and local levels after decades of federal decision making and policy guidance. This devolution of the national government's responsibilities was not accompanied by the transfer of fiscal resources, and it merely reflected the diminishing role of the federal government.

Prior to the late seventies, local governments were little more than administrative agents of federal programs for economic development. Federal initiatives, such as job training, urban development, and community renewal programs, flooded communities with federal monies, often bypassing state government. Consequently, programs sprang up and grantsmanship blossomed, all federally directed. In the late seventies, the situation began to change significantly. Although President Reagan is closely associated with the concept of the "New Federalism," he did not really initiate it, since—as it has been pointed out infrequently— many of the attempts to curtail federal direction in local economic development were undertaken by President Carter, who increased block grant usage. The basic reasoning for this transfer of responsibility for state and local economic development was established by the President's Commission for a National Agenda for the Eighties (1980), which produced a controversial study commissioned by President Carter. Yet it was President Reagan's budget cuts during the 1980s, coupled with retrenchment budgeting and fiscal constriction in the 1970s and the deep recession in 1981–1982, that convinced states and communities that they were on their own when it came to economic development.

This state of affairs most likely will not improve, regardless of who is president, because of the concern to reduce the national debt. As a result, interregional competition is growing while federal direction is declining and the international marketplace is expanding. Cities and communities are feeling compelled to enter the industrial marketplace to "buy" jobs and business activity from private enterprise. This has resulted in almost every city, county, and state in America competing fiercely to recruit industries. Unfortunately, the chances are nearly nonexistent that a community will land a new enterprise that is relocating or building a branch plant; over 15,000 state and local governments and economic organizations in the United States currently compete for fewer than 250 potential relocations and branch expansions. A stark example of this competition is the way states tried to recruit General Motors' Saturn plant. Economic development strategies must expand beyond industrial recruitment and consider the many crucial linkages that connect development policies with other public policies.

Policy Interconnections

Economic development policies are inextricably related to almost all other policy issues in state and local government. In higher education, for example, policies are being formulated that increasingly tie high-tech discoveries to local business development. Economic development goals are now considered an integral part of policy calculations in areas of local government responsibility such as public transportation, street widening, local tax structures, and a variety of quality-of-life considerations previously considered separate and unrelated (such as libraries, law enforcement, and parks and recreation). State policies on topics as varies as environmental regulation, water development and pricing, location of state corrections facilities, and educational reform all affect economic growth and must now be considered in the light of their effects.

At the national level, another policy interdependency concerns the relationship of manufacturing to services. Many economists argue that for the United States to address the balance-of-payments problem, it must revitalize its manufacturing share of world trade. Services alone cannot create a trade surplus. What is desperately needed is a reconceptualization of traditional economic and managerial thinking: a movement away from short-term, segmented economic policies toward an emphasis on long-term planning that focuses on adaptability and flexibility in designing policies for a broader, more interdependent economic environment.

Need for Public Managerial Leadership in Economic Development

In the absence of federal leadership, states and communities must begin initiating local responses. States must begin to set the pace for economic growth to maintain their competitiveness in an interdependent economic world. Rapid technological changes coupled with international competition have increased uncertainty and risk in many major industries and in urban and rural communities. Although uncertainty will always be present in an economy where no one has complete information, states and communities are attempting to be more innovative in their approaches in order not to become prisoners of swings in their economies. This particularly applies to one-industry towns and to regions that lack adequate economic diversification.

If global competition, rapidly changing technology, fiscal constraints, and future economic restructuring are to be confronted, new strategies must be implemented at the state and community levels. State and local economic development strategies need to change because the entire economy is undergoing a transition. The structural economic shift rekindles and fuels the issues that initially emerged during the recession of 1981–1982: declining competitiveness and productivity, unemployment and the need for job retraining, and plant closings and community decline. Some of these problems may solve themselves without major policy guidance through strictly market mechanisms. Others may not, and these are prompting local and state officials to invent economic development strategies custom-designed for their region.

State and local governments are entering a period of "generative development," a process in which new and sometimes experimental economic development approaches are generated, not just to create jobs, but in an effort to understand and harness the dynamics of local economies and the relationships with such governmental functions as education, social services, and infrastructure investment (Committee for Economic Development, 1986). As a result, some state and local public managers are learning that more shopping centers and incessant smokestack chasing are not synonymous with economic development. Many local communities are inventing new job creation strategies. To cite a few recent examples, Louisville and Baltimore have established venture capital pools to help finance struggling new businesses. Baltimore and Milwaukee are targeting their employee pension trust funds for small business loans. A San Francisco community action program used state grant money to purchase an ailing rent-a-car franchise, provided basic financing to make it economically sound, and began to use the business as a job training center. On a larger scale, several states, such as Indiana, Michigan, Ohio, Pennsylvania, Washington, and Wisconsin, have developed strategic economic plans.

Now that state and local governments are starting to engage in generative development, a central question must be posed: Will these new initiatives in economic development, regardless of their good intentions, result merely in disjointed programs that will do little to strengthen the community and will only accentuate competition among state and local governments for scarce resources? Will state and local managers merely pursue the same short-term economic goals with new vigor?

To keep new initiatives from being counterproductive, leadership is critical not only as a catalyst in promoting long-term economic growth but to bring together myriad key actors: business representatives, community and political leaders, and leaders from nonprofit organizations. Leadership approaches and economic development initiatives will invariably differ from one state to another, and from one community to another. Yet without active leadership in the public sector, even the best-conceived economic policy or set of policies can eventually undermine the efficacy of a strategic long-term view.

Conclusion

State and local policymakers are facing vexing economic problems that will require new approaches in building a more productive and viable state or local economy. A significant influence on state and local economic activity involves the complex interaction of national and international market forces. Nevertheless, state and local governments directly influence the foundations of economic growth within their boundaries, and leadership for economic development now falls most heavily on state and local public executives.

A central premise of this book is that economic development policies must be framed in accordance with what we refer to as the management of interdependencies. That is, the policies that are formulated must be connected with cultural, economic, political, and educational issues in order to be strategically linked to the unique and specific strengths of the state or local economy. This implies a reconceptualization of economic development in which the public manager or policymaker is compelled to think strategically about the real foundations of long-term prosperity. Encouraging capital formation, revising state and local tax systems, improving the educational system, and promoting economic diversification are all noble goals, but without a careful definition of the problem, an established set of strategic goals or vision, an implementation structure to coordinate initiatives, and a process for evaluating progress, economic policies can become static and thus ill-suited to political and economic changes that may occur in the state's future. The specific set of policies will, of course, depend on the state's or community's economic strengths; however, initiating a strategic approach recognizing the interdependency of issues will remain important for two basic reasons. First, decisions must eventually be made and courses of action taken at the state and community levels to enhance economic growth. The issue is therefore not whether to plan or not to plan; rather, it is to implement a management process that allows for an economic approach that is flexible in designing policies suited to particular situations. Second, the management process must be one that opens rather than limits a range of future choices. The important issue, then, becomes the type of management process that is most likely to achieve this end. A strategic management approach—one that builds on the rich network of institutions (public, private, and nonprofit), the citizenry, and the particular advantages of the state's location—offers the best way to revitalize the state and local economy for long-term growth. Although strategic management has been defined in numerous ways (Eadie and Steinbacher, 1985; Wechsler and Backoff, 1986), in economic development it has particular characteristics. First, it is future-oriented—it assesses political, social, and economic forces that will directly impinge on the future growth of the state or local economy and it adapts policies in recognition of such changes. Second, it is change-oriented—it reexamines traditional approaches to economic development and mobilizes organizational learning capacities in coordinating economic development activities; it evaluates enacted policies in order to determine program efficacy. Finally, it is intersectoral—it strategically links central public, private, and nonprofit actors in implementing policy goals; it uses an interdisciplinary approach involving various organizations in formulating economic policy (Eadie and Steinbacher, 1985).

Strategic management is a process that examines the state's or community's economic, political, human, and natural resources to identify long-range policy actions and goals while continuously evaluating their effectiveness in creating the economic wealth commensurate with the state's future strategic strengths. Strategic management is not a "cookbook" approach to economic development; rather, it provides the foundation needed for an analysis of possible strategies to be pursued. Moreover, this process does not negate the role of the market. The relevant concern from our perspective is to effectively coordinate, improve, and monitor policies that can help the market work even better. However, some prominent scholars are skeptical of such claims (Lawrence, 1984; Schultze, 1983). These economists contend that such policies will inevitably add a new layer of bureaucracy and may be predicated on a fundamental misreading of what is actually happening to the economy. Bluntly put, they question the assumption of the need for governmental intervention. For example, one economist has argued that U.S. regional economic disparity is a painful but therapeutic adjustment to macroeconomic changes (Norton, 1986). While it is not our purpose to discuss the validity of these claims here, we recognize the general merits of these arguments. Nonetheless, the economic stakes are too high for state and local policymakers wrestling with fiscal constraints, international competition, rapid shifts in technology, and unemployment to think that the market alone will resolve these complex issues. The pivotal concern is not the issue of governmental intervention but what kind of government intervention is warranted by specific economic situations. Traditional strategies predicated on outmoded assumptions of what constitutes economic development will be hard to break. The critical point in this book is that strategic management, and the interdependencies it implies, must be understood and acknowledged by policymakers in the economic development process. This is the real challenge confronting policymakers.

2

The Challenge of Stimulating
Economic Growth and Change

The broad shifts and major transformations in the economy require
states and cities to think strategically about the foundations of long-
term prosperity. Simultaneous structural changes in the U.S.
economy—a sudden shift from a national to a highly interconnected
global economy, severe adjustments in several key industries
(agriculture, mining, and timber, for example), and the uncoupling
of labor from organizational output—are creating urgent economic
dilemmas. America's economy is in transition, and, by most
accounts, state and local economies are also dramatically changing.
Traditional approaches to economic development are insufficient
in light of this transition. Historically, community and state
economic well-being have been synonymous with industrial
development or with farming and mining. Most of the 2,400 rural
counties nationwide have been dependent on these three economic
sectors (Henry and others, 1987). In a recent survey by the National
Governors Association, thirteen states said that overdependence on
one sector was a major economic development issue. Most of these
thirteen states are dependent on agriculture and mining industries
(Clarke, 1986).

Structural changes in the U.S. economy affect more than the
states and communities in the industrial Northeast and Midwest.
The timber industry in the Pacific Northwest, energy development
in the Rocky Mountain states, and agriculture in the rural Midwest
are all affected by economic transition. Yet studies of economically
distressed communities suggest that leaders and citizens fail to

connect unemployment, depressed income, and declining revenues with structural economic change. Instead, they perceive economic distress to be temporary and a problem that national countercyclical fiscal policies will solve. This perception leads to a wait-and-see attitude by many local leaders, or to economic policies that invest scarce public resources in outdated and inappropriate economic development strategies.

Why is it so difficult to stimulate state and local economic development effectively? Economic development and diversification is a slow and often painful process that requires some form of change, such as changing attitudes and perceptions regarding economic reality and removing institutional barriers to innovation and collaboration. As a result, economic growth now requires continuous strategic management. This chapter discusses why it is difficult for state and local governments to manage economic development strategically. The reasons include attitudinal barriers, outdated perspectives, institutional barriers, and difficulties in fostering collaborative decision making.

Attitudinal Barriers to Effective Economic Development Planning

Most traditional planning methods follow a "rational" approach, assuming that key policymakers only need accurate, up-to-date information in order to develop effective development policies. However, community attitudes often create barriers to rational planning; as a result, providing technical assistance to states and communities in decline does not necessarily stimulate change. Consultants to an Oregon community, for example, supplied decision makers with a series of technical studies explaining the types of new economic activities needed to counteract depression in the timber industry. Unfortunately, their suggestions were never implemented (Hibbard, 1986). Researchers in a rural Midwestern agricultural community reported a similar experience (Reed, Reed, and Luke, 1987).

The reasons that decision makers ignore technical assistance are twofold. One is that they are not sufficiently invested in the economic development plan because outside planning experts exclude them from the process (Feldt and Whorton, 1987). A second reason, however, is that state and local leaders have a characteristic set of attitudes and perceptions about economic reality that inhibit the potential for economic growth and change. These attitudes are variously characterized as "learned helplessness" (Hibbard, 1985) and economic "denial, withdrawal and blame" (Reed, Reed, and Luke, 1987).

Medical research over the last ten years has revealed a common process experienced by people with terminal illnesses. According to Kubler-Ross (1985), people react to their terminal illness in a typical way. First, they deny the illness. In this phase, they argue that the hospital mixed up their X-rays. They refuse to accept their coming death and talk of miraculous cures. This denial is the first, and very common, stage in a progression toward eventual acceptance of the situation. Anger and blame often follow denial; the person experiences rage and asks, "Why me?" Initial reactions of denial, anger, and blame are part of the process of letting go of physical and psychological attachments to people in the dying person's environment. The third stage is depression and withdrawal, where attempts to close oneself off to outside intrusion are common. Acceptance is the last stage in the process of dying, and typically generates a sense of hope. When a dying person accepts impending death, he or she undergoes a radical shift in perspective, seeing the possibility of a new form of life.

The stages of reaction to death and dying identified by Kubler-Ross are analogous to a community's psychological or attitudinal reactions to a crisis in the local or regional economy. The analogy helps to explain why it is so difficult for a state or community's leadership to accept the implications of strategic planning studies; even if strategic planning experts were to include them in external scanning and internal assessment of competitive advantage, decision makers would still tend to develop perceptions and attitudes about their economic situation characteristic of a person with a terminal illness.

Denial. Faced with a deteriorating economy, leaders may first deny the reality of the situation. At this stage, people may have the notion that "these are hard times, but things will work out." During the 1980s, state and local policymakers have been particularly vulnerable to this assessment. They erroneously describe the economic disruptions their communities are experiencing as the result of cyclical ups and downs in an industry, rather than permanent shifts in the economy.

Denial of economic change may actually exacerbate decline in small, single-industry towns whose economies have suffered from structural dislocations in the supporting industry. These communities need to make a transition from dependence on a single industry to greater economic diversification, and the consequences of inaction can thus be more harmful for them than for larger cities with more diversified economies. Small, single-industry towns are likely to react to economic decline by ignoring the underlying causes. This denial reaction runs counter to the expectations of many social scientists, who have assumed that small towns have a greater sense of their common fate than larger urban areas. Previously, researchers thought that a collective identity existed in small towns, creating conditions more conducive to effective mobilization in response to the need for action (Hibbard, 1986). While such generalizations may have been valid in the past, it is clear that the kinds of economic changes occurring now in states and communities can exceed the capacity of community leaders to comprehend and respond effectively.

Anger and Blame. At the stage of anger and blame, finger-pointing begins, and statements such as "Our Chamber of Commerce executive is incompetent—nothing is happening" and "It's the fault of the state's unitary tax/Japanese competition/the Sierra Club" are made. Responsibility for economic deterioration is often attributed to individual leaders, past or present, who have had a visible but often very general connection to a state or a community's economic troubles. A poignant example is Oregon. In the 1980s, many Oregonians blamed former governor Tom McCall for difficulties in attracting industrial firms. The neighboring states of California and Washington seemed to be considerably more successful at recruiting new firms. To promote tourism and to reduce development pressure, in the 1970s, McCall had invited Americans to "come and visit, but please don't stay." This statement remained in the minds of many Oregonians a decade later as the primary reason for the state's economic development problems.

Anger can provide the energy and impetus for policies and action. However, as long as state and local policymakers remain at this stage, a realistic assessment of their economic situation is unlikely. Effective strategies to respond to economic decline will be misguided and drain important human and fiscal resources.

Depression and Withdrawal. The third stage, depression and withdrawal, often follows the recognized failure of policies developed in earlier stages. Policymakers may withdraw from active participation in economic development efforts, having "burned out" from apparently fruitless attempts. Others may experience a sense of depression and withdrawal when they see that their control over their local destiny is limited or diminished. During this phase, policymakers see themselves as passive observers, rather than as active decision makers. They may be heard saying, "Little can be done to save our community," or "We have no control over our state's economy."

The reduction in federal aid, combined with the expanding global economy and the internationalization of markets, creates an immediate sense of helplessness in state and local policymakers. The New Federalism is shifting responsibility for economic development to states and communities without transferring additional resources, at a time when local policymakers are feeling hopelessly trapped in an uncertain global economic web.

Feeling helpless, pessimistic, and lacking faith in the future, policymakers avoid active planning efforts. Commenting on the impending shutdown of his town's second largest lumber mill, a mayor expressed his helplessness by saying, "It would hurt a substantial portion of our local economy, but it would not be the end of the world. We'd learn to adjust. It would be like cutting off a boy's arm or leg in surgery—he'd learn to live with it" (Hibbard, 1986, p. 192). Perceptions like these have the danger of creating a disabling "community ideology" or set of collective beliefs by which local residents represent their community to themselves and others (Marchak, 1983).

Acceptance, Hope, and Planning. In the final stage, acceptance, hope, and planning may arise from the realization that traditional economic development policies will no longer sustain local economic growth, and that state and local leaders can influence innovation and investment in the future. A gradual appreciation of the possibility of positive action can emerge at this time. Leaders may be ready for collaboration between government and business to plan effective economic strategies.

At this stage, leaders realize that solutions, not blame, are needed. They also see that success does not happen overnight. They look beyond the quick fix and frame their policies and programs to fit strategically with their unique circumstances. Unfortunately, there is no comprehensive economic theory to guide them once they reach this point. Nor is there one best way to stimulate economic activity.

Outdated Perspectives

State and local economic development policies have historically concentrated on recruiting large companies from outside the state. This industrial recruitment approach blossomed in the 1950s and matured in the 1960s and 1970s. In the 1980s, however, while the number of industrial attraction incentives increased, the competitive differential among states and communities dramatically declined because recruitment incentives pioneered by one state or community were typically emulated by others (Beaumont and Hovey, 1985). As a result, the importance of governmental subsidies to attract industrial prospects has diminished. In addition, there is considerable evidence that most new jobs are created by new and expanding local businesses, and that the few large firms that are attracted to a state or community are more likely to contract their work force than to expand (see Chapter Five).

Economic development is more than a series of industrial attraction and business retention activities. It is a process of identifying strategic goals that will stimulate and generate new economic activity. It is also a uniquely public process, requiring open discussion about opportunities and threats affecting the entire community. However, people are not accustomed to thinking about the economic value added to their community by recreation and cultural services or by locally traded products or services. They are used to thinking about economic value in terms of dependence on one or two large exporting industries. Naturally, this perspective discourages collective action and creates feelings of helplessness. Traditional policies have created a powerful barrier to local initiative and to community-based economic development strategies.

In the 1970s, encouraged by billions of dollars in federal grants and loans, many state and local governments focused primarily on one approach—industrial attraction. Now, federal dollars for local economic development are shrinking. Yet some states and communities have been slow to react to these changing circumstances. For example, economically distressed single-industry towns may be especially prone to cling to traditional industrial development policies, even though they are more vulnerable to shifting external forces. The deep-seated beliefs held by many about industrial development have become what de Tocqueville ([1835, 1840] 1945) and later Bellah and others (1985) would refer to as "habits of the heart."

Research has demonstrated the increasing influence of the formation and expansion of new firms on economic growth, yet many local community development offices lack the capacity to promote public investment in new, indigenous firms. They are unable to identify potentially successful businesses, to locate and package financing, and to assess the performance of new firms in the community. Thus, even in communities with a successful track record in industrial attraction, government staff may have difficulty acquiring the skills necessary for new entrepreneurial wealth creation strategies (Vaughan and others, 1984) that utilize approaches other than industrial recruitment. Although there is no single best way for a state or community to diversify and create new jobs, four generally recognized approaches are now available: attraction of businesses by recruiting enterprises from outside the region to relocate in the area, retention of companies that are considering locating in another area or closing their business operations, formation of new businesses driven by local entrepreneurs with good ideas and a business plan, and expansion of existing enterprises to facilitate the growth of indigenous businesses.

In short, there is mounting evidence of the need for states and communities to develop new economic development strategies that respond to the following situations: evidence of the wealth-creating potential of new business development, shrinking federal dollars for economic development (especially for industrial attraction), the expanding international marketplace, and, most important, the transition from a goods-producing to a service-based economy. The outdated perspectives of many state and community leaders, old "habits of the heart," can prevent the formulation of appropriate public policies to respond to unique situations.

Outdated Strategies	*New Strategies*
Industrial attraction and plant relocation	Local, "homegrown" business enterprise development
Reliance on federal policy guidance and financial assistance	Reliance on state and local leadership
Focusing on large manufacturing firms	Focusing on smaller and younger firms
Providing low-cost labor	Providing skilled and flexible labor
Providing low-cost land and tax subsidies	Providing accessibility to advanced technology and financial capital
Expansion into regional and national markets	Expansion into international, global markets
Increasing jobs and employment opportunities	Wealth creation and increasing the number of employers

Institutional Barriers

Several institutional barriers to strategically managing economic development exist. At the state level, for example, bureaucratic structures can be an obstacle to comprehensive policy development. While many governors and department heads now recognize the interdependence of economic development, community development, job training, transportation, and other functions of state government, implementation of a comprehensive approach is extremely difficult. A state government is organized by its specialized functions because of the complex array of programs and services administered at this level. Intergovernmental regulations and judicial mandates further complicate public administration. Consolidation of highly specialized functions will not lead inevitably to more cohesive, coherent economic development policies. On the contrary, there is always a danger that coordinating mechanisms such as super-cabinet departments, cabinet councils, and gubernatorial task forces will only add another layer of bureaucracy to an already complex structure.

At the department or division levels of state government, specialists in industrial development, business retention and formation, community development, and other areas of economic development are captives of standard operating procedures, federal and state program regulations, and interest group and clientele demands. Their day-to-day operating responsibilities make it very difficult to reflect on the broader implications of their programs and regulations for economic development. Attempts to create coordinating structures at the department level through either divisional consolidation or departmental cabinets do not automatically result in changes in the lower levels of the bureaucracy. These organizational barriers to effective economic development are not necessarily due to conscious resistance by government workers but are caused by the complexity of institutional structures created to oversee the many facets of economic development.

Other institutional factors directly affect the business climate in a state or community. Governmental legislation and regulation may limit competition or may emphasize industrial attraction over new business formation. In addition, federal and state economic development programs tend to support direct financial incentives, such as infrastructure loans and grants, when such assistance is premature for many small communities lacking a basic strategic planning capability (Paulsen and Reed, 1987). Despite increasing evidence that economic growth begins within a state or community through new business start-ups, institutional factors tend to perpetuate outdated development strategies and reinforce the "habits of the heart."

Organizational creativity and risk-taking behaviors are

uncommon in many public organizations (Benest, 1985). It is very difficult to get prior legislative approval for a public-private business venture if the project arouses political opposition or exposes the state or community to financial or legal liabilities. It is also very difficult for state or local agencies to get approval for research into new development opportunities. Government workers are often nervous about using their time for creative thinking, searching out and exploiting opportunities, because of citizens' stereotypes about lazy and unproductive bureaucrats. Government employees are typically too serious and worried about accountability to be creative and entrepreneurial. There are also few monetary or nonmonetary incentives for government employees to adopt new and uncertain economic development roles.

In many jurisdictions, economic policy is based on a short-term perspective connected with the election cycle. Although a comprehensive long-term perspective is extremely important, political agendas drive economic development policy decisions all too frequently. The pursuit of many conflicting individual and agency agendas makes it difficult to produce economic development policies beneficial to a state's or a community's economic health over the long run (Committee for Economic Development, 1986).

Difficulties in Collaborative Decision Making

It is virtually impossible for decision makers in the public sector to set economic development goals unilaterally. Public organizations are unique in the number and variety of key stakeholders to whom they must be accountable. Stakeholders—individuals or groups who are affected by or who can affect the future of an agency—are especially numerous and varied in economic development; they include developers, bankers, chambers of commerce, actual or potential employers, neighborhood groups, and environmentalists (Bryson and Roering, 1987). Effective economic development requires collaborative efforts among many organizations; diversifying the economic base requires broadening participation in economic development to include key leaders, such as state and local public officials, retail merchants, bankers, real estate brokers, utility executives, lawyers, and union leaders.

Managing economic development strategically now demands the active participation of persons not traditionally a part of economic development policy-making. Unfortunately, the more politically powerful stakeholders are typically not open to collaborative problem solving because their self-interest drives them to advance or thwart efforts at statewide or community-level economic strategies (Gray and Hay, 1986). Those that have the most to lose will be the least likely to support significant changes, making collaboration difficult.

Complicating the process is the fact that neither the public nor the private sector alone has the expertise, information, or resources necessary to enhance the vitality of state and local economies. Furthermore, the direct beneficiaries of economic development cover the entire spectrum of community residents, from the bank president to the unemployed laborer. Everyone is likely to benefit from economic development, either directly or indirectly. However, governmental and business leaders are not accustomed to working collaboratively to advance collective interests.

Traditional industrial attraction efforts did not require collaborative economic development strategies. Historically, local public officials relied on chambers of commerce and merchants' associations to promote economic development, and they did not participate actively in their activities. More important, industrial recruiters sought to retain and attract a winning mix of advanced industries, rather than targeting new enterprises that would initiate and accumulate capital in communities. It took corporate relocations and plant shutdowns in the early 1980s to alert public officials to the importance of governmental leadership and participation in new business development (Bergman, 1986).

Local business development strategies—formation, expansion, and retention—now require new roles for the public sector in economic development and generate new philosophical questions about public entrepreneurship. In New Haven, Connecticut, for example, the city government entered into a creative financing arrangement with a local developer to renovate the historic Shubert Theater. While the project was not a new business, it obviously contributed to the community by enhancing New Haven's cultural amenities and general quality of life. Yet the project provoked political opposition because of a perception that the city's participation in the project constituted collusion with the developer. Ironically, the financing arrangement with the developer cost the taxpayers less than a direct grant from the city to the Shubert Theater would have cost. In other communities as well, elected officials and the general public may feel uncomfortable with talk of return on investment, syndication proceeds, net distributable cash flow, and other aspects of private-sector financing (Kysiak, 1983). Traditional economic development strategies have not prepared elected officials or the general public for a public entrepreneurial role.

Conclusion

In order to respond to new economic opportunities and stem economic decline, state and community leaders need to be ready to manage their own economies. Readiness involves at least four key elements: changed attitudes, expanded perspectives, the removal of institutional barriers, and collaborative decision-making mechanisms. In order for economic growth to occur from within a state or community, attitudes about change need to be realistic and positive. The leadership of a state or community needs to be aware of how negative emotional reactions can hamper adjustment to changing economic conditions, and it must move policy-making beyond denial, blame, and withdrawal. Earlier industrial development strategies—attraction and retention—are no longer the most effective way to stimulate economic development. Successful economic revitalization and job creation now require an expansion of perspectives to include the formation and expansion of businesses as well. All four approaches must be combined with related public policies into unique strategies based on a particular state's or community's strengths and weaknesses. Institutional obstacles to effective strategic management, including disincentives to risk-taking behavior in governmental agencies, a conservative, short-term perspective by elected officials, political competition among key stakeholders, and powerful biases against the use of taxpayer dollars for investment in new business development, should be overcome.

Finally, new wealth-creating strategies that facilitate growth in the number of successful business ventures require government actors to be active partners with the business community.

The elements of readiness for strategic economic management are usually overlooked in the various guidebooks and process models of strategic planning. Yet mounting evidence suggests that attitudinal and institutional barriers prevent successful strategic planning and implementation. The dramatic curtailment of federal involvement in local economic development as well as the heightened awareness of the interdependence between the public, private, and nonprofit sectors create new requirements for collaborative efforts at stimulating economic development. Several guidelines emerge from this discussion. First, it is critical to form partnerships for action. Singular leadership and unilateral policy-making will seldom be effective; economic development strategies need to be far more interactive with public- and private-sector executives at the state and local levels than previously envisioned. Second, state and community leadership should transcend political changes and elections. Successful development requires time to produce observable results. Third, policy actors involved in economic development must improve communication. Too often, some key leaders don't understand what others have in mind, ignore the interests of key stakeholders, and fail to communicate their own personal agendas.

Leaders are facing a new situation in which economic reality differs fundamentally from past experience. Unilateral leadership and short-term economic planning cannot provide the necessary catalyst for development. A new planning process is required, one that is collaborative and stimulates strategic thinking. Such a process can best be understood as economic development strategic planning.

Part Two

Effective Planning and Implementation

State and local economic development is more likely to succeed if a strategic planning process is used that includes analysis or diagnosis of local strengths and weaknesses in an interdependent economy and a plan or vision of strategies that are likely to be successful. Chapter Three enumerates the steps in this two-phase process of identifying strategic issues and goals. Chapter Four describes the organizational and administrative units that must be established in order to implement the strategies. Either new agencies must be created or old institutions must be modified. Chapter Four explains how informal or temporary organizations, such as "blue-ribbon committees," can provide an excellent planning backdrop, while more permanent public, quasi-public, or private agencies can be established to sustain development efforts over several years. Chapter Four also addresses the issue of administrative centralization, which must eventually be dealt with. Decisions in this area should be guided by the types of strategies to be pursued as well as the existing institutional strengths of state or local government.

In any case, there are four general approaches to stimulating economic growth and diversity: formation, expansion, attraction, and retention of business enterprises. Chapter Five describes formation and expansion, which have become the most popular, largely because recent research indicates that small businesses generate the bulk of new jobs. Chapter Six examines attraction and retention strategies, which are potentially important, depending on the unique strengths of the local or regional economy.

Chapters Seven and Eight, respectively, offer information about two emerging arenas for potentially effective strategic action, international development and linkages with higher education. Although there are a wide variety of international strategies, the two most favored by state and local governments are (1) expanding local enterprises into the global marketplace and (2) increasing foreign investment into a region or community. State and local government leaders are reaching beyond the borders of the United States to respond more effectively to the expanding global economy. Public-sector involvement in the global economy is expanding through such specific activities as advocating exports of locally produced goods, helping local businesses obtain export assistance, coordinating trade missions and promotion workshops, providing direct export assistance to local businesses, joint venturing with private enterprise to promote export expansion or foreign investment, and establishing development corporations for stimulating international trade.

Institutions of higher education also provide a pivotal role in stimulating development in the postindustrial economy. Community colleges, four-year colleges, and universities can perform three important functions in conjunction with state and local government: education and human development, scientific research and technological development, and economic analysis and policy development. These areas for joint government-university efforts fit well with the traditional goals of higher education: research, education, and public service. However, the potential for partnerships between higher education and government remains unfulfilled, largely because of outdated images of adult learning held by some public policymakers and academicians' perceptions of challenges to their academic freedom. Nevertheless, higher education still remains a potentially strong resource for stimulating state and local economic development.

3

A Strategic Approach
to Economic Development:
A Step-By-Step Process

As the national economy shifts and the world economy exercises more and more influence over state and local business enterprises, communities are, in the words of the operator of a family-run sawmill in Oregon, "tightening their belts, getting a little smarter, and diversifying their economies" (U.S. Extension Service, 1987, p. 14). Unfortunately, no blueprint or single policy strategy for successful economic diversification exists. Similarly, no single factor explains why some states and communities are more successful than others in stimulating the formation, expansion, retention, and attraction of business enterprises. Several factors, however, increase the likelihood of success in state and local economic development planning: the identification of local needs and resources; adaptation to external constraints; local leadership that stimulates collaboration among public, private, and nonprofit organizations; and sustained effort over many years, sometimes decades.

The process that best integrates these factors is strategic planning. Business organizations use strategic planning to anticipate rapidly changing markets and to adapt organizational resources to external change. In this way, a business remains aware of its competitive position and its investment opportunities. Recently, governmental organizations have begun to use this process to help themselves adapt to technological change, fiscal stress, and the economic shifts described in earlier chapters.

A variety of different approaches to strategic planning exist, several of which are applicable in state and community settings (Bryson and Roering, 1987). Virtually all approaches contain some version of a three-step diagnosis-vision-action process (Committee for Economic Development, 1986). Diagnosis of economic trends seeks an understanding of how major economic forces are reshaping state and local economies; it requires information gathering and exploration of alternatives. Vision involves fundamental change from a narrow, short-term perspective to strategic initiatives that capture the dynamics of a changing economy and require choices among targets of opportunity. Action is realistic implementation of programs targeted to emerging economic opportunities.

Economic development strategic planning is action oriented, broadly participative, and emphasizes the need to understand a state or community's strengths, weaknesses, investment opportunities, and competitive threats. It is an effective planning process to facilitate the revitalization of local and state economies. The approach described in this chapter was originally developed in the 1920s at the Harvard Business School, modified by Public Technology, Inc., for use in the public sector (Sorkin and others, 1984), and further modified by the authors for community economic development. Like their business counterparts, community and state strategic planning teams can use this approach, shown in Figure 1, to analyze economic strengths and weaknesses and to devise economic development strategies and action plans. This chapter provides a step-by-step description of this process used at the local level. A more general version of this approach, adapted for state economic development, is then discussed.

Step One: Organizing for Community Strategic Planning

Before the strategic planning process begins, those who represent the economic development leadership must be convinced of the need for change. Community leaders may equate strategic planning with industrial recruitment strategies. This assumption is premature, however, without a realistic analysis of external opportunities and threats as well as internal strengths and weaknesses. To avoid premature decisions, those who represent the

Figure 1. Economic Development Strategic Planning.

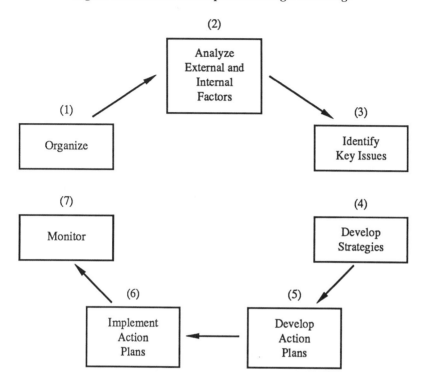

Source: Reed, Reed, and Luke, 1987.

economic development leadership of a community need first to understand the scope and possible impact of a strategic planning process.

Meeting with those actively involved in economic development is a good start. These leaders may be represented by city and county government, the local chamber of commerce, various development groups, or other committees and civic organizations. Leaving out a group or person who has been actively involved in economic development efforts in the past can make it more difficult to build support at the implementation stage. As part of the organization stage, these leaders need to make a commitment to undertake a comprehensive economic development program.

Commitment of resources is the beginning of the organization stage. The city council passes a resolution to support the effort. The chamber of commerce endorses the project. The county board and industrial development commission write letters of support. The process also requires financial and staff resources. Costs include computer time for data analysis, printing, postage, materials, meeting rooms, and other necessary items. Dollars may also be used to pay the expenses of private consultants, university personnel, or, in the case of a community project, staff from the state department of development. Staff resources from community or state organizations are needed to build a data base for later analysis. The commitment of money and staff time ensures that community leaders are prepared to participate actively in the strategic planning process.

Representatives from the economic development leadership constitute the steering committee. They are responsible for coordinating the activities of the strategic planning project and for appointing a local resource team from their own staffs to conduct the data collection and analysis. The members of the steering committee are the linchpin of the entire process. If they delegate their responsibilities to others on their staffs, attend meetings only intermittently, or allow pressing business to distract them from the project for long, support from others in the community will also dwindle. Their effective leadership is crucial to the success of the strategic planning effort.

Since leadership is the key, negative attitudes toward change held by leaders can be an obstacle to the development of successful economic policies. One approach to leadership development is to conduct a preplanning workshop before the analysis of the data and formulation of strategies and action plans begin. In Nebraska, for example, communities beginning a local strategic planning process participate in a pilot project funded by the state's department of economic development. In preparation for strategic planning, community leaders attend a retreat run by the Heartland Center for Leadership Development, a nonprofit organization whose mission is to promote strategic thinking and an entrepreneurial spirit in Nebraska communities (Reed, Reed, and Luke, 1987).

The Heartland Center attempts to develop community

leaders who understand the opportunities and constraints of the postindustrial economy. The retreat consists of a series of short presentations and small group activities aimed at creating a basic understanding of strategic planning, increasing awareness of how resistance to change can hamper strategic planning, and stimulating thinking about strategies for community survival. The center's staff use case studies to simulate the steps of the strategic planning process. Debriefing the case study exercise allows community leaders to reflect about their own attitudes and about the situation in their own communities.

Understanding the scope and potential impact of strategic planning and committing monetary resources and staff time help the economic development leadership of a community build the necessary commitment. All too often, strategic planning begins with the data analysis before participants are ready to assimilate the information. However, comprehensive and accurate information will not guarantee a realistic strategic plan. Therefore, it is important that the leadership workshop precede the building of the local data base and that all the members of the steering committee attend, as difficult as it may be for them to take the time from their other pressing responsibilities.

The components of a local data base include a survey of community attitudes, a survey of the business leadership, an inventory of the community's infrastructure, a profile of the manner in which the community is organized for economic development, and analyses of the economic base, population, and labor force. User-friendly software packages can be developed by private consultants or university personnel for data analysis. The local resource team is typically responsible for conducting the surveys, inventory, and profile, with assistance from outside facilitators. For example, staff from the state department of economic development can provide data on state and national trends. University personnel can offer examples of survey instruments. However, the local data are original information not likely to have been collected previously by a state agency. It is up to the local resource team to develop most of the data base.

The business leadership and community attitude surveys should be mailed or hand-delivered to all business firms and residents. Volunteers can pick up the completed questionnaires, or drops can be set up in local grocery stores, libraries, and so on. The typical business survey asks for information about the type of product or service provided, customers, the trading area, sources of competition, plans to expand or relocate, and attitudes about what the community or state can do to improve business (Council for Urban Economic Development, 1983). The typical community attitude survey asks questions about citizen satisfaction, perceptions of public service quality, and the quality of life.

The infrastructure inventory should include the broad categories of airports, streets and street lighting, wastewater collection and treatment, water supply, and solid waste management. Much of this information is of a highly technical nature, and the resource team may need help from state or local government employees in collecting and interpreting the data. At the community level, for example, information on wastewater collection and treatment should include operation and maintenance, permit limitations, provisions for emergency operation, preventive maintenance and safety, and sludge disposal, hauling, and spreading. Statistics are also needed on the wastewater treatment facility's conditions.

The organizational profile should contain a description of the present organizational structure for economic development. Although the resource team can gather the descriptive information, it should submit the data to a nearby university for evaluation and recommendations. A faculty consultant in public or business administration may suggest strengthening the existing structure, perhaps by creating a development corporation. Further organizational changes may take place after the steering committee actually develops a strategic plan (see Chapter Four).

Economic base, population, and labor force data provide crucial information for the external and internal analyses performed in the next stage. The economic information that goes into a typical software package includes the distribution of local employment among major industries; the local employment distribution for major industries compared to the national distribution; estimates of the trading area for retail businesses; employment growth and decline (shift-share); trends in population, households, and income; characteristics of the labor force, such as size, age, gender, educational attainment and training, and occupational distribution; trends in unemployment and labor availability; and statistics on hourly and weekly production, worker earnings, and productivity.

An accurate economic analysis can provide the steering committee with information about external and internal trends. However, concepts such as export base presume that economic growth occurs primarily through the sale of goods and services outside the local economy. Shift-share analysis measures the proportion of local employment growth due to national growth within basic industries and the proportion due to a local competitive share of an industry market. These analytic techniques are important, but measures of growth generated within a community from new business formation are also important. Indicators of entrepreneurial activity might include a well-planned business inventory or a measure of new business formation that uses ratios of new business start-ups to population and labor force and compares those ratios to the state or nation (Nebraska Department of Economic Development, 1987).

Step Two: Analyzing External and Internal Factors

Communities need to establish an economic intelligence system to help them understand the shifts taking place in the economy and how their local economy fits into the national and global picture. Such understanding enables a community to use its scarce resources for investment in strategic opportunities. Analyzing the factors affecting economic development thus constitutes an important second step of the strategic planning process. Members of the steering committee usually convene at this point for the first working session. Members of the local resource team also attend the first session because of their familiarity with the data base. Staff from the state department of development and university faculty act as project facilitators and technical experts because of their knowledge of the data base software package and their expertise in strategic planning generally.

The objective of the first working session is to use the analysis of external and internal factors to identify key strategic issues and to develop strategies appropriate to the community. This agenda usually takes an entire day, and, although it is not always practical, all members of the steering committee should try to attend the entire session. Holding the session during a retreat is helpful in screening out demands from daily routines. The agenda for the first working session typically follows five steps: a review and overview of the strategic planning process, presentation by outside facilitators and local resource team members of the data base, identification by the committee of external factors revealed by the data, identification of internal factors affecting development, and analyzing strengths and weaknesses, or resource capabilities, in light of opportunities and threats.

Review of the Strategic Planning Process. Several weeks may have elapsed between the leadership workshop and the first working session. It is helpful to start the working session by reviewing the steps of the process with committee members so that they know what to expect for the remainder of the day. Visual diagrams and charts help many people to conceptualize the process. It is also helpful to introduce the idea of export base and other economic terms; otherwise, confusion and frustration over the interpretation of the data will derail the session. With adequate preparation, the committee will be ready to digest the information about the local economy.

Presentation of the Local Data Base. The purpose of presenting the data base is to identify broad factors uniquely affecting development in the community. Summaries of key findings from the surveys, inventory, and organizational profile will be more helpful than long tables filled with statistics. Diagrams, charts, and bar graphs summarize the data and provide needed clarity.

Identification of External Factors. It is important to highlight and amplify those external factors or trends that appear to be especially relevant to the community. The National League of Cities (1979) provides an excellent analytic process for identifying external economic shifts. One external factor that might play a role in future development is the national growth or decline in an industry on which the community is heavily dependent. Competition from adjoining communities or states for local retail business is another external factor affecting development. In addition to the factors revealed by the data base, there may be others identified by the steering committee during the working session. Although community leaders may not be able to control such factors, they may discover strategies to capitalize on external trends or at least minimize their threat.

Identification of Internal Factors. Internal factors are strengths and weaknesses in location characteristics and resource capabilities that determine how effectively a community will respond or adapt to external change and to specific opportunities and threats. There are nine internal factors important for business attraction (Gregerman, 1984a):

1. Local labor market
2. Access to customer and supplier markets
3. Availability of development sites
4. Transportation service and networks
5. Education and training opportunities
6. Quality of life
7. Business climate
8. Capital availability
9. Taxes and regulations

These factors are considered by many to be the major factors influencing the location decisions of major corporations. Many of them are also important for business expansion within a community. The factors affecting investment in new indigenous enterprises, however, are very different (Gregerman, 1984a); they are:

1. Supportive fiscal, regulatory, and political climate
2. Supportive business community, including a pool of successful entrepreneurs

3. Skilled local labor force
4. Strong network of technical and professional services
5. Colleges and universities
6. Major corporation and government research and development centers
7. Access to capital; venture capital and commercial banks experienced in lending to nontraditional firms

Internal factors may also be outside the control of community leaders. For example, little can be done about geographical location and distance from a major interstate highway. On the other hand, an internal factor is considered to be a weakness only in the context of external opportunities and threats. There may be situations where strengthening an existing factor may help a community to capitalize on an emerging trend.

Listing Opportunities and Threats. After identifying the significant external and internal factors affecting development in the community, the steering committee proceeds to identify potentially positive or advantageous trends, such as the increase in service jobs, as well as the potentially negative factors, such as the decline in manufacturing employment in certain local industries.

In order to know their community's position, committee members need to systematically list the internal strengths and weaknesses pertaining to each opportunity or threat in a "SWOT" analysis. A community must be correctly positioned to capitalize on internal strengths (S) and to minimize internal weaknesses (W) in order to take advantage of external opportunities for investment (O) and to avoid external threats (T).

A "SWOT" analysis in a midwestern community identified the telemarketing industry as an investment opportunity. An existing strength to address that opportunity was the community's location in the Central Time Zone, which made it possible to cover both coasts during regular working hours. Other strengths were the number of part-time workers from family farms needing supplemental income, the comparatively low cost of land and utilities, and the neutral midwestern accent. An existing weakness was the small population, because most telemarketing firms have a high employee turnover and therefore depend on a relatively large employment base (a population of at least 10,000). In addition, this community was not organized to recruit a telemarketing firm.

The population size, of course, is outside the control of local decision makers. However, it is possible to devote local resources to developing a marketing effort. Ultimately, it is up to the steering committee to decide if this opportunity is sufficiently attractive to justify targeting resources to a marketing plan.

New resources may be needed to support new opportunities, while factors that the committee may regard as historic strengths may actually have become weaknesses because of changes in the external environment (Ansoff, 1985). This caveat underscores the importance of examining internal strengths and weaknesses in light of external forces.

Step Three: Identifying Key Strategic Issues

A strategic issue is a forthcoming development likely to hinder economic growth if no action is taken to address it. However, there may be external opportunities or threats that a community's leaders cannot realistically address, either because of internal factors that are beyond their control or because the investment of resources necessary to convert a weakness to a strength is deemed to be unreasonably high in relation to expected benefits. Thus, identifying strategic issues means identifying opportunities and threats that can be addressed by existing strengths or by converting weaknesses to strengths where feasible.

The steering committee may follow one of several approaches in listing its strategic issues (Bryson and Roering, 1987). For example, the city of Baltimore, joined by its five-county region and the state of Maryland, identified six strategic problems that needed to be addressed (Regional Planning Council, 1986): the changing structure of the industrial sector, the increased connections between education and employment, environmental quality, tax and revenue disparity, racial and socioeconomic disparity, and the condition of transportation and infrastructure.

Step Four: Developing Strategies

The last item on the agenda of the first working session is to develop tentative economic development strategies. The steering committee may have identified a long list of strategic issues, and they must rank those issues to ensure consensus and to avoid pie-in-the-sky strategies that try to accomplish too much with too few resources.

One excellent technique for ranking strategic issues is a matrix exercise, illustrated in Figure 2. The facilitators first assign a letter or number to each strategic issue. Then each steering committee member plots those numbers or letters on a matrix sheet according to two dimensions, first, the importance of the issue to local economic development and second, how well the community is currently addressing the issue. The facilitators then compile the results of the steering committee's "votes" for each issue. Strategic targets are those issues for which the votes are clustered in the top left-hand corner of the matrix: these issues are very important to economic development, but the community is currently performing poorly in addressing them.

Once the committee has developed its list of strategic targets, the final discussion revolves around the goals and objectives underlying those strategies. It is essential for committee members to reflect on what they are trying to accomplish with those strategies. In the midwestern town mentioned above, the strategic target of developing or attracting a telemarketing firm may reflect the broader goals and objectives of diversifying the economic base (an important goal if a community is heavily dependent on a single industry), stabilizing income for family farmers, and preserving family farms in the community.

Most approaches to strategic planning place goal-setting at the beginning of the process. While this sequence is very rational, in actual practice it is extremely difficult for a group of community leaders to reach consensus on values without first discussing concrete information about external and internal factors affecting development. However, after the group has worked through the arduous process of building consensus around specific issues, the goals and objectives implicit in those issues will be easier to clarify. Often, the steering committee will discover that its goals have changed since the beginning of the process.

Figure 2. Ranking Strategic Issues.

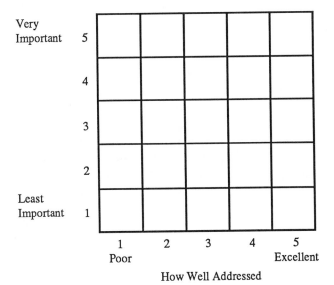

Steps Five and Six: Developing and Implementing the Action Plan

At the second working session, the task before the steering committee is to agree on the specific steps to carry out the most important strategies. First, the strategies identified at the first session are reviewed and modified if necessary. Then action steps are specified; the facilitators can draft an action plan for the committee's consideration, or the steering committee can develop the steps itself at the meeting. It is extremely important at this stage to set specific responsibilities for what will be done, who will do it, and how and when it will be accomplished. If the committee can't agree on these points, then the strategy is either too general or unrealistic.

The action plan may include steps to study a particular issue in greater depth. For example, support services to existing manufacturers may be an opportunity for future economic development; however, before steps are taken to develop such producer-service firms, it may be necessary to survey existing manufacturers in order to identify specific needs. A second example is industrial attraction: the committee may have identified this strategy as a priority, but the first step in implementing that strategy is a targeting study to pinpoint the types of industry that are most appropriate to the local economy.

Chapters Five and Six, which discuss new business formation, expansion, attraction, and retention, describe the steps required to target such opportunities effectively. The steering committee may find that its action plan repeats the strategic planning cycle with a more specific focus: organizing the appropriate individuals and groups for new business formation, assessing the internal factors conducive to new business development, and so on.

Step 7: Monitoring the Action Plan

The actual implementation of the action plan takes many months, sometimes years. During that time it is essential for the steering committee to meet periodically to assess the progress of the action plan, especially what is going well, what is not going well, and what midcourse corrections may be necessary.

Repeating the Planning Cycle

The strategic planning process is iterative in nature; experience gained during implementation will in most cases lead to modification of the action plan. Modifications may include dropping a particular action step because of difficulties marshaling internal resources or community support, or they may involve further targeting of strategic priorities. Three critical questions require assessment after the first strategic planning cycle: (1) What changes have taken place in the community's economic base or population? (2) What new information has been revealed about the community? (3) Which of the initial action steps have been successful or unsuccessful and why? Change in the action plan is not uncommon owing to high levels of uncertainty in the early stages of the process and the need to make assumptions about expected benefits and costs. As those assumptions are tested during the implementation stage, an action plan may prove to be ineffective in some respects. The first and succeeding iterations can uncover data that will refine, refocus, and amplify strategic issues.

State Economic Development Strategic Planning

States develop economic development strategic plans for the same reasons as communities: to understand better their economies, the external trends affecting them, and their competitive advantages and disadvantages compared to other jurisdictions, and to identify investment strategies most likely to promote economic growth. The recession of the mid 1970s prompted the first state strategic plans in Pennsylvania, Michigan, Indiana, and Wisconsin. The 1980s farm crisis was the catalyst for strategic plans in Nebraska, Iowa, and Mississippi. At least fourteen states have drafted some form of an economic development plan (National Association of State Development Agencies, 1987).

The steps followed by these states in formulating economic development plans are similar in many ways to the process described earlier in this chapter.

Organizing. Many states form a commission, executive planning committee, or state planning board made up of representatives from government, business, labor, and education. Some states have relied on a cabinet council or cluster representing different state agencies with responsibilities for economic development (such as labor, education, human services, and development or commerce). Frequently, these policy-level steering committees retain consultants to design the strategic planning process, contribute to the research, and even draw up a draft plan. For example, the executive planning committee in Indiana hired a consulting firm located in Massachusetts, while the cabinet council in Michigan used faculty from the university system to analyze the data and write a report.

External and Internal Analysis. The relevant factors are similar to those discussed earlier in this chapter—economic base, population patterns, industrial and technological trends, and new business formations. (A more comprehensive discussion of these factors is included in Chapter Ten.) The external analysis in Michigan, for example, revealed that the state's manufacturing base, not the service sector, was the key to its economic well-being. In Pennsylvania, on the other hand, the analysis suggested that the state's major competitive advantage was its strong university base and that internal factors were conducive to technology development (National Association of State Development Agencies, 1987).

Strategic Issues and Strategies. One of the major advantages of strategic planning is the identification of potential opportunities and threats to economic growth. For example, Pennsylvania identified in-state business creation and retention as key issues, while in Michigan, the analysis revealed that growth in the postindustrial service sector did not present an opportunity for that state. Nebraska's strategic plan identified its business climate as a strategic concern because of analyses suggesting that the state ranked relatively low in comparison to other states in support for small business (Nebraska Department of Economic Development, 1987). In Ohio, a senior management team from the Bureau of Employment Resources identified several strategic issues related to employment services and economic development, among them coping with federal funds reduction and improving planning and coordination between traditional employment services and the Job Training Partnership Act (Eadie and Steinbacher, 1985).

Action Plan Implementation. In some cases, state strategic plans include an extensive list of specific action steps. For example, the Pennsylvania plan contained sixty-nine specific recommendations. The Rhode Island strategic plan, called the "Greenhouse Compact," asked the voters to endorse twenty programs to revitalize that state's economy, including programs to expand firms paying above-average wages, create a Rhode Island Academy of Science and Engineering, and simplify state and local business regulations (the compact was eventually rejected by the voters). In other cases, the action plan called for more in-depth study of potential strategies. For example, Michigan established four policy/action groups to monitor the state's relative competitiveness with foreign nations, determine what state government can do to fill the competition gap, and develop a multiyear industrial competitiveness plan (National Association of State Development Agencies, 1987).

Important Factors. A review of a wide variety of states' planning efforts by the Oregon Joint Legislative Committee on Trade and Economic Development (1986) identified several key ingredients required for successful strategic planning at the state level:

- The governor's personal and visible commitment
- Private-sector participation, especially in the state's major industries
- Involvement of a wide range of interest groups and stakeholders
- Public and media acceptance of the strategic planning process
- Focus on issues related to the competitiveness and investment opportunities in key sectors of the state's economy
- Updating the strategic plan annually or biennially in step with the state's budget and legislative process in order to develop recommendations for the governor prior to the state agency budget cycle

Conclusion

An effective strategic planning process has broad participation by key stakeholders and promotes a shared understanding of strategic issues. Although there are many variations of the strategic planning process described in this chapter, there is usually a three-step cycle of diagnosis, vision, and action. States and communities must adapt this general process to their unique political and administrative circumstances. Some cities, for example, may take longer to complete this cycle than other cities. As a collaborative process, strategic planning provides a common language and policy framework for making strategic decisions. In addition, it builds commitment by participating leaders to the strategic action plan.

Strategic planning alone will not improve community or state economies. It can, however, greatly enhance the capability of decision makers to formulate and implement effective policies.

Participation and support will make the process work, and that means involving those who make a difference in the community or the state. As federal and state resources become more difficult to obtain, and as competition increases for scarce public dollars, those who are willing to make the effort to organize and target their economic development efforts will have a competitive advantage.

4

Organizing for Strategic Economic Development

Effective economic development strategies must suit a particular social, cultural, physical, and economic environment and must emerge from diagnoses of external trends and assessments of internal capabilities. Once the initial strategies have been formulated, states and communities must develop organizations with the responsibility to implement and evaluate these strategies. Some strategies are more easily pursued through informal organizational settings, others through more formal mechanisms. In either case, the choice of organizational form must be guided by the chosen strategies. The issue is how to organize or realign the state's or community's resources to achieve the strategic goals and objectives. There is no single right way to organize for managing economic development strategically. The organizational structure should be designed to fit the stages of development activity, the environment in which development is likely to occur, and the particular needs facing the state and community.

What makes the organizing effort so challenging is the complex set of interdependent relationships in which economic policy exists. State economic development departments, legislative policy committees, and economic task forces all interact with regional and local public and private agencies, development corporations, and even national and international organizations. This creates considerable overlap, duplication, and confusion over development activities. At the state and local levels, these relationships require new types of formal and informal organizational arrangements. No one agency is responsible for the economy, especially as state and local economies increase their interactions with national and international economic activity. In addition, successful development requires collaborative efforts and coordinated responses to economic opportunities. State and local governments cannot effectively pursue economic development unilaterally. Therefore, effective economic development organizations must facilitate planning with the wide variety of departments involved in economic development activities, integrating economic research with strategic action, and learning from experience.

Designing and managing the economic development organization emerges as a major managerial challenge following a successful strategic planning effort. An effective organization can assume a variety of configurations and can build on existing organizations, reorganize existing organizations to fit current strategies, or build new institutions to adjust to changing conditions and activities. This chapter will discuss approaches to organizing for economic development and factors to consider in building an effective organizational system to implement economic development activities.

Before rushing into creating a development group, an action team, or a line department, consideration should be given to the purposes of the organization and who should participate. An association created for improving downtown would be very different from one created to negotiate with industrial prospects. The first step is to ask what the purpose is to be served. Is it industrial attraction or commercial retention? Will it assist different geographical regions within the state or locality? Is it to facilitate cooperation or actually to package a particular project or investment? Once these types of questions have been answered, the focus should shift to who should participate. In some instances, business representatives would be the major actors. In other situations, a combination of public and private partnerships might be needed. Some organizational objectives can be served only by large umbrella organizations representing all segments of the business world, while others require the participation of only a particular sector of the business community. Organizing a statewide marketing program to promote tourism or product exports would require a broad organizational structure, while a community developing a business improvement district might have much narrower representation.

Advisory and Informal Organizations

Both states and localities use informal groups to achieve economic development strategies. Such groups are important where diverse interests are represented or where the voluntary nature of the project requires less formal structure. For example, several states and local governments are formulating entrepreneurial networks— networks of people that can coordinate the needed investments for new business ventures (Daneke, 1986). In fact, governmental investment in these new networks, according to a study conducted by the Office of Technology Assessment (1984), is a critical element in building a successful high-technology development. Other important elements include an organizational culture that promotes a common civic perspective and a positive attitude about the region's attributes and prospects; an environment that nurtures leaders, both public and private, who combine a track record for innovation with a broad view of their community's resources and promise; and a network of business/civic advocacy organizations that attracts the membership of top officers of major companies and receives from them the commitment of time and effort to work on issues of mutual concern.

Local chambers of commerce and state economic development agencies have created venture capital clubs that informally review prospects for entrepreneurial development and raise capital to provide funding for such efforts. Other informal organizations serve as advisory bodies to another formal body; in five states, governors have created staff task forces to advise on various economic development issues (Clarke, 1986). Ohio's governor uses cabinet clusters as working groups to focus on specific issues. States also have used blue-ribbon panels representing both public and private participants who can help develop strategies for development; state agency personnel often staff these panels. Subject-specific task forces have been used in states such as Nebraska and Alaska to focus on particular areas of concern, while advisory bodies representing particular business interests or particular geographic areas have been a popular mechanism in Arizona and Washington (Clarke, 1986).

Advisory bodies may help defer criticisms about creating another organization or duplicating efforts being made elsewhere. These organizations assist in building support for the strategic goals and objectives of the group when disagreement, dissension, or apathy exists among business or government leaders. Informal organizations also can carry out more traditional planning efforts that help set the stage for actions by the state or community and allow time for public resources to be thoughtfully committed for a longer-term effort.

As described in Chapter Three, strategic analysis and planning at the state and local levels provide a central organizing vision and an overarching framework for coordinating public- and private-sector efforts. Rhode Island, Washington, Michigan, and several other states have established temporary blue-ribbon commissions to develop strategic plans for their economies. The Rhode Island Strategic Development Commission was formed in 1982 with nineteen members and an advisory committee of fifty drawn from business, finance, organized labor, higher education, and government. The staff for the commission included seventy people loaned by their companies, unions, institutions, or government departments. The commission's goal was to develop a statewide consensus on a strategy for economic growth. The state of Washington created an Emergency Commission on Economic Development and Job Creation in 1983, which prepared a 160-page analysis of the state's economy and recommended several economic policy changes. In 1985, the Washington legislature permanently established the Washington Strategic Development Commission to institutionalize the strategic planning process. Washington's commission, appointed by the governor, includes public- and private-sector representatives, has its own full-time staff, and advises the governor and the state legislature on policies and programsto improve the competitive position of Washington's key industries. In many states, such as Nebraska, localities have also developed steering committees and resource teams to carry out community and regional strategic planning efforts (Reed, Reed, and Luke, 1987).

Informal groups do have serious shortcomings. They cannot effectively implement actions they propose. They have no legal standing and therefore cannot carry out development activities themselves. They have no way to raise funds directly and have no formal standing to ensure that their proposals are seriously considered. Nevertheless, temporary, informal associations may be the most effective vehicle for managing economic development when the issues giving rise to the group are narrowly defined, the effort is largely directed at planning and analysis, or the group is used to generate consensus, support, and interest in specific development activities.

Formal Implementing Organizations

Implementing organizations are structured to carry out strategies developed by policymakers. These organizations can be wholly governmental, wholly private, or a combination; yet they often work closely with other organizations at all levels to implement development goals fully.

Public-sector economic development agencies, whether part of the chief executive's staff or a separate line department, add certain strengths to a development effort. First, they can provide public-sector funding that otherwise would not be available to local projects or activities. Second, they can provide tax incentives to promote development efforts that otherwise would not be available to private business. Third, they can provide various types of relief from regulation, often considered a major stumbling block by developers. Fourth, public agencies provide assistance in quality-of-life factors, which appear to be increasingly important to business investment decisions. The quality of state and local school systems, access to cultural activities and recreational facilities, the quality and availability of public facilities and infrastructure, and the crime rate can all have an impact. Fifth, they can provide access to political and professional leadership for major development efforts. Without such support, many investment activities might be more difficult to achieve. Finally, public organizations can help orchestrate state and local government resources directed at assisting development efforts. This coordinating function might be difficult to achieve by limiting implementation only to private or quasi-private entities. Further, many federal, state, and local resources targeted toward development require the approval of state or local governments before they can be used to promote specific projects and activities.

On the other hand, state and local implementing organizations have both constitutional and statutory limitations. They often are constrained by the laws of the state or city; for example, most local governments have limits placed on general obligation municipal debt used to support private initiatives. States often have constitutional limits on their use of public funds for private gain; these limit the ability of public agencies to use such resources for stimulating private investment. Even where such measures are legal, political constraints can make it difficult to use local or state tax dollars for such efforts. Some states have been able to undertake such activities because of dollars made available from the federal government. Federal funding has been greatly reduced, however, and political opposition remains strong.

Local Governmental Structures

In the recent past, most local development efforts were directed by chambers of commerce. This began to change in the 1960s and 1970s as federal dollars were spent in increasing amounts to stimulate local development organizations. The Economic Development Administration funded efforts at the local and regional levels. The Small Business Administration helped support quasi-public and quasi-private organizations.

Localities also have created departments within city hall focused on implementing economic development activities. These departments may be highly specialized or they may incorporate a multitude of development efforts, from enterprise development to housing and community development. They may be a separate line department or part of the mayor's or city manager's staff. Specialized departments are attractive because they can focus their efforts and priorities on economic development. Such departments may lack the resources or interdepartmental coordination to accomplish their tasks, however, because these tasks are divided among several different agencies and departments.

On the other hand, there are several benefits associated with a combined line department. First, the community will have a more integrated development effort where all resources can be coordinated in the implementation of an economic development strategy. Second, it is more likely that public funds can be tailored to particular development needs so that federal, state, and local dollars can be coordinated to deliver a particular product or service affecting economic development. Third, the private sector will have a single focal point and a single source of information to draw on to help assist its efforts or deal with problems hindering its efforts.

The city of St. Paul, Minnesota, created an umbrella agency in 1977 with five divisions: community development, housing, business redevelopment, downtown development, and planning. This agency has had considerable success in implementing a wide range of development projects. Among the strengths cited by the director of this department are its responsiveness to public sentiment, its access to other departments in city hall that are necessary for implementing development activity, and its ability to take a "total development approach" to any area of need within the city (Bellus, 1983).

The major criticism of a combined economic and community development department within a public agency is the dilution of effort. Both public and private executives have argued that combining several functions with economic development in a single office reduces the effectiveness of all those functions. Economic development may need the full attention of a department. Conflicts often develop between housing and community development objectives on the one hand and economic development objectives on the other.

For example, if a city wants to revitalize a particular area, developers may wish to move as quickly as possible in order to reduce costs associated with planning and construction. An economic development department might agree to assist the developer in accomplishing this "fast-track" system. However, planning and community development interests might object to a speeded-up process because their job is to oversee land-use regulations associated with development, such as zoning, subdivision, building codes, and so forth. Placing the economic development function within such a broad department may dilute the advocacy function of economic development within the city or county and make that local government's efforts on behalf of development less effective. This is not to say that local regulations should be dispensed with, but a proper balance of development with local regulation may be difficult if both goals are advocated by one department. Although this concern has been expressed in communities throughout the country, large cities such as Minneapolis, Cleveland, and Omaha have moved toward centralization of their development, planning, and community development functions within one department.

A third approach, placing economic development responsibilities within a mayor's office, can be an attractive option because it clearly signals the commitment of the chief executive to the development effort. It also provides access to the executive that might be impossible to obtain through a line department. Still, many drawbacks also exist. First, this approach may overpoliticize the office and create credibility problems within and outside city hall. Second, it may make implementation difficult when the various line departments control the actual day-to-day operations of local government. Line departments may resent the demands placed on them by the mayor's office and become resistant to implementing activities on its behalf.

Cities in metropolitan areas have another difficulty—ensuring coordination among several jurisdictions pursuing similar development goals. Competition between cities for industrial prospects can waste scarce public resources. Similarly, duplication of small business assistance programs can cause expensive overlapping of services. In many cases, regional councils of governments can play a significant role as managing partners in regional economic development (National Association of Regional Councils, 1987).

An example of multijurisdictional coordination from the West Coast provides an interesting organizational solution to multijurisdictional competition and duplication. The metropolitan area that encompasses the cities of Eugene and Springfield, Oregon, established several interjurisdictional organizations to leverage their individual efforts better. One is the Metro Partnership, a quasi-public joint venture between the two cities and their chambers of commerce that seeks to recruit industries to the metropolitan area that are appropriate to the inherent strengths and weaknesses of the local economy. A second organization, the Business Assistance Network Group (BANG), coordinates the efforts of the cities' various small business assistance programs as well as the efforts of the state's small business development center, located at a nearby community college. These and other interjurisdictional organizations and joint projects can significantly reduce intercity competition while increasing the efficiency of development activities.

State Government Structures

Every state has established an economic development agency, although responsibilities, funding, and staffing patterns vary widely. Thirty-seven states have agencies that are independent of the governor's office and serve line functions. In seven states, the economic development activities are located within the governor's office. Three states have economic development functions organized within a larger organization, and four states use a board or commission to operate economic development activities (Clarke, 1986).

Traditionally, state economic development efforts are administered by one or more of three agencies or departments. The department of commerce is typically responsible for state banking regulations, small business development, insurance, corporations, and various professional and licensing boards; this is the department with which businesses come into contact most often. The department of economic development is typically the lead agency for industrial attraction, tourism, and state promotion. The department of community development is typically responsible for administering the Community Development Block Grant (CDBG) programs, state loan programs, and housing programs.

Line agencies appear to be the most popular implementing structure in state government for the same reasons as local government: they help increase visibility, they show a commitment to business activity, and they institutionalize economic development activities within state government (Clarke, 1986). Like local organizational efforts, line agencies can be specialized (for example, there can be separate agencies for community development, industrial development, tourism, and small business) or comprehensive. States such as Georgia and Pennsylvania separate economic development from community development. Recently, several states have pulled the administration of these functions into a centralized department. The Illinois Department of Commerce and Community Affairs is often cited as an example of a comprehensive development agency because it includes a broad array of functions and activities, among them business management support, export development, marketing, tourism, and job training.

One of the major problems associated with state development organizations is interdepartmental coordination. Intrastate coordinating agencies have been used to help improve cooperation among agencies that have some role in development. They can help improve policy development and policy implementation and they can coordinate resource allocations to various projects and activities. Some states have hired a single person to oversee economic development activity. In Massachusetts, for example, a person in the governor's office oversees the development and implementation of various development initiatives within several state departments (Clarke, 1986).

In addition to increased coordination efforts, state governments are attempting to improve their capacity to respond quickly to emerging developments in a state or regional economy. Neither a state department nor a blue-ribbon strategic planning commission alone can meet the increasing need for a centrally coordinated, rapid response to specific, large-impact economic development problems and opportunities, such as siting a major corporate enterprise or industrial plant. One approach is to establish a Governor's Economic Action Council, consisting of department heads in land use, economic development, transportation, and revenue, that is available at a moment's notice, at the call of the governor, to manage and coordinate the state's responses to large developments. Kentucky has established a "super cabinet" known as the Governor's Commerce Cabinet, a formal group of directors of departments that have the greatest effect on economic development implementation.

Private and Quasi-Private Organizations

There are numerous types of private organizations that have as all or part of their function the planning, development, or implementation of economic development. As with governmental organizations, private associations can focus on planning or on implementation or both. Private organizations are most commonly associated with business groups such as chambers of commerce. In Philadelphia, there are several such organizations involved with economic development. The community has recently created an organization called the Greater Philadelphia First Corporation that focuses local leadership in enterprise development and provides a pool of capital financing for specific development initiatives (Widner, 1983). Private groups may operate for a profit or act as a nonprofit corporation, and the goals and legal powers of the two types of organizations are very different.

For-profit firms must make money to be successful. Efforts that they undertake to spur economic activity should have a risk level low enough to ensure an adequate return on their investment that will produce dividends to their member stockholders. An exception would be a for-profit venture capital corporation, where risk is exceptionally high, but the chance for extremely high profits also exists. If, while the organization achieves its goal of an adequate return on investment, improvements to the local economy occur, this would be an added benefit. Some private organizations have been created for the purpose of stimulating economic development activity as well as to earn profits on their activities. These organizations must balance their public purposes (for example, stimulating state and local economic activity) with their need to earn a profit. A small town in Iowa, for example, held a fund-raising drive for a newly formed for-profit corporation to sell 135 shares of stock at $1,000 per share. The funds went toward the purchase and restoration of several stores downtown and the creation of a mini-mall. Clearly, this activity had both a public purpose and a profit motive. Nonprofit organizations, on the other hand, have as their major goal the promoting of a public purpose or activity. They use private skills and objectives without the overriding goal that spurs private actions in a profit-oriented firm.

Different resources and constraints on the two forms of private organizations are incorporated into state and federal law. Nonprofit organizations have clear tax advantages over for-profit organizations. Donations to nonprofit associations are tax-deductible in most instances, while donations to for-profit organizations are not. For-profit entities, unlike nonprofit agencies, must pay state and federal income taxes on their earnings. In addition, for-profit firms can issue dividends and use any excess assets over liabilities for private gain, while nonprofit organizations must use such resources to further their public purposes or goals. For-profit corporations can raise revenue to further their activities by selling shares of stock in the corporation. Nonprofit organizations raise funds through donations, membership dues, or other types of fund-raising activities, but they do not sell stock.

For-profit and nonprofit organizations also have some similar characteristics. They can obtain capital from private investors to further their activities, for-profit firms by selling stock, nonprofits by raising donations or selling products. Both have access to private bank financing. Both can carry out business-related activities benefiting private parties that public organizations cannot legally perform. For example, both types of private organizations can invest in a private business venture using their own funds. Public organizations would have to show a clear public purpose in doing so under many state laws, while these organizations would not.

Private for-profit and nonprofit corporations are an excellent way to achieve certain economic development goals because they provide flexibility that local public organizations simply do not have. In many ways, the nonprofit private organization may be more useful as an economic development vehicle simply because it may garner stronger public support and its tax advantages are more attractive to donors.

Private corporations also have disadvantages. Unlike governmental entities, private organizations cannot apply directly for many federal and state assistance programs even though they may become the beneficiaries of such programs. In addition, they have none of the taxation or regulatory powers that reside in local state or federal governments. They may also have serious public relations or political limitations in building public support. Local elected officials might find it much easier than a private association to rally public support behind a particular economic development activity.

Public-sector officials can play an important role in how private corporations provide direction to particular economic development strategies. One way to accomplish this is simply to create the organization. In some instances, state or local governments institute the creation of a private corporation. For example, Indiana's Economic Development Council (EDC) was created in 1985 to serve as an umbrella development agency to coordinate and evaluate all economic development policies. The EDC is a publicly chartered but privately incorporated corporation. Although the council includes key actors in the state legislature, it is independent of the state government. This strategy was used because it could facilitate public and private involvement and, more important, be free of political pressures in evaluating the efficacy of the numerous strategic efforts.

At the local level, a city council may also serve as a board of directors for a nonprofit development corporation. Problems can develop under this arrangement, however, if state conflict-of-interest laws are violated by such a relationship. The government can also have a say in who is appointed to the board of directors or a certain number of board seats can be reserved for public officials or public representatives. In this way the state or local government can maintain some control over the actions of the organization.

A second way in which public officials can exert influence over a private development corporation is through the structure of the by-laws of the corporation. In order for private organizations to incorporate, they must develop a set of by-laws or rules of conduct. State and local government officials can make sure that the purposes and actions of the corporation comply with their economic development goals and objectives by making sure the latter are included in the corporation's by-laws. Public officials can also specify how certain funds will be used, the advisory role that state and local officials can play in corporation activities, and the size and makeup of the board of directors through the by-laws.

Finally, control of the purse strings should not be overlooked when organizing a private corporate role for local economic development. Most private corporations that are actively pursuing economic revitalization or economic development strategies are eager to use the myriad federal, state, and local financing tools available for that purpose. Most of these tools require local or state government approval at a minimum and in many cases active government solicitation. This local function can be used as leverage to obtain cooperation by local development corporations in meeting governmental needs and concerns.

While governmental control of private development corporation efforts is not a necessary precursor to successful economic activities, some governmental role in such efforts is helpful. It will force cooperation and communication between the public and private sectors and stimulate joint efforts in creating and implementing development strategies. The government can also act to reduce duplication of effort created by unorganized or proliferating private corporations bent on certain development activities. Many different public and private organizations may exist and the danger of duplication and of operation at cross-purposes is a real and immediate one.

Development Corporations

Many different kinds of development corporations may exist within a state or community. Even though they vary in size, objectives, sources of funds, and specific targets, most share common characteristics: (1) they are incorporated; (2) they are locally initiated and controlled; (3) they have public- and private-sector representation; (4) they operate within a geographically defined target area; (5) they are small, flexible, and concerned with implementation; (6) they have more direct access to capital and fewer limitations on investing than strictly public or private organizations; and (7) they utilize their funding for activities that directly stimulate the formulation, expansion, attraction, or retention of business enterprises. Among the most common forms of development corporations are:

- Industrial development corporations
- Downtown development corporations
- Local development corporations
- Economic development corporations
- Community development corporations
- Housing development corporations

Industrial development corporations (IDCs) are interested in stimulating industrial attraction, retention, or expansion. They may be organized at the state or local level with a broad focus or a narrow focus on a particular geographical or industrial sector for development. Many of these organizations spring from local chamber of commerce efforts. IDCs also tend to be the oldest form of development corporation. The state of Connecticut operates a development authority to issue tax-exempt bonds to provide financing for land acquisition, construction, building improvements, and the purchase of machinery and equipment (Clarke, 1986).

Downtown development corporations (DDCs) are predominantly interested in the central business districts (CBDs) in communities and carry out a number of planning, technical assistance, and financing functions to stimulate downtown development. The Denver Partnership in Denver, Colorado, is an example of such a corporation. This corporation helped organize the financing and development of the 16th Street Mall project in downtown Denver and has worked extensively to increase the availability of housing in that area.

Local development corporations (LDCs) may be all-purpose, carrying out planning and implementation activities for both industrial and commercial projects throughout the community, or focused on particular geographical or business concerns. Many were created to meet the requirements of the Small Business Administration's 503 Program, which provides small business loans for capital where such capital would not be available otherwise. Others were created to carry out other financial packaging programs, including such programs as providing Industrial Revenue Bonds. Philadelphia has a corporation that focuses on a broad array of development activities, including industrial recruitment, financing, and marketing assistance. It has a thirty-two-member board of directors from both the public and private sectors. It acquires and develops business sites, provides financing through tax-exempt bonds and mortgages, helps facilitate private business loans, and helps package development projects (Adell, 1983).

Economic development corporations are similar in most respects to the other corporations discussed previously. These entities serve broad development objectives and are usually directed at service and retail rather than industrial activity.

Community development corporations (CDCs) were originally created as an element of a program funded under the federal Economic Opportunity Act of 1964 (Council for Urban Economic Development, 1984). CDCs have powers and responsibilities like those of other development corporations. Unlike the others, however, they are particularly responsible for spurring economic opportunities in low- and moderate-income areas and for fostering employment-generating development for the poor. According to the Council for Urban Economic Development (1984), CDCs have been organized in a number of different ways. Some act as cooperatives in which neighborhood residents buy shares of the corporation and share in its profits. Others act purely as nonprofit subsidiaries of for-profit corporations; resources from the for-profit entity may be funneled for tax purposes or for community service reasons to the nonprofit CDC.

Whichever organizing method is used, it is clear that these community development corporations are less concerned with profit and stimulating general economic activity than with targeting economic opportunities to the poor and low-income, unemployed and underemployed people within the community. Their mission is much more closely tied than that of other development corporations might be to traditional neighborhood community development efforts. They may also be more heavily subsidized than other organizations because of the nature of their clientele and the amount of assistance needed to stimulate private development in highly disinvested neighborhoods. The Toledo Trustcorp Bank operates a CDC that has invested over $237 million in local development efforts resulting in the creation of over 4,200 jobs. A consortium of Miami banks has organized a CDC to provide debt and equity financing to black-owned businesses in the Liberty City area and throughout Dade County (Sower and Vitarello, 1987).

Housing development corporations (HDCs) exist to stimulate both rental and owner-occupied housing in particular areas. These organizations often work on specific projects such as developing more housing for the elderly or stimulating downtown commercial areas. The tools and structure of the corporation follow the patterns discussed previously.

Conclusion

A multitude of different organizational mechanisms exist to assist states and communities in developing and implementing economic development strategies. No one structure is the right one for all communities. Both states and localities have organized in numerous ways in an attempt to stimulate economic activity. Some organizations are informal or are organized to develop plans and strategies. Others are more formal and focus on implementation. Whether these organizations are at the state or local level, they have certain common characteristics. They may be part of the mayor's or governor's office or they may be independent line agencies. They may be narrowly directed at particular economic development functions and activities or they may be more comprehensive and consolidate a number of activities. Coordination is stressed in many states and localities through the use of interagency task forces or committees. Some chief executives assign members of their staffs to oversee development.

Development organizations also operate through quasi-public and private corporations. These entities often serve to implement development activities that are difficult to accomplish within government for legal or political reasons. These corporations come in many forms, but all serve to help stimulate business activity.

No matter what organizational planning or delivery system is developed, it must be structured to operate within the particular economic environment that exists. These organizations are critical to any successful economic development effort and without them, strategies cannot be implemented effectively.

5

Fostering Small Business
Formation and Expansion

Small and young businesses have assumed a major role in state and local economies. A study done at the Massachusetts Institute of Technology in the late 1970s first drew wide attention to the significant potential of small businesses to generate jobs in the postindustrial economy (Birch, 1979). Since then, studies of state and local economies across the country have shown that the birth of new firms and the expansion of young firms are a significant source of job growth in the 1980s. During 1981 and 1982, for example, all of the 984,000 jobs gained by the U.S. economy were attributable to growth by small firms (White House Conference on Small Business, 1985). A study of the Long Island, New York, economy found that between 1976 and 1982, more than 99 percent of the new jobs created in the local economy were generated by the formation or expansion of small business enterprises (businesses with fewer than twenty employees). By contrast, during those six years, large firms were net job losers (Kamer, 1985).

The White House conferences on small business in 1980 and 1985 produced comprehensive lists of barriers and opportunities for small businesses, providing clarity to small business needs previously considered too diverse to be understood. What has followed is a dramatic increase in appreciation for the role small enterprises play in diversifying and energizing local and regional economies. This chapter will review the research regarding small business development. The benefits to the community's economy of small businesses will be discussed. Common barriers to formation and expansion will be identified, and examples of strategies for overcoming barriers will be presented.

Benefits of Smaller Enterprises

Since the late 1970s, small business enterprises have clearly been the major source of job growth. A survey of mayors of cities with more than 30,000 people concluded that small business is more important than big business to a city's overall economic health (Touche Ross, 1985). In addition to being the major source of new jobs, small businesses provide a number of tangible benefits to states and communities, creating ripple effects throughout the regional economy.

Job Generation. In a study of 5.6 million businesses between 1969 and 1976, David Birch (1979) found that two-thirds of all new jobs were created by firms with twenty or fewer employees and 80 percent were created by firms with 100 or fewer employees. Specifically, his research indicated that:

- small, independent firms, despite their difficulties in obtaining capital and their inherently high death rates, are the major generators of new jobs in the economy;
- employment growth in regions owing to migration of establishments from one state to another is virtually negligible;
- few of the net new jobs are generated by larger, well-known corporations;
- job losses each year are about the same in every region of the country; and
- small firms are almost four times more likely to expand than to contract, and larger firms are 50 percent more likely to shrink than to grow.

These findings confirmed earlier, less heralded studies by the Urban Institute that established that small, relatively young businesses dominate the marketplace in job generation. Investigating the decline of private-sector jobs in central business districts, Miller (1977) found that small companies expand more rapidly, usually experience faster growth in sales, and expand the number of jobs more quickly than larger firms. Small businesses are particularly relevant to central business districts because they operate on smaller parcels of land and can utilize older buildings, thus reducing the need for large industrial parcels. A 1976 study by the American Electronics Association aimed at measuring growth rates of electronics firms found new start-up businesses (less than five years old) had a growth rate 115 times that of mature companies (more than twenty years old). The average employment growth rate for developing companies (five to ten years old) was fifty-five times the growth rate of mature firms; and firms between ten and twenty years old had growth rates twenty to forty times the rate of older firms (Schweke, 1985).

In quick succession after Birch, others confirmed the importance of small business enterprises in the national economy. Stahrl Edmunds (1980), evaluating 1970–1977 data from the U.S. Department of Labor and the *Fortune* 500, concluded that 94 percent of the job generation in those years was attributable to smaller businesses. Armington and Odle (1982) found that small independent firms less than four years old created only 50 percent of the new jobs. However, when new subsidiaries of larger companies were counted with small independent enterprises, as in Birch's study, the figure jumps to nearly 80 percent. Data maintained by the U.S. Department of Commerce show a dramatic increase in the percentage of new jobs generated nationwide by small enterprises with fewer than 100 employees, from 51 percent in 1976–1980 to a high of nearly 100 percent in 1980–1984 (Kirchhoff, 1986).

Studies in several states have confirmed similar growth patterns in the state and local levels, in particular since the 1981–1982 recession. Between 1980 and 1982, for example, Oregon lost 5 percent of its total employment, mostly in large corporations, while companies with fewer than twenty workers grew by 9 percent (Cortwright, 1988). Another study of Seattle and King County, Washington, showed that 73 percent of new jobs were created by firms with nineteen or fewer employees and that 100 percent of all new jobs were generated by establishments in existence for less than four years and local in origin (Birch, 1985). Although the growth of small businesses varies among states and localities, many regional economies are based on small businesses with the bulk of new jobs generated by the formation of new businesses and the expansion of young businesses.

Technological Innovations. Small business enterprises play a critical role in stimulating technological innovations. An early study for the National Science Foundation found that smaller enterprises created two and a half times more innovations than larger companies (Gellman Research Associates, 1976). Follow-up research concluded that small businesses create more innovations per employee than large companies (Gellman Research Associates, 1982) and generate more innovations per dollar of research and development expenditure (National Science Board, 1977).

Economic Diversity. Adam Smith noted over two centuries ago that a regional or local economy is healthier if it consists of twenty firms each with 100 employees than if it has two firms each with 1,000 employees. Smith emphasized that the real wealth of nations comes not from the size of firms but from their numbers. Smallness tends to create diversity and competition, whereas largeness tends to stifle them (Whitelaw, 1986). Diversity reduces the vulnerability of a state or local economy to unforeseen events and helps attenuate economic downturns during normal business cycles. During times of stagnant regional economies, smaller, younger firms are a particularly important source of employment growth.

Responsiveness to the Community. Homegrown, locally owned industries tend to have a stake in the city and to identify with the surrounding community, leading to more involved corporate citizenship. Industries recruited from outside are absentee-owned and play much smaller roles in local affairs. The greater activism of smaller, locally owned businesses is particularly important to governments, especially in an era of diminishing government revenues, when the private sector is more willing to help address public problems.

Local Spending. Profits from smaller, locally owned businesses typically remain in the state. On the other hand, recruited industries, not locally owned, export large shares of their company profits back to their corporate headquarters (Raab, 1987).

Stability. Branch plants and corporations with out-of-state headquarters are more likely to relocate than smaller enterprises. They are more footloose, less tied to a geographical location, and subject to continual recruitment efforts by other states. In addition, larger companies can be more vulnerable to corporate restructuring and adverse effects of mergers and acquisitions. A recent study of the lumber industry also found that locally owned small manufacturing firms are less likely to close their plants during recessionary times (Hubbird, 1987). Locally owned firms, especially employee-owed enterprises, showed significantly more stability because of a greater willingness to accept marginally lower profits rather than close their doors.

Changes Favoring Younger, Smaller Enterprises

It is easier to understand this recent surge in the importance of new business formation and expansion when it is examined within a larger context of recent economic and political changes.

Deregulation. The deregulation of major American industries, begun in the 1970s and accelerated during the Reagan administration, stimulated the formation and expansion of many businesses. In the trucking industry, for example, more than 13,000 new companies have started since 1980. The deregulation of airlines resulted in the formation and expansion of many small commuter carriers, as well as the more visible mergers between the larger airlines. A notable example is the deregulation of long-distance telephone services and the breakup of American Telephone and Telegraph (AT&T), which stimulated the rapid development of competing long-distance carriers, a multiplicity of regional phone companies, and a wide variety of advanced technology- and communications-based spin-offs. The number of start-ups in deregulated industries increased 25 percent between 1980 and 1983, more than double the 11 percent increase in new start-ups in all industries (Levinson, 1985).

Delayering and Displacement. Stimulated initially by the recession of the early 1980s, larger corporations eliminated significant numbers of middle-level managers and executives. Companies forced to tighten their belts reacted first by laying off the middle-level employee, a strategy considered much less disruptive than closing down entire divisions or branches ("The Shrinking of Middle Management," 1983). For example, the shakeout in the telecommunications industry that resulted from the AT&T divestiture caused a significant decline in middle-level employment at Northwest Bell (Boyle, 1986a) and other telephone subsidiaries. This trend of "delayering" in the industrial or corporate hierarchy released scores of middle- and upper-level managers into the workplace of self-employment and new venture creation. New companies were increasingly formed by business and professional workers who had lost their jobs and were forced to take advantage of their early retirement.

Both technological forces and economic necessity have forced a significant cut in middle-management staffs of such traditional industries as Firestone (a 20 percent cutback), Crown Zellerbach (a 20 percent reduction), and Chrysler (a 40 percent cut) ("The Shrinking of Middle Management," 1983). Compounding this was an exodus of women from larger corporations. The number of new businesses started by women increased 74 percent in the ten-year period ending in 1984, compared to a 24 percent increase in new businesses started by men. Women have become increasingly disenchanted as they bump up against the "glass ceiling," an invisible barrier that keeps women from senior-level positions in large corporations.

New Work Force. The 1980s also witnessed the emergence of a work ethic that placed individual opportunity and reward ahead of corporate loyalty. A new breed of "gold-collar workers" has emerged (Kelley, 1985), "knowledge-workers" who are skillful in managing information. The gold-collar worker creates wealth through the use of his or her mind and typically jumps at new opportunities. This new work force is in stark contrast to the "organization man" who gravitated to the large corporate organizations in the 1950s (Whyte, 1956).

Expanded Service Sector. The service sector has been, and will be into the 1990s, the fastest-growing employment sector. Ninety-seven percent of services-producing businesses have fewer than 100 employees; one out of every two service workers is employed by a small firm, whereas only one out of every four manufacturing employees is in a small firm. In addition, services-providing enterprises can start and grow with less start-up capital. It is far easier to finance a new computer software firm than it is to form a new machinery or production firm.

Reduced Economies of Scale. Large manufacturers are increasingly subcontracting to smaller companies. Large government agencies are similarly contracting with smaller, private firms to produce public services. This trend is fueled by the expectation of lower labor costs, reduced overhead, and increased flexibility. Economies of scale historically achieved by expanding a firm's size seldom emerge today, when companies must be quick to adapt to rapidly changing markets and new developments in technology. Although economies of scale can still be found, largeness no longer automatically means reduced costs. This is one reason that the number of businesses with fewer than twenty employees increased while the number of large firms actually declined in the early 1980s.

New Venture Creation and Enterprise Development

Enterprise development refers to the formation and expansion of small business entreprises by an individual or a group, ranging from self-employment to companies that employ up to twenty people. The process of new venture creation, however, is complex. Small businesses vary widely and can be structured as sole proprietorships, family-owned businesses, joint ventures, new profit centers within corporations, cooperatives, and new independent corporations.

Essentially, venture creation is the organizing and managing of new organizations and usually follows six steps. A person or group locates a business opportunity, accumulates resources, builds an organization, produces products and services, markets the products and services, and responds to government and society

(Gartner, 1985). The process of starting a new business is, however, not a single, well-worn path followed by all entrepreneurs (Hartman, 1983). There are nearly a dozen different types of entrepreneurs (Vesper, 1979), and entrepreneurs in certain industries are different from those in other industries (Cooper and Dunkelberg, 1981). The old perspective—that entrepreneurs and their ventures are a homogeneous population following an unvarying course of enterprise development—has not held up under close scrutiny during the 1980s.

There are many definitions of entrepreneurship, and none is commonly accepted. There is widespread agreement that entrepreneurs are different from nonentrepreneurs and that what distinguishes entrepreneurial from nonentrepreneurial firms is the rate of innovation and new product introduction. Not every new small business is entrepreneurial, however; only enterprises that introduce an innovation are considered entrepreneurial (Drucker, 1985). Small business enterprises thus vary considerably, and the environments and markets they respond to are similarly diverse.

Research on new business start-ups by both entrepreneurs and nonentrepreneurs has identified three key dimensions in venture creation. First, persons with expertise initiate a new venture (the personal dimension). Second, an organizational entity is established that evolves over time, taking more than a year (the organizational dimension). Third, the new venture seeks out resources and responds to its environment (the ecological dimension) (Van de Ven, Hudson, and Schroeder, 1984). State and local policy can most easily influence the ecological dimension—the environment—of new venture creation. It is certainly less able to affect the personal dimension—the psychological traits, leadership styles, and management goals of the entrepreneurs—and the organizational dimension of a new venture.

In a review of seventeen research studies on environmental variables, Bruno and Tyebjee (1982) found twelve factors that influenced new venture creation:

- Venture capital availability
- Presence of experienced entrepreneurs
- Technically skilled work force

- Accessibility of suppliers
- Accessibility of customers or new markets
- General governmental influences
- Proximity to universities
- Availability of land or facilities
- Accessibility of transportation
- Attitude of area population
- Availability of supporting services
- Quality of life

These twelve variables provide an excellent starting point for assessing the climate for enterprise development. All small businesses, however, do not necessarily have the same strengths and suffer from different constraints. State and local policymakers may tend to lump all small enterprises together. To get an accurate assessment of influences on formation and expansion of enterprises, policymakers must look at individual sectors in the local and state economy. Such tools as export base analysis, shift-share analysis, and business formation trends, discussed in Chapter Three, can provide useful sector-oriented information.

Barriers to Formation and Expansion of Business Enterprises

Policymakers who have identified small business formation and expansion as a strategic goal must first identify the unique problems of younger, smaller businesses located in their community and state. In general, national and regional studies indicate that the most frequently cited barriers to formation and expansion of business enterprises depend on Bruno and Tyebjee's (1982) first two variables: they are the shortage of both debt and equity capital and the need for managerial and technical support.

Capital Availability. Unfortunately, persons starting new ventures find it difficult to obtain sufficient start-up capital through debt or equity financing. The most common sources of start-up capital are personal savings and loans from family, friends, and associates. A nonrandom national survey conducted by *Venture* magazine that collected the responses of 1,305 entrepreneurs found that start-up capital for 54 percent of their new businesses came primarily from personal savings. Bank loans accounted for start-up capital in only 14 percent of the new enterprises; loans from friends and relatives were used to finance new ventures 11 percent of the time; and in the remainder, start-up capital was provided by venture capital investors (4 percent) or other finance sources (Madlin, 1985). These figures closely resemble the responses of a more scientific university survey of a cross-section of 1,805 small businesses, in which 47 percent cited personal savings as the most important source of start-up capital (Cooper and Dunkelberg, 1981).

Other studies confirm these findings. Because of the inherent risks involved in new business formation, most financial institutions are reluctant to invest in new or young enterprises. Newer, smaller businesses are often unable to satisfy their capital needs through conventional private-sector financial institutions; new businesses are therefore heavily dependent on personal savings, loans from family, friends, and associates, and traditional forms of collateral such as home ownership. Clearly, insufficient availability of capital is a critical stumbling block to enterprise development. But the capital needs of new enterprises depend on a variety of factors that make it difficult to make generalizations that can guide public policy.

One factor is the economic sector of the business. Some industrial sectors are more capital-rich than others, which must be taken into account. Electronics-related business firms receive nearly 60 percent of all venture capital invested in the United States; health care businesses receive 11 percent, and the rest is spread rather thinly across other sectors (Daniels, 1985).

A second factor is the geographical region. States are usually characterized by several distinct economic regions, each with different levels of population, income, employment growth, and business sectors. Capital needs are, of course, higher in regions experiencing economic shock or decline. New firms starting in regions with healthier economies will have easier access to financial capital than those in depressed regions.

A third factor is the firm's stage of development. Small firms require different kinds of capital during various stages of their development. Therefore, an analysis of capital needs for new enterprises in a state or community must consider the demand for and supply of different types of capital. These include:

- Research and development capital for the development of a new product and process technology
- Seed capital to move the innovation from initial research to commercial application
- Short-term capital (generally for one year or less), including working capital for financing inventory and accounts receivable; this is particularly critical to rapidly growing firms that have difficulty generating working capital with personal sources
- Intermediate-term capital (generally for one to ten years) used primarily for permanent working capital or for equipment purchase
- Long-term capital (generally for ten to twenty-five years) to finance the acquisition of land, plant, and equipment (Daniels, 1985)

A fourth factor is local variation in capital markets. There are four capital markets that influence business formation and expansion, and these four markets vary from state to state. The commercial lending market—the publicly regulated commercial banks, thrifts, insurance companies, and pension funds—contains the bulk of the investment capital. The generally conservative nature of commercial lending practices, however, reduces the amount of risk capital made available to start new business enterprises. Commercial lending institutions are less willing to finance small, new businesses, often citing "undercapitalization" as a reason for denying credit for start-up capital. The formal venture capital market is limited to certain advanced technology sectors, such as computers, electronics, and biotechnology. It is often limited to metropolitan regions, and it has narrow financing targets, generally investing $2-3 million, and seldom less than $500,000, per enterprise. Venture capital firms have recently become less venturesome. They are putting a smaller share of their new investments into new enterprises and more into seemingly safer leveraged buyouts (Jacobs, 1985). The public equity market, financing enterprises through public offerings of stock, is similarly limited and narrowly focused.

The informal investment market typically fills many of the gaps in the capital market left by the formal venture capital and public equity markets. Recent research in the informal investment market yields an informative glimpse of the investors who choose this market. Informal investors invest smaller amounts than other segments of the risk capital market, $50,000 on average. Because they frequently invest in conjunction with other informal investors, they can also meet the need for somewhat larger financings. The total amount of investment in a single firm often approaches $250,000 to $500,000, the minimum investment of professional venture capital funds. Informal investors are more likely than other segments of the capital market to invest in start-ups and very young firms. However, a significant minority also invest in established firms. They tend to invest close to home, usually within 300 miles. They prefer the manufacturing sector, particularly high-technology and industrial products, although they show interest in a wide range of industrial sectors. Informal investors tend to be more patient investors than professional venture capitalists, exhibiting a willingness to maintain their holdings for longer periods, frequently in excess of ten years. Finally, individual investors often are influenced in investment decisions by such nonfinancial considerations as creating jobs, developing socially useful technology, supporting female and minority entrepreneurs, and assisting entrepreneurs to build successful enterprises. In some cases, they are willing to accept lower returns in exchange for these nonfinancial rewards (Daniels, 1985, p. 41).

Management and Technical Assistance. The second most significant cause of small business failures is lack of entrepreneurial or managerial expertise. Such expertise can become the missing link that ensures sound investments of start-up capital. New business owners often require assistance in developing their markets and taking advantage of local, state, and federal resources aimed directly at small business. Most new and expanding companies need two specific types of assistance: general management assistance and scientific or technical assistance. Managerial knowledge and capacity include such diverse areas as personnel, marketing, accounting, finance, and business law. The particular type of expertise required is specific to each company and sector. A lack of expertise in these areas, however, often leads to constraints on the formation and growth of firms. Scientific knowledge and ability cover specific areas such as engineering, product design, and materials testing. The differences between management assistance and technical assistance can become blurred to the business owner. Nevertheless, managerial problems are distinct from scientific and technical problems and require different types of assistance. Two common strategies used by state and local governments to provide both kinds of assistance are the establishment of business incubators and small business development centers.

A small-business incubator provides an environment designed to increase the survival and expansion rates of new and young small business enterprises. Incubators typically provide management assistance, rents below the market rate, flexible space, and shared services. Successful facilities "incubate" a business for a certain period of time, perhaps from two to four years; the businesses then move into the community. Incubators are springing up around the country, using abandoned warehouses and farm-equipment stores, vacant school buildings, or newly built industrial park facilities to provide low-cost space in a cloistered environment for start-up firms. Usual incubator services include a receptionist, a janitor, and secretarial help, often included in the price of the rent. Some incubators build into the base rent a little "draw-off" to be placed in a revolving loan fund or venture capital fund for incubator tenants. According to many incubator managers, on-site technical and managerial services such as bookkeeping, accounting, and loan packaging are the most critical forms of assistance.

Another key characteristic of successful incubators is a high degree of tenant interaction. Informal discussions among tenants allow the exchange of information and support. These linkages also extend beyond the incubator; in St. Paul, for example, incubator enterprises are given first opportunity to supply city government purchasing needs through targeted city procurement. In this way, the incubator enterprises can provide products that the community might otherwise import (Evans and others, 1985).

There are generally four types of incubators: private non-profit, private for-profit, university-affiliated, and local-government-operated. No two incubators are alike; each is tailored to the unique economic conditions and small business needs of the community (Temali and Campbell, 1984). While most were started in urban areas, many have been successfully established in small cities and towns, such as Bennington, Vermont (population 16,000), Binghamton, New York (population 55,000), Meadville, Pennsylvania (population 15,544), Rolla, Missouri (population 14,000), and Greenville, Mississippi (population 41,000) (Atkinson, 1986).

Small business development centers (SBDCs) are one-stop shopping centers for the new small business owner as well as the successful entrepreneur. There are several hundred SBDCs at community colleges and universities across the country, jointly funded by federal, state, and local governments. They provide individualized consulting and assistance as well as broader educational programs to small business owners. SBDCs typically provide counseling by college faculty and professional consultants, business training through a wide variety of workshops and seminars, technical assistance and support through print and electronic resources, and referral services. Counseling and information are usually free, while fees are often charged for classes, seminars, and workshops (see Chapter Eight).

Identifying and Removing Strategic Barriers

Business formation and expansion are most often constrained by the lack of two resources, knowledge and capital. Barriers to formation and expansion, however, vary from community to community and from state to state. Each region must identify region-specific barriers to enterprise development and strategic goals for encouraging new business formation.

Statewide Assessment. One approach to stimulating formation and expansion is to remove barriers that hinder all small businesses in a state or community. Oregon provides an example of an assessment by private-sector representatives to identify barriers to small business development. As a part of a statewide economic development summit in 1986, discussions were held by the state's industry representatives, chamber of commerce executives, and small business owners. Small business formation and expansion were identified as one of six key issues for statewide economic development. An assessment by this private-sector group identified several issues of concern to small business owners and managers in Oregon (Council for Economic Development in Oregon, 1987), many of which were later addressed by the state legislature.

According to their assessment, general business liability insurance appeared excessive, particularly product liability insurance. Insurance premiums seemed prohibitive to many small businesses, causing the loss of product lines and unemployment. Solutions identified for further examination included tort-law reform and changes in the state regulation of the insurance industry.

Worker's compensation was ranked as another deterrent to job creation. A nationwide survey showed that Oregon ranked high in worker's compensation benefit costs as a percentage of total wages. Solutions suggested for policy discussion included stream-lining paperwork requirements, increasing the flexibility of regulations applied to small firms, developing tiered rates for assigned-risk pools to reflect the real risk of individual participants, allowing the grouping of small businesses for insurance purposes, and replacing the schedule of benefits for injured workers with a formula that would compensate them on an actual wage-loss basis.

The federal tax reform of 1986 broadened the base of taxable income, causing substantial differences between state and federal tax law. In addition, business owners felt that government too often looked to taxpayers for additional state revenues rather than reducing public expenditures. Solutions discussed as possible alternatives included enacting legislation to bring Oregon tax law into conformity with federal law, identifying high-cost state government services and seeking audits to identify cost-saving reforms, and repealing the statutory limit of $7,000 on the deduction of federal taxes from Oregon personal income to avoid double taxation.

Barriers to the formation of private capital funding identified at the statewide summit include unrealistic and complex security regulations, limitations on the use of revenue loans and development fund loans, the high cost of administering complex state and federal loan programs, and the lack of incentives for private investment. It was generally agreed by the private-sector representatives that increased attention was needed for encouraging capital formation for start-up or expanding firms. Solutions suggested for possible policy changes included simplifying government security regulations and requirements for Oregonians investing in Oregon enterprises, enacting legislation enabling Oregon businesses to market their securities in capital-rich states, modifying tax laws to create incentives for investing in Oregon securities, and changing the requirements for borrowing from the Oregon Business Development Fund.

Targeting Specific Sectors. Some small businesses are budding large businesses. Some, however, will forever remain small. Every state has its premier homegrown company that grew out of one resident's garage or storefront to be a national or multinational corporation. California has TRW; although its corporate headquarters are now in Ohio, it began in a garage in a Los Angeles suburb as a spin-off from Hughes Aircraft. Oregon has Nike Inc. running shoes, and Nebraska has Godfather's Pizza. But the reality is that the majority of small enterprises will remain small. Although people tend to lump them all together into a homogeneous group, small businesses do not necessarily have much in common. Smallness by itself does not necessarily identify those enterprises that have potential for growth. Stimulating economic diversification through enterprise development eventually requires targeting certain sectors or types of small businesses that have high potential for growth in the state or community.

First, economic development should build on local strengths. Predicting which economic sectors and enterprises will generate high-growth businesses and which will not is difficult. Identifying the right targets for small enterprise development requires a community first to assess the strengths of its existing economic base. The city of Omaha, for example, is one of the few cities in the world that has its major downtown corporations, medical center, and university linked by laser-powered fiber optics. These provide a fertile telecommunications infrastructure for spawning small enterprises that rely on such fiber-optics technology. Policies in Omaha that target this type of telecommunications enterprise can build on local strengths and stimulate business formation more easily than policies targeting, for example, petroleum-based enterprises (which might be more appropriate to Tulsa or Houston) or timber-based enterprises (which would be more effective in the Pacific Northwest).

Second, communities should not become preoccupied with high-tech enterprises. In the rush to stimulate new business formation, many localities may prematurely focus on high-tech development. Led by the glamour of high-tech entrepreneurial firms like Apple Computer, Inc., policymakers can turn too quickly to high-tech development. Small businesses, however, include health care agencies, frozen or packaged food producers, and family-run shoe stores as well as innovative computer software companies. Small business development is not synonymous with high-tech development. Although most high-tech firms start out small, relatively few small business start-ups are in high-tech areas such as software and biotechnology. Between 1982 and 1984, the bulk of small business start-ups nationally were in such industries as child care, construction, and trucking. Computer and data-processing services accounted for 120,000 new jobs nationwide, while nearly four times that number were generated by bars and restaurants (Levinson, 1985).

Third, communities should target specific companies. In addition to targeting certain sectors that have high potential for new enterprise formation, communities need to identify local enterprises that have high potential for exports, reduce the need to import goods into the region, or generate innovative products and display potential for accelerated market penetration. Goods and services sold outside the local economy bring new money and wealth into the region. This export expansion strategy can accelerate the creation of new wealth locally. Goods and services that are currently being imported from outside the region can be replaced with locally produced goods and services. This import substitution strategy reduces economic "leakage" from the community or state (Jacobs, 1984). Finally, enterprise growth occurs when business owners discover innovative goods and services that can enter markets previously dominated by larger companies and destroy current market shares. This process, first described by Joseph Schumpeter (1934), is known as the process of "creative market destruction": the creation of wealth by destroying existing market structures.

Small, innovative companies form and grow by creatively destroying current market shares. A good example is Godfather's Pizza, initially owned by Willie Theisen, which developed a combination of innovations—a new pizza recipe, self-serve style, and a unique and consistent restaurant motif. With this combination, Godfather's entered the restaurant franchise business in 1976 and became the fastest-growing restaurant franchise in the United States in just six years. During that time, large pizza chains such as Shakey's Pizza and Pizza Inn experienced considerable loss of market share, and the other industry great, Pizza Hut, was forced to reorganize. At the same time, the entire pizza restaurant industry experienced a spurt in growth. Godfather's stimulated creative destruction; it entered the market with successful innovations, changed the market structure by eroding the market share of established large firms, and expanded the pizza restaurant market by appealing to a larger segment of the population (Kirchhoff, 1986).

Efforts to stimulate formation and expansion of enterprises must aim at reducing constraints on growth to allow smaller businesses to grow more rapidly. Whereas general strategies for formation and expansion are appropriate at the state level, as in the example of Oregon discussed above, localities may focus efforts on potential high-growth businesses. In 1983, St. Paul, Minnesota, started its Homegrown Economic Project to diversify its economy through stimulating and nurturing local homegrown enterprises. The city identified strategic industry sectors and from ten to twenty-five potential business enterprises that could be developed or expanded.

Cleveland provides another example of such targeting. In 1982, Cleveland Tomorrow developed a four-point strategic plan for stimulating the city's revitalization (Shatten, 1985). The plan's goals were to retain the existing manufacturing base through improved productivity and quality of work life in area factories; foster new business development through advanced technology and entrepreneurship; assist in the physical rebuilding of the central city through better planning, organization, and support of catalytic projects; and assure essential public support in education, economic development, public financing, and infrastructure.

In developing action plans for the second strategic goal, Cleveland developed a list of prospective growth businesses by assessing private-sector industry forecasts and government analyses. From this assessment, it was concluded that a new business formation plan must include two components: targeted efforts to strengthen dramatically the communities' science and technology base, and a sustained commitment to foster a more entrepreneurial environment in the community.

Technology development was considered a critical factor in the region's economy. Although Cleveland already possessed a substantial research and development and knowledge base, it was largely in mature industries such as the rubber industry and in automotive research, rather than in growth sectors such as pharmaceuticals, electronics, and aerospace.

An innovative, entrepreneurial environment was identified as a necessary part of technology development to capture locally the commercial spin-offs of scientific research. Further analysis indicated that for an environment supportive of new business formation in advanced technology, four specific elements were needed: research facilities with a culture that facilitated spin-offs, a support system (artificial or market-driven) that encouraged entrepreneurs, ready access to early risk capital, and a critical mass of similarly oriented companies to nurture and sustain growth.

Small Local Government-Small Business Collaboration. Smaller cities and towns in particular should examine small business development in their strategic planning. Small businesses and small local governments share certain characteristics that facilitate active collaboration and cooperative ventures. These include a grass-roots status that allows both local governments and small businesses to maintain close contact with the public; a smallness that encourages experimentation with new ideas, products, or services; a feeling that their position or rank is at the bottom of their respective sectors and, at times, a feeling that they are forgotten; a lack of financial resources that creates significant barriers to growth, and an awareness of their resources' limits; and a frustration brought on by interaction with the larger bureaucracies in the private and public sectors.

Five significant barriers to small business growth—limited access to capital, discriminatory taxation, the high cost of government regulation and paperwork, inflation and high interest rates, and shortage of management personnel—are faced by many local government agencies as well. Certainly, the tax-collecting abilities of small cities are greatly overshadowed by the income tax at the federal and state levels. While small firms claim a disproportionate impact from business taxes, small cities increasingly face the problem of constitutional and statutory restrictions on their revenue-generating capacity. Similarly, city officials would agree that the costs associated with government regulation and paperwork at the state and federal levels are high. Small businesses face problems of competitive disadvantages (for example, volume discounts by larger companies). Local governments face a similar problem of limited powers relative to state and federal government.

The shared characteristics of limited size and power suggest that a closer and more productive alliance might be formed between small cities and small businesses. Community leaders need to gain insight into the problems of the small business entrepreneur to develop a foundation for working together.

Conclusion

Young enterprises are the key to generating economic growth. They can provide a state or local economy with the bulk of its job growth and innovation. During the 1960s and 1970s, states' development strategies typically centered on large businesses or big industries. Today, states and localities must stimulate greater diversity with increased numbers of small businesses. Small business enterprises are now an important investment for cities and towns, and tapping their potential to create jobs and wealth is the challenge for state and local economic development.

This challenge suggests a more active role for local government in enterprise development. Targeting local government resources and regulations to stimulate new business formation and expansion requires a strategic analysis to determine the appropriate sector or types of firms on which to focus. Assistance should be provided to enterprises that are more likely to grow, such as innovative businesses that have high potential for creative market destruction. This expanded role in small business development, although it appears to be a dramatic departure from traditional industrial recruitment, does not require a major reorientation of perspective at the local government level. Similarities between local governments, especially small cities, and small businesses create tremendous potential for understanding and partnership.

General interventions to increase the spirit of entrepreneurship can enhance the small business environment. There are a variety of actions that can be taken locally: enhancing the climate for small businesses by targeting city policies and streamlining local permit processes to encourage business expansion, stimulating investment by the private sector in new and growing business enterprises, and establishing incubators to facilitate small business development. At the state level, general interventions into the business climate can be aimed at improving access to financial capital through deregulation of commercial finance institutions and new tax policies aimed at the informal investment market. It is extremely difficult to assess accurately the success or failure of these public policy interventions. However, it must be emphasized that any strategic action must be tailored to the state and local economy and based on an analysis of economic strengths, weaknesses, and barriers to enterprise development.

6

Attracting and Retaining
Business Enterprises

Among the most common goals of economic development is the attraction of new businesses into the state and community. Since the 1930s, creating new jobs by industrial recruitment has enjoyed considerable favor as a way to stimulate economic development. Interest in attracting new industrial manufacturing firms has continued because they provide goods that are largely exported outside a region and they therefore can have a dramatic, sometimes immediate, impact on employment and income levels.

However, as pointed out earlier, industrial attraction may be the least effective approach for many states and communities because of the changing nature of the U.S. economy and the smaller number of industrial relocations in the 1980s. Industrial attraction has been recently criticized for several reasons. One criticism is that subnational industrial attraction merely moves industry from one location within a region to another and thus does little to actually create new jobs. Another criticism is that it creates competition among cities and states that can ultimately damage the local tax structure and shift business costs to state and local governments or to existing local businesses. Such costs often outweigh the economic benefits gained from an industry's relocation in a state or locality. For example, if the practice were carried to its logical conclusion, states would eliminate corporate taxes so they could compete for manufacturing firms on an equal basis. While the benefits of such a strategy are open to question, the costs are substantial. There is considerable evidence that "as the bidding wars among states and localities heat up, it is not clear that the increased economic activity which the industrial location incentives attract pays its own way" (Rubin and Zorn, 1985, p. 334). On the other hand, if a state does not offer an inducement to attract firms, it can be at a disadvantage compared with other states. These findings have led to a renewed interest in two areas: the enlargement of attraction efforts to include service and wholesale/retail trade businesses, and increased attention to business retention.

Service and retail/wholesale trade attraction is particularly appropriate where firms have the potential to export goods and services outside the region. There are two general problems in attracting service enterprises, however. First, the service sector is difficult to define. The U.S. Census Bureau treats it as a residual category that includes all employment sectors except manufacturing, mining, construction, and agriculture. Second, many service firms do not export, but rather recirculate local wealth. An example of such a business would be a local accounting firm that serves only local clients. If, however, that firm expands its business to include individuals and corporations beyond its community, it can become a net exporter of services and thus bring new dollars and jobs into the state. Retail services tend to be local in nature and therefore are seen as having less influence on local economic conditions. However, regional retailing efforts such as direct mail can provide a major expansion in local economic activity.

State and local governments are also finding the retention of existing businesses increasingly important. While this is more difficult and less visible, the local impact may be substantial, especially in areas facing serious economic decline. Retention is an attractive economic development goal because it can maintain jobs and income for the community and it can open the opportunity for expansion should the productivity of these businesses increase in the future. Although the bulk of new jobs are created by new and expanding businesses, the closing of a company in a small community can be devastating. This chapter discusses the necessary steps in a successful attraction and recruitment program for traditional industries, service industries, and high-tech enterprises. An analysis of retention efforts is then provided.

Attracting Manufacturing Firms

Industrial manufacturing recruitment or "smokestack chasing" has provided the basis for much of the economic development activity at the state and local levels for the past fifty years. This did not begin to change until the mid 1970s and early 1980s. While most development efforts now include many more elements, industrial attraction is still a major focus. The steps in industrial recruitment are fairly standard and include creating a formal organization for the purposes of attracting industry, targeting a particular set of industries, developing a financing program, assembling land and buildings, developing a marketing strategy, and prospecting.

While not all state and local governments may follow these steps, they constitute the model that most economic developers recommend.

Organization. The first act of an industrial attraction program is to create a formal organization. In most instances, this is a nonprofit industrial development corporation that acts as an extension of the local chamber of commerce. As discussed in Chapter Four, this organization has many powers, including the power to raise money, to carry out negotiations in private, to remain tax-exempt, and to buy and sell property.

Targeting. Targeting specific industries is an extremely important goal-setting step in the recruitment process. There are various ways this can be accomplished. Among the factors that a state or locality might want to consider in developing criteria for choosing industries are its income mix, natural resource base, current infrastructure condition and potential for expansion, and labor skill levels. While it may seem self-evident that everyone wants high-paying jobs, the state or locality as a whole may not require them if current skill levels will support only moderate incomes. Likewise, if serious underemployment problems exist, industries whose pay scales would help alleviate this problem would be prime targets. An analysis of current employment characteristics is helpful here.

While most states and localities are open to an expansion or upgrading of their existing capital facilities, at some point the ill effects of such an expansion can outweigh the benefits. If the expansion or introduction of an industry would change the entire physical character of a community, as the new Saturn automobile plant is doing in Spring Hill, Tennessee, some localities may decide that the cost is simply too high. Finally, a community with a high concentration of a particular industry may decide to capitalize on that concentration in order to add to the existing base, or it may decide to diversify the industrial base so that its economy will not risk collapse should that industry sector decline.

This type of review helps the state or community to focus on its needs from its own point of view. The next step is to determine the industries most likely to be attracted to the area; this step is based on the strengths and weaknesses analysis made as part of the strategic planning effort discussed in Chapter Three. Targeting must also include some clear understanding of the changing trends in industrial expansion of the past several years and the internal and external factors that affect expansion. A market analysis of trends nationally, regionally, and statewide is very useful. External factors might be revealed by the following questions: What types of industry are growing nationally? Are they capturing a larger share of employment? Is this trend true for the state or region? Which industries are growing more rapidly in the state or region than nationally? What is the potential that this growth trend will continue?

Internal factors need to be reviewed as well. How skilled is our labor force? Is our infrastructure condition adequate to handle particular types of industry? Is land developed and under the control of the community's economic development organization? On the basis of this profile, the next step is to identify industries that might be interested in the mix of advantages that the state or community has to offer. Industries targeted with this level of detail can clearly direct a state or locality's recruitment efforts. This list of industries is further and further shortened until a handful of most likely candidates remains (Boyle, 1986b).

By evaluating the state or community's needs and capabilities as well as the potential market of industries that fit those needs, the state or locality can focus its interest on a few high-potential firms that would be likely candidates for a recruitment effort. It makes little sense to focus on industries that are declining, or on industries that are growing but require resources that the locality is unable to provide. It would not make sense for most states to recruit firms dependent on high-technology research facilities that only a few locations in the country can currently supply. However, it may make considerable sense to focus on industries dependent on agricultural research (food-processing techniques, for example) where an existing capability (local agriculture production, for example) needs only to be channeled in that direction.

Financing. Financing a recruitment effort can be expensive: staff are needed to carry it out, marketing costs will be high, and industrial sites will need to be acquired and developed. This may be only the beginning. In 1985, the state of Illinois, McLean County, and the city of Bloomington worked jointly to recruit a new auto assembly plant to be built jointly by Chrysler and Mitsubishi. The resources committed by these governments were extensive and included expenses for land, facilities, and services in excess of $80 million (Elder and Lind, 1987). Before a state or locality develops a recruitment program, it needs to evaluate the potential sources and amounts of funding that will be needed. As discussed in Chapter Nine, federal and state grants and loans may be a potential source; however, traditional funding agencies such as the Economic Development Administration (EDA), Title V Regional Commissions, and the Farmers Home Administration (FmHA) have either disappeared or greatly reduced the amount of dollars committed to such efforts. States may be able to assist, but it is likely that dollars will also need to come from the local business community or from local taxes.

Various tax incentives can be used for industrial recruitment. The most common are tax increment financing, tax abatements, industrial revenue bonds, changes in tax structure, changes in tax base, and enterprise zones that combine several tax incentives. Tax increment financing and tax abatement are both linked to the property tax. Industrial revenue bonds are linked to federal and state income taxes. Changes in tax structure and tax base are incentives that can be linked to any tax source.

Tax increment financing (TIF) provides a method by which a locality can use increased property tax assessments to retire bonds issued to help finance projects directly linked to some type of business investment. An example might best illustrate how TIF works. If an industry was interested in locating in a particular community but felt the site it would occupy needed major capital improvements (sewer, water, and road improvements, a rail spur, and so forth), TIF bonds could be issued to pay for these improvements. The payment of principal and interest to retire these bonds would come from increased property tax revenues. If the land identified for the new industry is undeveloped, little tax revenue is being produced. If its value increases dramatically as a result of the industrial development, the difference between the predevelopment tax earnings and the postdevelopment tax earnings is used to retire the bonds. Minnesota, California, and Florida have been leaders in the use of TIF, and today numerous states have enabling legislation allowing its use.

Criticisms of TIF focus on the property tax base itself. First, concern exists over the possibility that voters could limit future increases in property tax assessments and that such limits could threaten the repayment of TIF bonds. This fear has not greatly affected the use of such financing and these risks can be incorporated into the interest rates charged on the bonds when they are sold. A second criticism of TIF is that it diverts future tax revenue away from other uses that might be considered at least as important as the economic development investment. This is referred to as "opportunity costs." Property taxes are used to finance a number of local activities, from county and city governments to public schools and various nonprofit activities. Money earmarked for bond repayment is a direct loss of revenue to support such activities. Despite these criticisms, most state and local officials appear to strongly support the use of TIF and this can be seen in its growing popularity in the last decade.

A very popular twist on tax increment financing is the creation of business improvement districts. While predominantly used in central business district areas, this method has also found acceptance in industrial attraction. The concept is quite simple. If state law allows, a number of businesses will join together within a particular area of the community and agree to place a surcharge on their current property tax assessments. The increased revenue derived from this surcharge is then used to help improve the physical appearance and competitive environment of that area. How the funds can be used is determined by state law, but often they can be used for personnel and marketing expenditures as well as physical improvements.

Little opposition has arisen to this tax incentive, largely because it is imposed on local businesses rather than on the general public and because it requires a majority of those businesses affected to voluntarily approve its use. Some have questioned its effectiveness in retail projects when funds have been used for cosmetic improvements rather than to implement more tangible investment strategies.

Tax abatement is the flip side of tax increment financing. In this case, the locality agrees to freeze the property tax assessment for a particular parcel of land at a predevelopment value for a specific period of time. This allows the industry or business to enjoy the improvements made to the property without paying higher taxes that result from those improvements. This tax incentive has been used extensively in Missouri and Ohio.

As with tax increment financing, opposition to the use of abatements have focused on the opportunity costs of lost revenue for other activities dependent on property taxes. Abatements also have been criticized along with other tax incentives for their tendency to give some new businesses unfair competitive advantages over existing firms that did not receive such financial assistance. This complaint has been particularly visible with respect to industrial revenue bonds.

Industrial revenue bonds (IRBs) and industrial development bonds (IDBs), while greatly curtailed by the 1987 changes in the federal income tax law, still provide an attractive incentive for industrial development. Simply put, these bonds are approved for issuance by a state or local government, but they are actually marketed and sold by private businesses. The bonds are attractive because they are tax-exempt and therefore sell for less than taxable bonds. This reduces the cost of capital to business and thereby serves as an incentive for investment. Current law limits each state's use of these bonds to an amount equal to $50 per capita or $250 million, whichever is greater. In addition, their use is limited to small issues until December 1989, water, sewer and solid waste bonds, mass transit bonds, student loans, single-family mortgage bonds, multifamily rental bonds, district heating and cooling projects, local electric and gas furnishing projects, tax-increment financing, and construction of hazardous waste facilities.

The major reason for the federal government's increased restrictions on the use of IDBs and IRBs is the high level of criticism they have received. Many believe that these tax-free bonds give unfair advantages to new firms over existing firms that made business investments without them. For example, a hotel firm allowed to issue IRBs could reduce its costs sufficiently to provide rooms at rates below those that an existing hotel could offer. Another objection to IRBs is their indiscriminate use. Many states and localities have granted permission to issue bonds to any business that requested it, thus providing no control over their use or linkage to the states' economic development goals and objectives. Iowa City, Iowa, made headlines several years ago by actually adopting a policy on how IDBs would be used. Unfortunately, it is the exception rather than the rule.

Changes in tax structure that reduce the tax burden on business firms and their employees take many forms: reduced corporation tax rates, corporate tax credits, sales tax exemptions, revisions in how various taxes are computed (this has recently been a heated issue in the case of statewide unitary sales tax programs), and changes in individual income tax rates for higher-income wage earners.

Only Nevada and South Dakota have no corporate income taxes. However, many state policies reflect a perceived trade-off between the revenue derived from these taxes and the possibility that such taxes cause firms to locate outside their borders. While most of the literature indicates that taxes do not play a decisive role in locational decisions, many states use low corporate tax rates as an incentive to attract industry. The competition from other states in this area makes these incentives difficult to ignore. Companies looking for locations will certainly use these incentives as a bargaining chip even though their real importance may be marginal.

Many state sales tax policies reflect concerns about the economic impact taxes have on economic development. Few states have sales taxes on services, at least in part owing to the economic impact such a tax would have on service businesses. States may exempt certain products from the sales tax because of the importance of those products to the state; for example, in agriculture-based economies farm equipment is often exempt from sales taxes.

In some instances the definition of a tax base or the way taxes are computed can play a role in attraction efforts. The recent furor over how several states computed income for corporations—the unitary tax—was a good example of the use of computation methods as a tax incentive or disincentive. The unitary tax provision provided for computing tax liability on the basis of worldwide business (sales, payroll, and property), rather than only that business that took place within the state. The net effect was to increase taxes for many multinational firms. Many states, such as California and Oregon, repealed their unitary tax provisions because of business pressure and corporate threats to relocate or stop investment. Other states have proposed changing the tax computation formulas so that corporations headquartered outside the state would pay a higher rate or have a larger base for taxation than businesses with headquarters within the state.

In another example, states with highly progressive income tax structures have found businesses with a larger number of highly paid executives to be very negative because of the tax liability suffered by those executives. A recent example occurred in Nebraska, where the business community advocated substantial reductions in state income tax rates at higher income levels because of the perceived reluctance of high-salaried employees to move to a state with a very progressive tax structure.

Over thirty states have recently adopted enterprise-zone legislation. These zones vary greatly from state to state, but all the legislation combines a series of tax reductions with regulatory relief in an attempt to lure investment to geographical areas suffering from serious disinvestment. Much of it is directed at new investment and provides tax advantages tied to start-up costs. Such things as the rate at which property or equipment can be depreciated and tax abatement are much more useful to new firms than are tax reductions that require substantial profit margins—something few new firms have. Also, new firms are often the least able to cope with the myriad rules and regulations that can affect start-up costs. States have attempted to greatly reduce the costs and delays afflicting businesses that might wish to expand or start within a designated zone. This is not to say that tax incentives for existing firms wishing to expand are not included in zones; rather, many states believe new firm development is the key to meeting many of their goals, particularly in blighted areas. The state of Illinois provides a comprehensive illustration of enterprise zone incentives:

- Investment tax credit (0.5 percent) on new investments
- $100 million in revenue bonds for construction in enterprise zones
- State income tax exemption on dividends for corporations conducting all their business in enterprise zones
- $500 income tax credit per eligible dislocated worker hired in an enterprise zone
- Sales tax exemption on building materials used in enterprise zones
- Utility tax exemption for business investments that create 200 jobs or retain 1,000 jobs
- Machinery and equipment sales tax exemption for businesses that create 200 jobs or retain 1,000 jobs
- Local property tax abatement on building improvements or new construction
- Local sales tax relief on building materials purchases (Augustine and Elfine, 1986)

The actual effect of these tax incentives is hard to measure. Corporations threaten to leave if tax policies are not changed, and industrial recruiters often argue that several (unnamed) firms have declined to locate in the state because of the lack of tax incentives. Proving, however, that the tax policy was the major factor or even a major consideration in locational decisions is almost impossible because corporate decision making is not open to public scrutiny. Businesses will try to maximize profits by reducing external costs associated with taxation. Whether their inability to get tax policies changed will cause them to locate someplace else is always difficult to assess. This being the case, states with few competitive advantages and fearful of losing out to states that have such advantages may change their tax code in an attempt to protect themselves against the possibility that locational decisions will be made on this basis.

Attracting Service and Retail Businesses

Many of the steps used to attract manufacturing industries can also be used in attracting service and retail businesses. The focus is different, however, and in most cases service and retail attraction is more difficult. First of all, the state is dealing with a larger number of smaller firms. Industrial attraction allows the state or locality to narrow choices to a handful of potential prospects and to direct efforts toward recruiting the one or two that appear to be most likely to locate within its borders. Service recruitment, however, entails an enormous number of options. Attraction strategies may therefore be unable to focus on any one type of service or trade business; rather, they must focus on several different types of firms that fit niches within the local economy.

A second difficulty, closely associated with the first, is the number of people that will be involved in the process. For example, in recruiting a manufacturing firm, the community may organize a single team of local leaders to work with that firm, organize information, handle the prospect's site visit, and deal with various other aspects of the attraction effort. With a service recruitment, however, several different teams may be needed. One team works to hire new doctors or bring a medical clinic to town. Another works to locate an accounting or investment firm. Another directs its efforts at filling vacant space on Main Street with a new fabric shop or five-and-dime store. The diversity within the service sector makes it more difficult to work with.

Another major difficulty in service and trade recruitment is that there is no one place to find businesses intending to relocate.

In the manufacturing sector, several publications are available that describe the various firms and their characteristics. No such list exists for service firms; therefore, states must conduct their own specialized research and develop targeting lists by collecting information on specific sectors and industry trends.

The larger amounts of state and local resources needed to organize a large staff and undertake thorough research may be difficult to obtain. At the same time, the payoffs associated with service and trade recruitment may appear small in comparison with industrial recruitment. The total benefits to the state or locality might be as high or higher with a service-recruitment program, but this can be difficult to prove to those who may not understand the recent changes in business activity.

Owing to these difficulties, many states and communities have no direct attraction program for services and trade. Most states have ongoing industrial recruitment programs; they are familiar with the topic and know how to carry out various recruitment activities. Service-sector recruitment, on the other hand, is less familiar to development officials and less information is available about how successful recruitment efforts can be undertaken. This uncertainty and lack of familiarity can make development officials uncomfortable and reduce their desire to work toward developing a specific program aimed at service attraction.

Nevertheless, it is necessary to understand the importance of a service industry attraction program, especially if it is a part of a focused economic development strategy. Attracting services may prove to be an effective complement to industrial attraction in the long term. The number of manufacturing businesses that are expanding or relocating is very small, while the number of states and localities recruiting such firms is very large. According to one report, over thirty-five states competed for the General Motors Saturn plant ("Kalamazoo May . . . ," 1985). The expansion of service firms, however, has been significant.

The first step in recruiting service firms is to develop an appropriate organization that can plan and implement a service attraction program. If the locality's needs include revitalization of the downtown area, creation of a Downtown or Central Business District Development Corporation is critical. On the other hand, if the needs are more by sector than by geographic area, a different nonprofit agency directed at these sectors may be more useful. For example, communities may create a nonprofit group to help expand their health care facilities or to recruit new health care providers.

A second step is to evaluate internal and external factors affecting service recruitment and to obtain information on local needs. A local government, for example, must ask the following questions: What is the current service/retail mix? Where outside the community do citizens go to shop? Why? What is the retail/service trade area? Where are the business "gaps" in this area that could be filled with a new firm or firms? Are there geographical concerns (for example, a deteriorating downtown) that need to be addressed? What space is available for retail and service business uses? What is the cost of this space? What is the current vacancy rate of this space? By answering these questions, the community can begin to target particular sectors of the service and retail sector most likely to succeed and increase the local economic base.

A third step is targeted marketing. This requires an understanding of existing service markets and potential markets outside the state or city. If a city has an existing base of health care providers, it may find that this sector is a major exporter of services throughout the region. Targeting specific health care services to help expand or fill gaps in this sector can be a viable marketing strategy in this instance.

A final element is financing. It may be more difficult to raise money for this type of recruiting effort because of its relative newness. Tax districts, dues surcharges, selling stock in a for-profit corporation, enlisting donations, applying for grants, and fund-raising projects all hold promise.

Attracting High-Technology Businesses

One of the most visible industrial recruitment areas in the 1980s has been high-technology industry. This is true for several reasons. The success of technology-based industries in areas such as Silicon Valley in California, Route 128 in Massachusetts, and Research Triangle in North Carolina have led others to try to emulate their accomplishments. Recruiting high-technology firms is seen by many public officials as a way to create new jobs while increasing wealth, since this area is expanding compared to other types of industry. Finally, many states and localities see high-tech businesses as sources of ideas and innovations that will increase the likelihood of new business start-ups (Weiss, 1985).

Attracting high-tech businesses, however, is considerably more difficult than attracting other types of business and should not be pursued without a sound analysis of the local economy's strengths and weaknesses. First, high-tech industries in general are a very small part of the country's employment base. Although some high-tech occupations will grow remarkably—computer-related jobs are projected to increase 45 percent during the 1980s—they nonetheless represent only 1.5 percent of the labor force (Perelman, 1984). Because of this, high-tech is not a strong job-creating sector. Second, recruiting advanced technology industries does not require the same strengths in the local economic base as traditional attraction strategies. While states might score high on a traditional industrial recruitment effort that focuses on such things as cheap land, low state taxes, and nonunion work forces, they are likely to do less well in recruiting high-technology firms interested in highly skilled labor, risk capital, and strong research and development capabilities.

Unlike traditional industrial development strategies, high-technology recruitment involves three major areas: improving state and local educational systems, making direct investments in research and development, and providing technical assistance in moving research and development ideas into production (Clarke, 1986). Most state and local initiatives directed at industries that produce advanced technology products therefore focus on five areas: technology research and development, human capital, small-business training and assistance, financial capital, and physical capital (Office of Technology Assessment, 1984). While there is little empirical evidence that these initiatives work, favorable experience in some states provides a broad outline of potentially successful high-tech recruitment.

University-based research centers can be a strong source of technology development. Arizona operates an Engineering Excellence Center within Arizona State University, while Michigan has developed an Industrial Technology Institute associated with but separate from the University of Michigan (Clarke, 1986). Iowa has committed $25 million in government bond funding for laser research through its university system. The state of New York hopes to attract technology directly through businesses themselves by providing grants to existing firms that can take existing research and move it toward production. Other states have utilized grant-in-aid programs focusing on applied technological research.

Human capital is important in a number of ways (see Chapter Eight). States and localities must be able to recruit "gold-chippers" capable of leading research and development efforts. More important, they must also have access to the highly skilled labor force that high-technology firms require. The most important criterion high-tech industries use to select new plant sites is the local availability of skilled technical and professional workers (Joint Economic Committee, 1982). While some states and communities focus on computer science and engineering programs, effective efforts are likely to encompass a much broader group of disciplines.

Small-business training and assistance are particularly important in high-risk, high-technology fields. Many states are working with their colleges and universities to expand training and assistance programs for small businesses. North Dakota, for example, has created a center for innovation and business development through the University of North Dakota specifically for this purpose (Clarke, 1986).

Financial capital is extremely important to high-technology development, and it is often difficult to obtain because of the unknown risks associated with many of these business ventures. State and local venture capital financing programs are directed toward advanced technology enterprises; more than twelve states now operate such programs (see Chapter Ten). The state of Indiana, for example, allows a tax credit on individual investments for those willing to place capital in a venture capital pool administered by a state-created development corporation (Brody, 1985). Another example is Connecticut, which provides funding to help move research prototypes into production.

Physical capital includes such things as access to land, buildings, and other facilities necessary for product research, development, and production. Perhaps one of the most visible forms of physical capital is incubator facilities, which are springing up all over the country. These provide low-cost office and laboratory space as well as office staff assistance, thus reducing the start-up costs and management problems that often plague new small business ventures (see Chapter Five).

Retention

Retention programs are imperative for communities facing economic decline, but they should not be ignored by healthy communities. Appropriate policies and public support must be generated so that retention efforts are given the same consideration as attraction programs. Strategies to retain local businesses and maintain existing jobs are essentially strategies to reduce barriers to local business development (Vaughan, 1980). Barriers to retention are thus similar to the barriers to formation and expansion discussed in Chapter Five.

Factors that particularly influence plant and business closings, and that increase the need for retention efforts, are declining demand for a firm's goods and services, increases in energy prices, capital market gaps, and increasing taxes (Vaughan, 1980). In addition, retention strategies must focus on preventing local companies from moving for the sake of expansion opportunities they perceive in other localities. Factors that influence companies to move include inadequate transportation, low availability of land, lack of public services, lack of capital, and high labor costs.

Successful state and local retention efforts therefore focus on at least three objectives (Vaughan, 1980). The first is to increase the demand for a firm's products and services and thus expand its market penetration. "Buy local" programs, for example, can help stimulate local sales. A second objective is to reduce the cost of operation so that profits may be increased. Businesses that have high operating or debt costs and lack cash flow will be likely candidates for a business retention program. Such firms can be assisted through such things as refinancing existing debt, negotiating cover utility costs, reducing rental costs of land and facilities, and automating their businesses. The key here is to work with the firm to make its production costs low enough to remain competitive in the marketplace.

A third objective is to spread information about the product so that external markets can be created or enlarged. Marketing and promotion programs operated by states and localities may be of considerable assistance in this regard. Many states promote products that are produced within their borders. Such programs can have an effect in both national and international markets. Trade shows, visiting with major buyers of these products, and export development offices can all assist in improving product markets.

When a community is faced with a crisis—an imminent business shutdown or plant closure—retention efforts are best focused in three areas. First, discussions must be held at once to assess what is immediately needed to prevent the closure. Negotiations with the local plant manager or the corporate managers can help identify critical steps that can be taken collaboratively to either postpone or prevent the closure. Second, state and local governments can encourage or facilitate a buyout of the company to prevent a closing. The state of Oregon, for example, provides funding and technical assistance for conducting feasibility studies of employee buyouts of firms intending to close. Third, if these attempts fail, steps must be taken to deal effectively with the laid-off workers and their families through employment assistance and retraining if necessary.

Retention programs are difficult to implement. One reason for this is the invisibility of the successes. Retaining a 200-employee firm within the community has as much and probably more impact on a community's economic health in the long run than recruiting a 200-employee firm. Still, the public's perception is that resources should be used more for attraction than retention. Attraction strategies tend to have more public support because the results are easy to measure (see the new firm we just recruited!) and many believe the benefits of a retention program do not justify its costs (Nathanson, 1980). Yet retention efforts have a number of direct benefits. First, jobs otherwise lost and the multiplier effect that they generate stay in the community. Second, businesses that reaffirm their desire to stay offer the potential for expansion and increased income. Third, people who work for a retained firm may be the best sources of new business start-ups, thus offering the potential for spin-off benefits. Finally, retention says a great deal about the image the community will project to new or expanding firms outside its borders. This image can play a critical role in recruiting new firms.

What factors are included within a business retention program? First and foremost is a strong analysis of the business environment within the community. The locality must have a clear understanding of what the barriers to retention are, how they manifest themselves, and whether they can be changed through local action. If small business failures are an increasing problem, the community can act to institute strategies to assist businesses before they fail. If a shortage of skilled labor is a barrier, action to provide skill training can be instituted before a firm looks elsewhere to meet this need.

The state of Minnesota has developed a business retention program for its communities that includes several steps. First, an awareness is developed within the community itself of the importance of business retention. Second, the community organizes its effort by selecting a task force that can spearhead the retention effort. Third, the community determines which businesses it is most important to retain. Fourth, a survey is developed and given to local businesses to determine potential problems or opportunities that state and local agencies can use to establish an assistance program. Finally, a volunteer network is created to help carry out the survey and interviews and then analyze the results (Wolf, 1986).

In order to retain firms that might leave or fail, states and localities must learn to anticipate; there is little that can be accomplished after a firm has made a decision to relocate. Managing economic development strategically requires an early warning system that anticipates failures and relocations so that action can be taken before the decisions are made. Effective warning systems have several characteristics, including reliability, clear priorities, manageability, and a strong data base (Nathanson, 1980).

Reliability refers to the ability to locate with some degree of accuracy where the problems are or are likely to be. This can include identifying firms with plans to close plants or small businesses with weak financing or management. The key is to locate problems in the making and to address them in the early stages of development. A business assistance program for young firms is one way to identify problems and assist in retention.

Smaller communities will have little trouble ranking their targets because they are dealing with small numbers. Larger communities and states, on the other hand, will need to concentrate their efforts on those firms that are likely to have the greatest impact should they leave or fail or on firms in industries that are shrinking nationwide.

A locality can find itself trying to do too much with too little; retention programs should be manageable and strive to match internal capabilities with program objectives. If it is impossible to locate and assist every young business that might need help, a smaller scope can focus on the high-risk businesses or those with the greatest impact.

The success of an early warning system largely depends on a strong data base. Three differing levels of data are needed: secondary, primary, and informal (Nathanson, 1980). Secondary data includes information published by standard sources such as the Bureau of the Census, Dun and Bradstreet (a firm that supplies data on new business starts), and Polk (a firm that tracks business activity by census tract). Primary data include direct data collection by the state or locality. Phone or questionnaire surveys, file reviews, interviews, and so forth belong to this category. Finally, informal data, or the grapevine, can be an important source of information. Although the benefits must be measured against the rumor control problems that exist, certain inside information can be a valuable source of knowledge about future actions. The locality should also look for trends over time and how external economic conditions may affect local businesses. In any case, the data must be as comprehensive, accurate, and timely as possible.

Conclusion

Attraction and retention strategies will vary greatly among states and communities depending on their current needs, their competitive advantages and disadvantages, and the changing nature of business activity itself. Clearly defined goals and objectives, strong organizational commitment, and proactive activities are all important.

Attraction efforts can focus on a number of areas, including manufacturing, high technology, service, and retail and wholesale trade. Each requires different strategies, organizational commitment, and resources. What works effectively in attracting manufacturing may not be successful for recruiting service industries. The costs and benefits of any attraction program should be carefully scrutinized to determine whether it is worth the public investment required.

The attractiveness of a recruitment program should not overshadow the importance of serving the needs of the state's existing businesses. Retention programs may be the most important part of any state or local development strategy. Although saving jobs is less visible and harder to sell to policy officials, it must be a priority. A mixture of attraction and retention can provide a solid base for successful economic development if it is structured within a clearly defined strategic management program.

7

Examining International Trade
and Investment Opportunities

In 1959, Governor Luther H. Hodges of North Carolina traveled to
Europe for the purpose of attacting direct foreign investment to the
state. At the time, his trip attracted only a modicum of interest.
Today, however, it is regarded as an important turning point for
gubernatorial involvement in international economic affairs.
Governor Hodges's travel marked the beginning of a growing
realization among state officials that their regional economies do
not exist in an economic vacuum. State and local economies have
become inexorably intertwined with the world economy, and
international trade and business development have become prom-
ising strategies for economic growth. This new reality has, in many
respects, expanded the role of the governor, who is now not only
the chief executive of the state but a diplomatic negotiator abroad
in promoting state exports and in attracting direct foreign
investments. The National Governors Association (NGA) created
an International Trade and Foreign Affairs Committee in 1978.
Now, according to its most recent survey of state involvement in
international affairs, forty-nine states hold export seminars for
small and medium-sized businesses; forty-five states use publications and computerized systems to assist local exports to find
potential markets; thirty-eight states have overseas representatives
in seventeen countries; fifteen states have initiated export finance
legislation and ten states already have similar programs in operation; and all fifty states have sister-state relationships with governments around the world (Clarke, 1986).

Similarly, local governments are becoming increasingly active in international economic affairs. In fact, it was local governments, not state governments, that first recognized the importance of foreign relations. In 1956, President Eisenhower initiated the U.S. Sister Cities program, which encouraged exchanges between American and foreign cities. This program has grown more important as American cities have become interested in trade development. For example, in 1981 the U.S. Conference of Mayors organized an "Invest in American Cities" program in Zurich that gave 180 U.S. cities the opportunity to discuss with foreign cities the possibilities for foreign investment and trade. Presently, 750 American cities have trade development agreements with over 1,200 cities in 86 countries.

City and county government officials have recognized that their local economies are not just local anymore, but global in scope. As a result, the National League of Cities established an international economic development task force in 1982. Their groundbreaking report, published in 1984, charted a new international course for local economic development strategies.

This new participation by state and local governments in international economic affairs has been characterized as "global microdiplomacy" (Duchacek, 1984), in which new contacts are developed beyond the borders of the United States by state and local officials in order to respond more effectively to the expanding global economy. During the 1960s, the American economy was relatively free from foreign competition. In the 1980s, however, over 70 percent of American industries are competing with foreign businesses. Foreign competitors, for example, have captured 90 percent of the U.S. cutlery market, 30 percent of the machine tools market, and over 20 percent of the steel market. America's share of world exports in manufacturing has dropped from 25.5 percent in 1956 to about 17 percent in 1985. Imports increased 30 percent between 1973 and 1981 alone. Since 1981, over two and a half million jobs have been lost to foreign competition. One of the most recent developments—and hardly a surprising one—is that U.S. companies are shifting their production overseas to take advantage of lower costs. One out of eight U.S. jobs in manufacturing is tied to exports, one-third of U.S. corporate profits are derived from international business activities, and one out of three acres of farmland is for export production (Kline, 1984). With the increase in foreign investments in U.S. business enterprises since the 1970s, it is no wonder that states and communities are developing strategies to respond to the internationalization of their economies.

Nearly all states and communities have been drawn, willingly or not, into the international economic arena, where each must fend for itself with its own unique set of problems and mix of goods and services (Duchacek, 1984). In response, legislatures nationwide are either studying or enacting new approaches to spur state exports and to attract foreign investment or tourism. The devolution of federal economic development programs to state and local governments, the continuing federal budget crunch, the deleterious effects of the 1981-1982 recession, and threat of plant closings and worker dislocation have all prompted states to step up their trade and foreign investment efforts. States and local communities realize that they cannot wait for federal action (whatever that might be) to rectify this situation; rather, their fates now rest, for the most part, in their own hands.

This chapter will discuss the various strategies available to community and state officials to stimulate international trade linkages and foreign investment, including the recent findings of the National League of Cities International Economic Development Task Force and research compiled by the National Association of State Development Agencies. Several case studies will also be highlighted. Finally, there will be a discussion of whether every state and locality should be involved in formulating an international economic program, or set of programs, given that such programs are often devised without considering carefully the strategic needs of the state or local government.

State Strategies for Expanding State Exports

Local and state economic development strategies are increasingly linked to the formulation of a state or local foreign economic policy as a means to strengthen the state's economic base, preserve and increase job opportunities, lower unemployment, and increase tax revenues. Ninety-eight percent of all states conduct export seminars and conferences; 96 percent sponsor trade missions; 94 percent disseminate sales leads to potential exporting firms; 92 percent offer one-on-one export-oriented counseling; 88 percent sponsor trade shows; 74 percent provide referrals to local export services; 66 percent provide foreign office representatives; 62 percent prepare international market studies; 60 percent publish international market newsletters; and 56 percent publish handbooks for international trade and export (National Governors Association, 1987).

Export promotion that is directed primarily at existing firms within the state is important to small and medium-sized businesses. For example, in 1983, one-fifth of Iowa's manufactured goods were for exports that resulted in an increase of state employment of 130,000. Furthermore, it has been estimated that every dollar of state spending to promote exports by small businesses has led to about $260 in export sales. However, state governments face a precarious problem: small and medium-sized businesses in the United States have generally been more insular in exporting their products than firms in other industrialized countries. It is estimated that over 20,000 small firms have the capacity to export their products. Presently, 300 firms account for 80 percent of all U.S. exports. There are a variety of reasons that small firms would export if they were given adequate assistance. Exporting could increase their pool of customers, offset reduced sales at home, extend the life of a product, extend production schedules, and generally expand markets (Posner, 1984). States have the capacity to assist small and medium-sized firms to expand into the global market. The specific export promotion strategies employed by states can be divided into three broad categories: technical support, export finance, and information brokering (Clarke, 1986).

Technical Support. State technical assistance includes, among other things, providing potential exporters with appropriate documentation, dealing with persons who perform export-related tasks, and assisting with licensing procedures. Some states, like Indiana, have created private nonprofit institutions that work closely with firms to expand exports. Technical assistance also includes specific information pertaining to detailed economic data on particular countries, potential market demand, financing, political and cultural factors in other countries, and how to promote a product for foreign markets. More recently, assistance has included giving an exporter the opportunity to conduct a seminar for business executives in a foreign market. Equally important is the assistance that universities can offer in international business, foreign languages, and international law.

The state of Virginia's technical assistance program provides an excellent example. Recently, the Virginia department of economic development created the Virginia International Trade Institute (VITI). As one of its key functions, VITI has attempted to identify general trading companies in the state and to distribute a comprehensive list to the state's manufacturers specifying the products that each trade company handles. It has also taken the lead in serving as a referral service for information on higher education activities in international trade and legal assistance in export-related activities. Along with these traditional assistance programs, VITI has conducted workshops in Virginia on a company-by-company basis, instructing firms on how to market goods for selected foreign markets and matching state companies to suitable foreign countries. In addition, VITI coordinates overseas marketing visits by state businesses.

Connecticut's department of economic development created an international division that prides itself on providing technical assistance with a personalized approach, including identification of the products sought, specific information on the manufacturers' products, and personal contact with individuals interested in international business (this contact is on a per-trade-lead basis). Both Virginia's and Connecticut's technical assistance programs involve a trade partnership between the state government and businesses. Oklahoma, on the other hand, is unique because it is the first state to establish a formal federal-state partnership in order to coordinate technical assistance programs more effectively. The state of Oklahoma and the federal government jointly provide such technical assistance as trade data and investment opportunities overseas, identification of overseas buyers, trade fairs, market research, and airport licensing information. This program is serving as a model for other pilot programs in Alabama, California, Connecticut, Maryland, Minnesota, New York, and North Carolina.

Export Finance. Export financing is regarded by most small businesses as a critical factor in their success in international trade activities. Not surprisingly, state export finance programs are structured to assist small and medium-sized firms. States' involvement in export financing typically includes loan guarantees and, in certain states, direct loans. Some state governments help subsidize business expenses dealing with overseas trade (including tax incentives for selling products, subsidies for business travel, and financing of trade booths). In addition, a number of states offer export credit insurance, often in conjunction with the Foreign Credit Insurance Association, a group that works closely with the U.S. Export-Import Bank. In general, state export finance programs usually include the following strategies: providing guarantees to banks for working capital loans made to firms before an export shipment is made; providing postshipment guarantees to banks for short- and medium-term loans made to foreign buyers; helping arrange insurance for the banks from federal or private sources against the risk of default by a foreign buyer (the state usually purchases reinsurance to protect itself from loss); acting as a delivery mechanism for some programs of the U.S. Export-Import bank; and advising businesses and banks of federal and state export finance programs (Klauser, 1985).

State governments have been actively experimenting with combinations of these activities, and although it is too soon to assess their success, they help illuminate possible strategies. In 1984, for example, Michigan committed $500,000 within the Office of International Development to start an export financing program. It was specifically designed to "piggy-back" on the private bond markets to "buy down" the interest rate, thus making export financing more accessible. Minnesota, on the other hand, created an Export Finance Authority that guarantees bank loans for preshipment and postshipment borrowing (ranging from $25,000 to $250,000). California started an Export Finance Office (located within the California World Trade Commission) that not only makes loan guarantees, as well as providing insurance and coinsurance, but provides counseling and coordinates federal and private financing. In 1983, Indiana amended its Employment Development Commission to provide seed monies for export financing. As presently structured, this export finance program will cover 80 percent of the balance on the loans being guaranteed to small and medium-sized firms. Finally, Wisconsin issues bonds in order to finance its program for export promotion. Close to $550 million was raised in 1986 to assist small businesses with export sales financing. This program is administered from the Wisconsin Housing and Economic Development Authority. Similarly, in 1986 the Illinois Export Development Authority (IEDA) authorized a $15 billion bond issue to help Illinois's state exporters. This bond issue, which is backed by a $650,000 debt service appropriated by the state legislature as well as a credit letter from the Bank of Tokyo, has already supported about $2.5 million worth of state exports. The IEDA offers its assistance to any state exporter; the only stipulations are that the company maintain jobs in the state and that at least 25 percent of the final value added to the product (minus profits) take place in the state ("Illinois Export Authority . . . ," 1987). It is estimated that 200 new jobs have been created thanks to the IEDA's export financing. Eventually, the IEDA would like to be authorized to issue up to $100 million in bonds.

Information Brokering. A major obstacle for any effective export promotion policy is the prospective state exporters' lack of key information. Almost every state now holds seminars or conferences or distributes export handbooks and newsletters to foster more state exports. New York, for example, created Export Opportunity Bulletins (EOBs), which consist of inquiries received from foreign buyers. Every month sixty EOBs are distributed statewide to about one-quarter of the manufacturers within the state; they have been credited with facilitating an estimated $43 million in exports from 1980 to 1982. In addition, the state has started a "Products from New York State Index," which lists products available from New York manufacturers and is printed in English, German, Spanish, French, and Japanese.

Presently, forty-five states provide trade leads to business enterprises interested in exporting. The leads include trade information gathered through personal contact, from overseas offices, and through the U.S. Department of Commerce's Trade Opportunities Program. While the provision of trade leads varies from state to state, there has been a steady trend by states to provide a comprehensive data base linking firms, their products, and their resources with specific export opportunities. Fifteen states have such a program, but few offer foreign importers more than a general product description used by the federal government. California has recently started a computerized system that uses a detailed tariff code classification that can identify products and their match overseas. This automated trade lead system is being implemented to collect and store information from up to 10,000 California producers, along with an equal number of foreign buyers. In sum, information brokering by state governments offers two kinds of market information. States try to provide export information related to specific companies that want to export their products and information that attempts to alert the state's industrial firms to the realities of international trade.

State Strategies for Stimulating Foreign Investment

While the emphasis of many states has been, for the most part, on export promotion, direct foreign investment is also a crucial factor in job creation. Presently, foreign companies have invested close to $1 trillion in the U.S. economy: $450 billion in banking assets, $250 billion in manufacturing and assembly plants, $200 billion in Treasury bills, and $100 billion in real estate (Tolchin, 1987). This capital influx, however, has changed the role of the United States' international investment position. In 1987, for the first time in seventy years, the United States became a debtor nation, owing the world a staggering net amount of about $357 billion (Ventriss, 1986). On the positive side, investment by foreign companies in the United States since 1980 has generated from 1.5 to 2.5 million jobs. Foreign investment is critically important to large state economies, such as those of California, Illinois, New Jersey, New York, Ohio, Pennsylvania, and Texas. Some of the most recent examples of significant foreign investment can be found in smaller states, such as Tennessee (a Nissan plant), Kentucky (a Toyota plant), and Oregon (a Fujitsu plant). As reported by Kline (1984), foreign firms have outpaced domestic companies in annual growth both in compensation paid (13.2 percent to 9.9 percent) and in employment (3 percent to 1.6 percent) in the mid seventies. States are trying to create an array of financial incentives ranging from tax abatements to repeal of the unitary tax (recent examples include Indiana, Oregon, and Florida). Other strategies employed by states are trade missions and visits by representatives from foreign companies. Thirty-four states have conducted more than 300 trade shows, trade missions, and fairs from 1980 to 1985, aiming at attracting foreign investment into state and local economies. Some states have implemented new incentives such as direct subsidies for "infant" technology industries and the development of industrial parks to compete for foreign investment. Interstate rivalries for foreign investment are emerging, however; and, as more and more incentives are promoted by different states, many economic development experts are openly questioning whether these new incentive packages are excessive and offset the potential benefits of new jobs. Many economists have argued that such financial incentives are wasteful from a national perspective; they contend that these state strategies influence only the choice between competing U.S. locations rather than the basic decision to invest in the United States itself (Kline, 1984). Moreover, critics have argued that tax incentives give an added advantage to foreign companies in competition with domestic companies (Tolchin, 1987).

Unfortunately, there has been little careful analysis of foreign investment incentives, since most state governments do not calculate the cost of attracting new investment on a case-by-case basis. Doubts have also been raised about whether foreign investment actually translates into more jobs. According to the U.S. Department of Commerce, acquisitions and mergers can account for half of all foreign investments, and acquisitions seldom create new jobs. Regardless of these drawbacks, statewide politics will still propel policymakers to continue in their attempts to attract foreign investment by offering corporate income tax incentives, sales tax exemptions for equipment, and loan packages for constructing new plant facilities. The pivotal question for states is how much they are willing to up the incentive ante in what has been aptly called "the new War Between the States" (Grady, 1987).

Local Strategies for International Economic Development

No analysis of international economic development would be complete without examining how American cities are increasingly looking overseas to create new jobs and foster economic growth. Local government interest in international economic affairs is not surprising, considering that trade and investment activities often directly affect local communities. In general, most local government interest has been focused on stimulating foreign investment in a community. For example, in Tulsa, a European machinery firm called Hilti added 1,200 jobs. In Massachusetts, with the assistance of the Massachusetts Foreign Business Council, a Central Cities Investment program was created to stimulate foreign manufacturing investment in distressed urban areas. A Los Angeles trade corporation assisted the Aluminum Body Corporation to formalize a deal with Saudi Arabia for medical and dental gear that resulted in sales of $1.5 million. These examples of international development in American cities show that cities are often better salesmen than the federal government for the particular needs of their local economies, primarily because local business leaders and officials have a better sense of their local products and markets than higher levels of government.

While major American cities have gained more attention with their international economic activities, smaller cities are also increasingly becoming involved. Colorado Springs, for instance, sent a delegation to West Germany and Hong Kong in 1984 and has been trying to promote more trade by creating foreign-trade zones where imported goods can be distributed under reduced U.S. tariffs. In 1984, there were sixty-five foreign-trade zones nationwide that generated about $12 billion in business and created 112,000 U.S. jobs. Norfolk, Virginia, has recently taken the bold initiative of forming public export-trading companies that assist small firms with export-related activities.

All of these examples are indicative of a recent trend—a trend that was clearly reflected in a report published in 1984 by the National League of Cities (NLC) and entitled *International Trade:*

A New City Economic Development Strategy. This report is note-worthy because it is the first time a major association representing American cities has acknowledged openly that local economies are now interdependent with a global economy. More important, the report argues that while most city officials formerly played a minor role in international economic affairs, they can no longer do so. New realities are forcing local officials to adapt new economic strategies in this global economic environment. This report identifies local government strategies to promote international business development, recommends services that the NLC should provide for cities to build their international business development capacities, and identifies ways cities can strengthen ties with private enterprises that operate internationally. The report emphasizes, however, that export promotion and direct foreign investment are not panaceas for local economic woes, but rather are important strategies among others to generate new jobs and diversify local economies. Policies outlined by the NLC include:

- *Providing leadership to encourage and assist local businesses to initiate or expand international business activities.* Local leadership should encourage businesses to think internation-ally, and cities should provide counseling and financial assistance to local enterprises intending to expand into foreign markets.
- *Considering encouragement of direct foreign investment.* Local marketing promotions should be conducted to highlight community assets and emphasize comparative attractiveness. In addition, communities can provide job assistance programs to provide incentives for an investor's location decision.
- *Considering conducting trade missions.* Local officials can lead a delegation of private and public leaders to conduct prelimi-nary meetings with foreign buyers.
- *Considering formation of foreign-trade zones.* This is a popular approach because no customs duties are levied on foreign companies in foreign-trade zones and the companies find these zones attractive for reexporting purposes.
- *Considering formation of an export trading company.* Such trading companies can help reduce the cost of exporting and can

assist local businesses in market research, export promotion overseas, pricing, distribution, and credit lending.

- *Considering development of a local business assistance center.* Local agencies can assist businesses in finding financial resources necessary for exporting, identify business enterprises that can export products, and assist businesses with an array of pertinent market information in conjunction with federal and state information-brokering programs.

- *Considering establishment of ties with universities.* City officials can encourage local universities to offer courses in international law, international business, and foreign languages and can stimulate universities and community colleges to provide training to meet potential foreign investors' job skill requirements.

- *Providing information on trade fairs, exhibits, and government-sponsored trade missions.* Cities can provide salient information to local businesses regarding selling opportunities overseas and can link businesses to a network of services that may be provided by the local chamber of commerce or local business assistance office.

- *Considering increasing international tourism.* Local governments can promote local assets attractive to foreign tourists and develop special services such as multilingual hotel staffs, tour guides, and other amenities.

- *Considering better utilization of the popular sister-cities program.* This can encourage trade development and close collaboration by local officials with world trade clubs and foreign embassy offices (National League of Cities, 1984).

These proposals constitute a policy checklist for formulating local strategies in the global marketplace. However, while it briefly defines the elements of an international city (that is, a city with an international airport, port of entry facility, businesses involved in international transactions, and foreign-trade zones), the report offers no assessment of whether every American city can realistically get involved in these ambitious endeavors. Unfortunately, not all cities can make effective use of export development programs; financial and budgetary constraints, political philosophy, and occasional overbureaucratic government structures can all reduce the feasibility of international activities. More important, a city's economic base and the types, sizes, and ages of its indigenous business enterprises actually determine whether an export development program makes sense (Levine, 1986).

State and local governments are increasingly involved in the internationalization of their economies. According to the National Association of State Development Agencies (NASDA), states have nearly doubled the average appropriation for international development initiatives, from $590,142 in 1984 to $980,125 in 1986 (untitled mimeographed data report, 1987). Average staff size has increased from nine to twelve persons in the same period and the number of state foreign offices has also increased significantly. Although these programs are valuable in giving a sense of just how active governments can become in global economic affairs, careful analysis is required before state or local governments venture out; international strategies must be based on an assessment of local strengths and weaknesses. Recent programs developed by California and Maryland provide illustrative examples of how state governments can stimulate international economic activity.

California: A Globally Interdependent State Economy. California's economy can best be understood in relation to the Pacific Basin countries. Three-fourths of California's $80 billion annual trade is with Pacific Basin nations, primarily Japan ($7.4 billion in 1986). California is Japan's leading trade partner ($2.8 billion in 1985) after the United States as a whole. Compared to other states, California has by far the largest number of export-related jobs; one of every five manufacturing jobs and one of four agricultural jobs is directly related to trade. California's economy is therefore critically linked to development in the Pacific Rim.

Other indicators underscore California's interdependence. For example, 487 Japanese plants employing 62,000 people are situated in the state—over 40 percent of Japan's total investment in the United States. There are nine Japanese-affiliated banks chartered in California, employing 10,500 people and holding assets in excess of $10 billion. Of the 2.3 million jobs created since 1981 as a result of direct foreign investment in the United States, some

241,000 were in California. Moreover, approximately one million jobs in California—over 8 percent of total employment—are now attributable to foreign investment. California leads the nation in foreign investment: over 2,125 affiliates of foreign companies— nearly 25 percent of all foreign affiliates operating in the United States—have property, plants, or equipment in the state, with a gross value exceeding $27 billion.

Certain factors in this state of affairs have become troubling to policymakers. First, many policymakers have become alarmed at the erosion of the competitive advantage of several Californian industries. A 1985 report of the California Senate Select Committee on Long Range Policy Planning spelled out the erosion in each industry:

- *Agriculture.* California's exports of agricultural products declined by 2 percent between 1981 and 1984, causing a decline in farm incomes. The value of farm exports dropped by nearly $1 billion between 1980 and 1984, causing a $3 billion drop in statewide economic activity and a loss of 96,000 jobs.
- *Advanced technology manufacturing.* California's preeminence in this area is being eroded. California has been losing its productivity advantage in computers; a 12 percent productivity advantage in the manufacture of computers in 1972 had become a 7 percent disadvantage by 1982. The Japanese are gaining larger market shares in world exports of high-technology products. While California has increased its research base, it is losing its manufacturing base in high technology.
- *Basic manufacturing.* While specialty manufactures in such areas as apparel and printing have been growing to serve new markets, California has lost much of its traditional manufacturing base. For example, a 9 percent productivity advantage in automobile manufactures in 1972 had become a 9 percent disadvantage by 1982.
- *Aerospace.* While defense spending has promoted the growth of this sector, California is losing its ability to compete in commercial aircraft. California's share of commercial jet deliveries declined from 41.5 percent of the total market in 1972 to 21.1 percent in 1982; its productivity advantage in aerospace

fell from 28 percent in 1972 to 22 percent in 1982. The industry may thus be vulnerable to the next slowdown in defense spending.

- *Finance.* Deregulation and interstate banking have created great turbulence in this industry. While some institutions are taking advantage of the new environment, the overall productivity of California's financial industry has lagged behind the rest of the nation. In 1972, California gross profit per employee (an equivalent measure to productivity) was 8.3 percent less than the U.S. average; by 1982, that gap had widened to 10.2 percent (*California and the 21st Century*, 1986).

This erosion is taking place as California is facing enormous trade deficits of more than $29 billion, much of this with nations of the Pacific Basin. While California industries are still world leaders in the invention of new technologies and the development of new products, they fall behind in the application of technologies in production and the marketing of new products in the international arena.

A second factor making policymakers nervous is California's business climate, ranked thirtieth among the fifty states in 1982. According to the California Senate Select Committee's report, 46 percent of industrial site selectors believed California had a negative business climate, 45 percent believed the state had high state taxes, 32 percent believed it had high labor costs, and 28 percent felt it had high land costs. The survey also concluded that of the firms that had looked at California and elected to go elsewhere, 48 percent cited as their reason a negative state business climate (*California and the 21st Century*, 1986). While California is the country's leading export state, most businesses in the state are relatively unaware of possibilities for international trade; it has been estimated that at least 1,100 California small businesses could become new exporters if they were given adequate assistance.

In response to these circumstances, and because California's leaders have acknowledged the tremendous stake they have in worldwide economic and political developments that affect California's international competitiveness, state legislators enacted legislation in 1983 that led to the creation of the California State World Trade Commission (WTC), the agency responsible for international trade. The WTC's strategies for dealing with the new international interdependency are to favorably influence public policy regarding international trade and inward investment, to create an increasing demand for California's exports and promote inward investment and tourism, and to tap the export potential of California's small businesses (Mentor International, 1985).

The WTC represents a definitive break from California's previous trade efforts. First, the WTC was designed as a partnership between public and private interests. About 80 percent of the original fifteen-member board (since reduced to eleven members) was from California's international business community. Second, the WTC was designed not as a state agency but as a nonprofit organization in order to utilize private funds for the promotion of international trade. Finally, the WTC elevated trade functions from the responsibility of a department to that of a high-level committee whose members include the governor, lieutenant governor, and secretary of state.

To pursue its strategies, the WTC focuses on four basic functions: export finance, information and assistance, trade promotion, and trade policy advocacy. The California Export Finance Office, a unit of the WTC, was created in 1985 in response to California companies' increased loss of overseas sales to foreign competitors, the reluctance of commercial lenders to lend to new-to-export companies, and the large potential for California to enter the export market or expand export operations (*California and the Pacific Rim,* 1986). The California Export Finance Program (CEFP) provides access for state exporters to such institutions as the Small Business Administration (SBA), the U.S. Export-Import Bank, and commercial lenders for financing of California exports. This program is specifically designed to assist small business exporters and strengthen their financial relationship so they can qualify for government and commercial loans. In 1986, this program was funded with $2 million, which is expected to be increased to $5 million. CEFP also covers loans to purchase materials, services, and labor to prepare products for export sale and loans that finance export sale terms for foreign buyers. Another

important function of this program—one that is often overlooked
by states that have designed similar programs—is to provide
businesses with current information on economic and political
conditions in the buyers' country.

In 1986, the WTC introduced a computerized automated
trade lead system that identifies California producers of specific
products and matches them with buyers overseas. The WTC also
distributed over 10,000 copies of an export guide that helps small
and middle-sized businesses market their products overseas. It also
sponsored agricultural trade seminars that focused on particular
export opportunities in specific countries. The seminars were
viewed as especially important, since overseas sales of the state's $14
billion farm industry have dropped dramatically in recent years.
The WTC is now assisting the farm industry by keeping it informed
about a bill passed in 1986 that makes matching funds available to
exporters for a program intended to stimulate overseas promotion
and marketing as well as technical research.

The trade promotion program involves two approaches. The
first involves California trade shows and exhibits in such countries
as China (agricultural production and packaging equipment),
Taiwan (technology and industrial products), Hong Kong (alternative energy), Japan (specialty foods), Korea (technology and
industrial products), England (aerospace equipment), Mexico
(technology and industrial products), and Singapore (computers
and office automation equipment). In a single trade show held in
Paris, from 150 to 200 California companies were linked with
foreign buyers. The second approach is the creation of overseas
offices. In 1986, the WTC opened offices in London and Tokyo.
These offices have a $700,000 budget with which to seek a greater
number of export leads and to stimulate a larger amount of foreign
investment. These overseas offices were selected in part because
Britain and Japan are among the largest foreign investors in
California, with $2.7 billion and $2.2 billion respectively (Canada,
the leader, has invested $5.6 billion). These offices report directly to
the governor, thus giving them added prestige abroad and ensuring
more effective coordination among the several California agencies
involved in trade and investment promotion. Stimulating foreign
investment is critical to California. Although California leads the

nation in foreign investment, as described above, from 1977 to 1981, employment related to foreign investment grew faster in twenty-eight states than in California. California accounts for 12 percent of the U.S. gross national product (GNP) and 11 percent of U.S. employment; with its extensive natural resources, abundant human resources, and proximity to the Pacific Basin nations, California would be expected to attract a far larger share of direct foreign investment than other states. Yet it received only 10 percent of direct foreign investment in the nation between 1977 and 1981.

Historically, the WTC has urged reforming the unitary tax (which was done in 1986) and has identified potential problems in bilateral trade proposals with Israel. In addition, as part of its advocacy role, the WTC has exerted pressure on federal legislators to dismantle trade barriers to California products ranging from advanced technological equipment to agricultural commodities. More important, California was the first state to send a special international trade representative to Washington, D.C., to work with the Office of the U.S. Trade Representative, the State Department, and the California congressional delegation in order to promote California's international economic interests. This unusual kind of advocacy on the part of a state government is understandable, given that California's gross national product is the sixth highest in the world. California is the only state with a representative at the meetings of the General Agreement on Tariffs and Trade (GATT), an international organization governing international commerce. California's representative at the GATT negotiations will try to influence other nations to strengthen laws pertaining to intellectual property rights, patents, and computer software, as well as to reduce agricultural export subsidies that have hurt California growers.

California's funding for initiatives in international affairs increased from $460,000 in 1984 to almost $6 million in 1986. The various strategies pursued by the state, managed predominantly by the WTC, reflect the economic strengths identified through a strategic analysis of the state's economy. The state of Maryland provides an example of a smaller state pursuing international strategies.

Maryland: An Aggressive Trade Initiative. To comprehend why a small state with few natural resources would mount one of the most aggressive international economic efforts of any state, it is necessary to analyze the economic challenges facing Maryland. In 1981, Maryland's $1.2 billion worth of manufacturing exports accounted for the direct employment of about 13,000 workers. Another estimated 28,000 jobs existed in nonmanufacturing companies that supplied various materials and services supporting manufactured exports. A majority of these manufacturing jobs were concentrated in primary metals, chemical industries, nonelectric machinery, and electric/electronic equipment. In all, Maryland's total employment related to exports amounted to 53,800, or 10 percent of total state employment.

According to state policymakers and business leaders, Maryland was in a strong position to attract international trade and market its own goods abroad, given its proximity to Washington, D.C., and the strategic advantage of the Port of Baltimore and Baltimore International Airport. Yet Maryland's economic performance was substantially below the national average. Maryland ranked thirty-third in manufactured exports in 1983 and thirty-fifth in agricultural exports in 1982; Maryland also ranked last in exports among states with a major port facility and forty-fifth among all states in average per capita export value in 1982.

In 1983, state policymakers implemented an international trade initiative designed to fill a gap in Maryland's international trade efforts. Past efforts had emphasized attracting firms to Maryland (not promoting exports), since this was the responsibility charged to the Department of Economic and Community Development (DECD). The international trade initiative focused on developing international markets for Maryland's products and encouraging business activity overseas. It called for three basic strategies: creation of a trade policy council, strengthening of current programs, and creation of an international trade office.

The first strategy established a coordinating mechanism to improve participation and communication among different key public and private actors. The trade policy council, chaired by the lieutenant governor, would advise the governor and the general assembly about the state's role in international trade. More important, it would serve as a vehicle for private-sector input and for public-private coordination. Since the council is made up of federal, state, and local government officials, it helps ensure better coordination of international marketing efforts, overseas offices, and information and assistance to state exporters. The trade policy council meets quarterly and is attended by all department directors.

The second strategy included the strengthening of transportation facilities and the promotion of Maryland's port and other transportation assets through the state's department of transportation.

The third strategy, and the primary thrust of the international trade program, was the establishment of the Office of International Trade (OIT) within the DECD. The OIT's central purpose is to facilitate job creation by increasing exports and by providing assistance to potential state exporters. Six areas are outlined within the OIT: export program, barter and countertrade, joint-venture assistance, sister-state relationships, regional and international marketing efforts, and overseas operations. The export program consists of counseling and serving as an "information filler" to distribute appropriate information to small businesses. Related activities include assisting small businesses in market entry by trade exhibitions and assistance with documentation, publishing a newsletter and channeling leads to Maryland firms, and providing financial guarantees to assist businesses by expanding the Maryland Industrial Development Financing Authority (MIDFA) for export financing. Barter and countertrade is a unique program that attempts to assist export efforts when an overvalued dollar would normally prevent exporting. Countertrade is a technique for obtaining goods or services without having to use money and usually involves a set of agreements between two countries. According to the *California and the Pacific Rim* (1986) report, countertrade accounts for 40 percent of world trade. Maryland's program is structured to involve the state in this growing trade development.

Joint-venture assistance is specifically designed to help small and medium-sized businesses that do not possess the in-house expertise to carry out such export efforts. Sister-state relationships— an important strategy used by many states—were promoted to assist international efforts by providing a trade advantage with three regions: Nord Pas Calai Region, France; Kanagawa Prefecture, Japan; and Anhui Province, China. OIT's marketing efforts consist of assisting counties in establishing international trade programs, helping to further the development of foreign-trade zones, and emphasizing Maryland's geographical advantages to foreign countries. Finally, overseas offices, currently operating in Brussels and Tokyo with a budget of $485,000, are intended, in part, to promote reverse investment. It will also be the responsibility of these overseas offices to provide export assistance to Maryland firms.

For its size, Maryland has the most extensive international program in the country. In 1986, it appropriated $1.4 million for its international activities and employed a full-time staff of eighteen. Only nine states have appropriated more funds than Maryland, and only eight states have allocated more staff to their international departments.

Are International Strategies Cost-Effective?

The effectiveness of state and local trade programs and initiatives in attracting direct foreign investment is difficult to evaluate empirically, since they are relatively new efforts. The problem of evaluating programs is further compounded by the wide variety of international approaches found among states. Ohio, for example, has initiated a strategic plan that is designed almost exclusively to boost state exports, targeting financial, insurance, legal, and professional services for assistance. Illinois, on the other hand, not only encourages export-specific goods (particularly steel and corn) but has one of the strongest programs in the country to encourage foreign investment (it conducted twenty-five international trade shows in 1985 and 1986 alone). Maryland is relying heavily on port expansion in Baltimore, while Kentucky is promoting agricultural products by the creation of an export trading company. In the Pacific Northwest, Washington and Oregon are initiating aggressive international marketing programs. Oregon's recent repeal of the unitary tax responded, to some extent, to California's dominance in attracting foreign investment. Following a different strategy, Washington generated $43 million in additional sales from 1981 to 1986 through its export promotion programs. According to state estimates, this accounted for nearly 7,000 new jobs and about $300 million in capital investments (Clarke, 1986).

As a result of these diverse strategies employed by states, and because presently there is a lack of empirical evaluation to determine the effectiveness of these programs, the following questions must be used as a policy guide to assess the appropriateness of state and local international economic strategies:

- Do the state and local governments possess the financial resources they need to engage in international affairs and, more important, the commitment by the state, local, and private-sector leadership they need to ensure a successful program?
- Have tax incentives to recruit domestic and international firms (for example, repeal of sales tax on production machinery) made the state or locality more competitive than a strategy emphasizing infrastructural and human capital investments would have made it?
- Can an international economic approach be strategically linked to substantive policies dealing with education, job retraining, and capital finance?
- Are policies designed for the strategic long-term needs and strengths of the state and local economy?
- In developing international programs, have state and local leaders carefully assessed the economic global forces outside their control and how their policies could be undermined by these forces?
- Finally, as part of an overall strategy for economic development, does a focus on international affairs merely reflect a knee-jerk reaction to what other states are doing to create jobs?

Is International Recruitment Worth It?

Most states are interested in engaging in a global industrial recruitment program to increase foreign investment. Unfortunately, some agencies rush to implement such programs without carefully ascertaining whether the strategies are appropriate to their local economies, or whether they help diversify their economic base.

Although tax concessions have become a popular tool to attract foreign firms, empirical research indicates that a domestic or international firm's decision to locate in a certain region is only minimally influenced by taxes. Firms typically take into consideration three key cost components when making a location change: transportation, labor, and energy. Other salient factors include such issues as quality of education, recreation, and size and accessibility of markets (see Chapter Three). More important, job growth is associated more with the growth of existing firms than with the recruitment of new firms and with small businesses rather than large ones (see Chapter Five). Foreign investment programs may offer short-term benefits, but their cost may force states to raise taxes or lower the quality of existing public services; in the long term, this can become so burdensome to small and medium-sized local firms that they actually look to move elsewhere.

New Jersey's effort in state promotion to attract investment is an example of the competitive spiral that can occur between states. New Jersey sees New York as a formidable competitor in providing incentives to prospective foreign firms. New Jersey's strategy in this regard is straightforward: whatever they may want in New York, they can get it cheaper in New Jersey. For example, New Jersey in the last couple of years has repealed the unincorporated business tax and has eliminated the corporate business tax on regulated investment companies (it imposes instead a set fee). These state promotion efforts are questionable, however, because they depend on factors that are less salient than other market forces in determining location decisions. The loss of tax revenues due to these international incentives can also deplete the public funding needed to provide a quality labor force and infrastructural investments that actually influence business location decisions more directly. As a result of efforts like these, strategic needs for the long-term growth of a state or community can become secondary to questionable short-term goals of job recruitment.

Is Export Promotion Worth It?

Export promotion strategies assume that community income will increase as more firms export their products outside the state's boundaries, diversifying the economic base, particularly in regions that are experiencing a serious decline in goods-producing industries. It has been argued that a strong export promotion program can serve as a critical buffer against cyclical downturns in the national or regional economy (Kline, 1983). The difficulty in designing effective export promotion strategies, however, is that export industries are not always easy to identify. Conventional economic wisdom asserts that services-producing enterprises serve primarily local demands, while goods-producing enterprises, such as manufacturing and agriculture, are more likely to export goods.

This does not fit with the current economy for two basic reasons. First, a large part of the manufacturing sector may exist to meet local demands, including printing, food processing, and the production of some fabricated metals and certain types of mechanical and electrical equipment. Second, important services-producing enterprises can be export-driven, even though they would be difficult for a development agency to identify in advance. For example, since 1980, legal services have surpassed apparel as New York City's largest export industry. It is therefore difficult to assess generally the effectiveness of export promotion programs without examining the specific local or state economy involved (Vaughan and others, 1984).

More important, there are data regarding the effect of state export expansion activities and job generation. On the one hand, Carlino and Mills (1987) question whether economic policies such as export-related activities contribute to employment growth. After a review of existing empirical evidence, they conclude that these state strategies may have no noticeable effect on employment. On the other hand, however, a more recent time-series analysis of all fifty states' export-expansion activities indicates that state policies that affect state exports positively influence job creation (Coughlin and Cartwright, 1987).

Effective International Economic Development Strategies

Not every city or state can initiate international economic strategies. Those that do pursue foreign investment initiatives and export promotion programs must consider, first, whether the area's business enterprises and economic base are appropriate for increased trade and tourism, and second, how the investment and export programs fit with other economic resources such as human capital, public infrastructure, and capital availability. Effective international initiatives must be a part of a larger set of development strategies. No state or local international policies, regardless of how ambitious they are, can offset deficiences in human resources, infrastructure, or capital. A one-dimensional policy that measures economic wealth solely in terms of gross investment and export gains is a policy that will most likely ignore the long-term strategic advantage of its community's unique economic strengths.

Seattle provides an excellent example of a city that is trying to strategically design related development policies that take advantage of its unique strengths. Since Seattle's port acts as the gateway for imports and exports passing through Washington State (trade accounts for one out of five jobs in the state), the city officials are building on what they call "the interconnectedness of economic and cultural issues" as a strategic step in promoting Seattle as an international city (Crowley, 1984, pp. 1–3). Their methods include making Seattle more comfortable for foreign visitors, especially those from East Asia, and learning that cultural issues are essential to social contact; developing a network with universities and colleges to apply their knowledge and resources to international contacts; supporting nonprofit and citizen-based efforts to stimulate foreign exchange; pursuing the concept of Seattle as world trade center; and creating international trade parks and designating international zones with multilingual signs. Furthermore, Seattle has linked its eleven sister-city relationships to its international relations activities as a means of complementing its own short- and long-term goals in promoting trade and tourism. The creation of an Office of International Relations was an important step in coordinating this new activity.

If an export promotion or foreign investment policy fits with a state or locality's economic base and other economic resources, how should the state or locality proceed in order to maximize its unique assets? There are three general guidelines that can be useful in promoting programs that strategically fit the state's or city's needs and abilities.

First, before any international development program is

started, a comprehensive analysis of the state's or city's economic base must be made to pinpoint the strategic weaknesses and strengths of the local economy. This rather simple notion is often overlooked by state and local officials who feel compelled to put together quickly a set of international programs (partly because of competition with other states or localities). This feeling is understandable. The danger in this approach, however, is that an investment or export promotion program that is appropriate for one state or region may be inappropriate for another. The determination of which policy is most congruent to the particular economic needs of a state or locality can be assessed by a careful analysis of some of the following factors:

1. The existing imports and exports of the local economy.
2. The existing linkages between the service sector and the manufacturing sector. For example, 25 percent of California's service employment is directly connected to manufacturing (Borrus, 1985). Since the growth of services-producing enterprises is integrally linked to the success of goods-producing industries, any export promotion policy must be sensitive to the relationship of these two sectors in order to sustain the growth of the service sector.
3. Potential international markets for small business exports and which businesses can compete best in a particular market niche.
4. External and internal factors affecting local export companies in the global economy. External factors include trade (for example, a strong dollar, foreign competition), the business cycle (for example, interest rates, disinflation, recession), federal policies (for example, R&D tax credits, tax treatment of international operations, tax subsidies), and changing markets (for example, increased world supply of certain goods, differential labor costs in other countries). Internal factors include technology (for example, impact of process technology, adoption of technologies), human resources (for example, human capital investment, role of public universities), financial capital (for example, cost of capital, availability of public and private lending, debt problems of companies), and

management (for example, management practices in response
to market changes, efficacy of existing marketing strategies in
the world markets).

While this analysis may initially seem ambitious in scope, it is
nevertheless helpful in assessing where to allocate public resources
strategically to initiate successfully an international development
policy.

    Second, after analyzing the economic interdependencies of
the local or state economy, an assessment of the institutional
capacities and the governmental role most appropriate to achieve
international objectives is needed. The institutional framework that
is ultimately implemented will obviously depend on how ambitious
the strategic goals are and on the financial resources that are
available. According to a Community Development Training
Institute (CDTI) study, most American cities cannot afford to
administer adequately an aggressive international policy (Tigan,
1986). Assuming that some international approach is warranted, the
institutional framework decided on will largely be contingent on
the level of involvement the local and state governments want with
the business community. The levels of involvement can be grouped
into the following broad governmental roles (Levine, 1986):

- *Advocate.* This role is perhaps appropriate for most cities and
  for less wealthy states, such as Vermont, South Dakota, Maine,
  Idaho, Montana, Nevada, and North Dakota. The local or state
  government generates state or local exports by increasing the
  awareness of the business community, perhaps by sponsoring a
  conference on the opportunities of exporting goods in selected
  overseas markets, or by generating media support for trade
  efforts. This approach requires a minimum of public funds and
  expertise.
- *Service Access Provider.* Essentially, a government agency acts
  as an exporter facilitator, referring businesses to the proper
  export assistance. This role also entails serving as a liaison to
  the federal government and other public- and private-sector
  organizations.
- *Coordinator.* This role incorporates the first two. The local or

state government coordinates activities such as export seminars and trade information workshops in preparing businesses for export promotion. The government may also coordinate trade missions and visits from foreign governments. On certain occasions, this coordinating could entail specific agreements between local, state, and federal programs.

- *Direct Service Provider.* The government provides appropriate funding in order to deliver specific governmental technical services to exporters. These include export counseling, market studies, trade mission shows, financing, language banks, how-to books, and dissemination of trade leads to ensure more effective state or local exporting. This approach is expensive, but it can be effective in reaching new businesses that would find it difficult to export their goods without direct assistance. However, because nonprofit or private organizations can be helpful in some of these areas, a local government should be cautious before undertaking this rather expensive and ambitious endeavor; only large cities and states should carefully consider this option.

- *Service Funder.* The government provides a service through a service vendor (public or private). This role is similar to the preceding one, except that the city or state is relieved of the administrative burden (although not of the financial burden) of implementing the program. An example of this approach is when a sponsoring local government hires an export management firm to identify potential export buyers and link manufacturers with certain clients overseas or to assess the exportability of particular local products.

- *Joint Venture.* This approach is a unique joint governmental effort by complementary local or state agencies that pool their efforts and resources in the pursuit of an international policy. Such joint efforts are occurring in New England, the South, and the Midwest. The Mid-South Trade Council, for example, formed by the export offices of Mississippi, Tennessee, Arkansas, and Alabama, in 1984 conducted a catalogue show in Latin America to promote investment. A similar regional approach to international trade was developed by Georgia, Indiana, Iowa, Kentucky, Missouri, and West Virginia and called the Mid-

America Trade Council. At the state government level, this approach is a way to ameliorate the competition that often occurs between states. It can also be applied with cities. The Metropolitan Partnership of Eugene-Springfield (Oregon), for example, combines one city with a strong service sector and an adjacent city with a manufacturing base, building on their different economic strengths without causing intercity rivalry.

* *Foundation.* This role is the most comprehensive approach, since it combines most of the other approaches with the creation of a new organization for export promotion and foreign investment. This new organization (a development corporation, for example) combines both public and private resources in order to coordinate all local or regional international activities. This organizational framework may also be capable of engaging in profit-making endeavors. It is rarely utilized by either local or state government, particularly since it may not be allowable under some state or local laws.

No single export development approach is appropriate for all localities or states. The determination of which option to choose will depend on the city or state experimenting with different approaches, or combinations of approaches, that are suitable for achieving its short- and long-term strategic goals. In general, a developmental process should occur, building from the basic Advocate approach to more administratively and financially ambitious options like Direct Service Provider and Service Funder. Any program should be considered an experiment and have a mandatory three-year evaluation review. This review is critical, first, because few data exist to predict which approach is more cost-effective, and second, because many of these approaches may be found to be better implemented by existing private or nonprofit organizations. A recent example is the use of export trading companies. Export trading companies, modeled somewhat after Japan and the Western European nations, have been developed by the ports of New Jersey and New York, North Dakota, and more recently by Mississippi, New Jersey, Oregon, and Virginia. These export trading companies (created by the Export Trading Company Act of 1982) have had major difficulties: current law limits their ability to trade, and there is little public-sector expertise in operating them. Thus, it may be more appropriate for this approach to be managed by more experienced export-management firms, financial and insurance companies, and freight forward companies, rather than a public export trading company. However, without a few years of actual experience, the cost-effectiveness of this approach cannot be fully evaluated.

Finally, the effectiveness of an international program will be determined by whether it is commensurate with the short- and long-term strategic goals of other economic development efforts; hence a "strategic fit" must be achieved among the developmental goals of infrastructure investment, human capital, natural resources, and capital investment. Surprisingly, the issue of compatibility of economic development goals is ignored by most states and localities. Even California—with its economic base so interdependent with the world economy—has been accused of formulating an international economic program that lacks cohesion (*California and the 21st Century*, 1986). International policies are interdependent with overall economic development goals and cannot be separated from other issues, such as the educational level of the work force, the transportation and telecommunications infrastructure, and the availability of financial capital. Specific suggestions for this strategic fit between an international program and related development programs might include:

- combining an export promotion or investment approach with policies related to business retention, regulation of finance industry, and job retraining programs;
- assessing foreign investment strategies for their effect on employment in specific companies and industries and whether such investments—given the fact of capital mobility—can be beneficial in the long term; and
- combining international activities with improvements in basic education and skills of students in the primary, secondary, and university systems. This includes exposing students to foreign languages, geography, foreign cultures, international studies, and trade.

This is only a partial list of possible linkages between international economic activities and other economic development strategies. The critical issue is that without these linkages, states and localities will find their international approaches, regardless of how well conceived, divorced from the interdependency of issues that policymakers must face in designing an economic development program compatible with their specific needs and abilities.

Conclusion

The relationship of domestic economies and international affairs has been called by one scholar "intermestic politics" (Manning, 1977). Intermestic politics have become particularly important for governors and mayors who find their economies vulnerable to changes in the global economy. Interestingly, the U.S. government has encouraged states to promote foreign trade and reverse investment in the belief that objectives at the domestic and international levels are basically aligned, although nuanced differently. This enthusiasm about state and local involvement in international affairs has not been without its critics. For example, the U.S. Trade Representative and the Treasury Department have been alarmed regarding state powers of taxation. The potential uses of taxation to help state export trade and investment could lead to trouble with GATT and its standards. Furthermore, the State Department worries that states' various commercial initiatives, such as Kentucky's desire for trade with South Africa, will take on disturbing political overtones. Moreover, U.S. negotiators will have to consider that any multilateral agreement with other countries must also address the issue of state government investment strategies (Kline, 1984). This could force the federal government to maintain control over state policies in this area.

The issue is even more perplexing on the trade side. This is illustrated, in part, by state governments that have initiated "Buy America" provisions, contrary to the open trade policy of the United States (Kline, 1984). Some countries have argued that such state government action is contrary to international trade practices in that it forces other countries to deal with fifty states as if they were fifty different countries.

These issues are real, since state and local involvement in international economic affairs is not a passing phenomenon. The pivotal issue is how to coordinate effectively international activities with a strategic economic plan, and, more important, what should be the scope of state or local involvement in this area.

8

How Colleges and Universities
Can Enhance Development

A dynamic economy requires well-educated people and new ideas. Higher education is a source of both. Community colleges, four-year colleges, and universities have an important contribution to make to a state's and a region's economic vitality, and in many regions of the country they have become the cornerstone of state and local economic development. States' economic futures, and the vitality of the American economy itself, are increasingly linked to universities, colleges, and community colleges.

Education, training, and human capital development have historically been the primary activities of universities and colleges, and they have contributed directly to economic development through higher levels of personal income. The relationship between the general education level of the regional labor force and economic development has been known for many years. High levels of educational attainment are clearly associated with high levels of personal income and low unemployment rates. Similarly, low levels of educational attainment are associated with low income and high unemployment. Generally, educated workers earn substantially more than workers with less education. Related studies indicate that the quality and quantity of postsecondary education influence the personal earnings and economic growth of a region. For example, the median household income for "baby boomers" (the bulk of the current and future work force) rises steadily with education, from $12,000 for high school dropouts to approximately $32,000 for householders with some graduate-level education (U.S. Bureau of the Census, 1985). Higher family incomes increase local and regional economic activity because they allow increased spending.

Adam Smith, in his classic *The Wealth of Nations* (1937), first asserted that human capital is the principal resource of economic growth and wealth creation. The goals of human capital development, however, have changed. New fields, such as biotechnology, have emerged, requiring new skills. In addition, technological advances affecting established industries are creating new demands for skilled employees; owing to robotics, for example, the auto industry now requires more computer engineers and fewer mechanical engineers. Today, corporate leaders are concerned that current institutions of higher learning are a barrier to, not a generator of, economic growth. The 1983 study *A Nation at Risk* (National Commission on Excellence in Education, 1983) concluded that the nation is in peril and that our economic vitality and survival are in danger because the educational systems are not adapting. Top corporate executives are saying that the nation's businesses are not competing effectively in world markets because of the inadequacy of the country's educational system. States' economic futures, and the vitality of the American economy itself, are increasingly linked to universities, colleges, and community colleges. President Reagan's Commission on Industrial Competitiveness, in 1985, concluded that universities and schools have a crucial role to play in revitalizing the nation's economy and that strong educational institutions are needed to capitalize on key strengths in technology and human resources. A growing number of reports have documented the inadequacies of elementary, secondary, and postsecondary education and strongly suggest that human capital inadequacies can be a significant brake on state economic growth over the next decade. The educational attainment of the population of a state or community is an important measure of its capacity to sustain a vital economy; in many regions, human capital inadequacies are a significant barrier to economic development.

The recognition of the strategic importance of human capital fundamentally changes the way state and local policymakers must think about a region's colleges and universities. Higher education can now play a more prominent partnership role in promoting and enhancing long-term economic wealth. States and communities must learn to utilize colleges and universities as an integral part of their development strategies. This chapter will examine the relationship between education and the postindustrial economy that is increasingly information-based and global. It will also explore the three broad roles colleges and universities play in state and local economic development: human development, technological development, and policy development. This will be followed by a discussion of the implications for state and local government in forging appropriate development programs.

Higher Education and Economic Development

Recent studies suggest a critical link between local and state economies and institutions of higher education. At the local level, five key factors were found to be critical for economic development in America's cities and towns: a highly educated and trained work force; high-quality university research; high-quality transportation and communication infrastructure; a physically attractive environment; and professional management and efficient provision of local public services (Birch, 1984). At the state level, recent business climate research shows the decreasing importance of traditional, industry-related business factors such as low wages. The most recent analysis by AmeriTrust (a Cleveland-based bank-holding company) and SRI International (formerly the Stanford Research Institute) found that rapid technological changes experienced by the American economy and the crystallization of a global, internationalized economy have transformed the factors necessary for healthy state business climates. This research identifies the three most important factors in today's state economies, two of which are closely linked to higher education institutions; they are:

- A skilled and adaptable work force—the extent to which an area possesses a skilled and adaptable work force (its human capital), maintains strong education and training institutions, and encourages public-private collaboration to meet the skill needs of business and the training and retraining needs of individuals
- Accessible technology—the extent to which there are adequate

science and technology resources, accessible research institutions, and mechanisms for commercialization of technologies

- Capital availability—the extent to which capital is available for all types of business needs (from new enterprise formation to corporate venturing by large firms) through a variety of lending sources, including regional financial institutions and venture capitalists, and the extent to which the availability of capital is encouraged by state regulations and other policies (SRI International, 1986b)

Many of the recent state economic development strategic plans, based on assessments of the states' economic strengths and weaknesses, place substantial emphasis on education. The report of the North Carolina Economic Development Board (1986) identified education as a critical strategic issue. Two of its top three issues were adult illiteracy and work force training (the third was infrastructure). A report by the Commission on the Future of the South (1986) similarly concludes that investments in educational systems are fundamental. Four of its ten recommendations for the southeastern states concerned education; other goals were increasing the South's capacity to generate and use new technology and developing leaders with a global vision. A review of a variety of states' economic reports and strategic plans shows a strong similarity in their emphasis on training and education (Liner, 1987).

A distinguishing characteristic of the postindustrial economy, and a major reason for the renewed attention to higher education, is the increased importance of information versus labor and energy in the production of goods and services. Information has become the most important raw material, and it is through information processing that economic value is added to goods and services. It is through information processing and knowledge development, for example, that agriculture and manufacturing continue to produce more with fewer employees. Generally speaking, the current information-based economy is characterized by the following factors: the development of information-intensive products (such as biotechnology and computer software), the ability to send and receive information from nearly any place on earth, the almost instantaneous communication that is possible between one place and another, the amount of information that can be transmitted, the miniaturization of computer and communication technologies, the increased utilization of telecommunicated messages compared to transactions requiring physical movement, the ability to select from expanding data banks the precise information needed for making economic policy and investment decisions, and the ability through artificial intelligence to solve problems in ways beyond individual human capabilities (Dillman, 1986, p. 45).

One result of the increased importance of information is that the need for human capital development has shifted from production skills to information-processing and problem-solving skills. In addition, most of the jobs now being created require a capacity for working with other people; and few of the new jobs require manual or physical skills (except for word processing). Most of the new jobs demand an ability to adjust to forces requiring continual changes in products, processes, and management structures. A comparison of the past and emerging economies' needs shows the course that human capital development must take:

Historical Needs	*Emerging Needs*
Developing skills for agricultural and manufacturing industries	Developing skills for information, knowledge, and service industries
Knowledge about local and regional markets	Knowledge about national and international markets
Developing technical expertise	Developing skills in learning how to learn
Raw materials and financial capital as strategic resources	Knowledge and information processing as strategic resources
Training for highly predictable work force	Training for a highly flexible, learning work force
Slowly changing skill requirements	Skill requirements that can change every four to ten years
Workers working primarily with their hands and by themselves	Workers working primarily with their minds and with other people

States are recognizing the link between higher education and economic development and are beginning to invest in a wide variety of research-oriented programs. A study for the National Conference of Lieutenant Governors (Tucker, 1985) found a common set of strategies being used in states across the country. These strategies included increasing salaries at the state's leading engineering school, building advanced technology research centers with close industry ties at the leading research university or a consortium of research universities, creating centers of excellence, establishing a research park to attract private firms engaged in targeted enterprises, establishing a mechanism for improving the communication of research results produced by state universities to private entrepreneurs, improving coordination between state agencies responsible for jobs programs and those responsible for vocational education, and offering free or low-cost vocational training to firms relocating in the state or expanding existing facilities.

Local governments are utilizing universities and colleges to a lesser degree. A survey of twelve medium-sized cities nationwide with universities and colleges (City of Eugene, 1987) provides a glimpse of local government utilization of higher education institutions in economic development planning. Over 40 percent of the cities did not use or minimally used their local universities as resources in local economic development. Three of the twelve cities surveyed (25 percent) did not involve their local university or college in any of their economic development efforts. Two of the cities (18 percent) were involved with higher education only minimally for real estate purposes; their university or college owned parcels of land that they were trying either to buy or to sell for redevelopment purposes. Another one-fourth of the cities engaged the university or college in the development of research parks. In addition, three of the twelve cities used their local university or college to obtain economic and demographic analyses. Only one city of the twelve surveyed worked with a university to spur technology transfer.

None of the cities in this survey developed any formal process for evaluating the effectiveness of joint university–local government efforts, making any empirical assessment impossible. Nevertheless, there is certainly increased movement by state and local governments to utilize colleges and universities in stimulating economic development. In addition, nearly 40 percent of universities surveyed nationwide now include economic development in their mission (SRI International, 1986a). Colleges and universities provide three resources for state and local economic development: stimulating adult learning and human development, stimulating scientific and technological development, and providing economic analysis and policy development.

Adult Learning and Human Development

Although increased interest has recently focused attention on higher education's role in stimulating scientific research and technological development, human capital inadequacy, not research transfer, is likely to be the brake on state and local economic development into the twenty-first century. The educational attainment of the population of a state or community is often the clearest measure of its capacity to sustain a vital economy; in many regions, human capital inadequacies will become the biggest barrier to job creation. Employment rates and business incorporation rates are influenced by the quality of a state or community's human capital.

Higher education develops skills and imparts knowledge to the work force of a state and region. Human capital is roughly the stored human productive potential of a region's work force. It is defined not by the number of available workers, but by their capacity, that is, by what they are capable of doing with their knowledge, skill, and experience (Schultz, 1971).

Human capital is difficult to understand, and difficult to give financial meaning to, because it is largely invisible. Public investment in human capital development is hampered by vagueness and uncertainties in outcome. The intellectual currency and products of a person's brain are not easily counted. The processes that produce and enhance this invisible resource are, therefore, not well understood. For these reasons, the strategic connection between human capital development and economic development often remains invisible.

Not only is this resource invisible, but considerable time is required to develop and maintain it. It is subject to depreciation in two ways: first, lack of practice and idleness cause degeneration of human capital, and second, it can be made obsolete by new knowledge and skills. The development of human capital thus requires state and local policymakers to pay attention to an invisible resource.

Most of the current discussion on educational reform focuses on primary and secondary schools. As the requirements increase for an internationally and technologically literate work force to compete economically in the global marketplace, educational policy discussions remain fixed on youth, not adults. Although reforms in K–12 education are very important, the critical relation between adult learning and economic development also must be recognized as a critical priority for several reasons. First, technological and economic changes will require the average worker to change careers from two to four times during his or her adulthood. Second, from 75 to 80 percent of the people who will constitute the American work force in the year 2000 are adults today. Third, an estimated 20 percent of the current work force is functionally illiterate; in the United States, there are more adult illiterates than there are students in private and public secondary schools combined (Perelman, 1984).

Basic Adult Education. The definition of basic education—the skills a person needs to participate effectively in society—has changed. To eliminate irrelevant curricula, and to avoid educating people in obsolete skills for a society of the past, college and university curricula must be reassessed. Simply offering more of the same sorts of education may not produce the required human capital. Curricular change is needed not just to respond to industry's needs; the primary mission of higher education is not to assist industry, but to educate and to seek knowledge. A shift in basic adult education is particularly needed to maintain our capacity for self-governance in a global economy.

By 1987, fueled by a number of reports critical of higher education, 95 percent of America's colleges were changing or considering changing their core curricula. Three-fourths are instituting or are considering the establishment of new general education requirements that focus on improving students' mathematical, computer-related, and writing skills. In addition, there is increasing attention to making the interdisciplinary linkages between subjects more visible, improving skills in critical thinking, increasing foreign-language proficiency, and broadening the students' perspectives by offering courses in international studies as well as the study of women, minorities, and the disadvantaged (Heller, 1987). The thrust of these curricular reforms is to expand students' capacities to live in the more complex, interdependent world that now exists.

Familiarity with science and technology is increasingly necessary. In many regions of the country, however, there are serious and growing shortages of high-quality faculty in the fields of computer science and engineering. In addition, there are fewer students entering graduate school to pursue advanced degrees in science and engineering programs. Complicating this situation is the blurring of the line between the disciplines of engineering and computer science. As a result, basic science education may be obsolete or lacking. California, attempting to deal with part of this situation, has proposed an engineering and computer science doctoral assistance program to reduce the faculty shortage in these two fields. The National Governors Association (1987) has recommended increases in scholarship programs for science students and is encouraging new interdisciplinary programs in science, engineering, and business.

There is an increasing need for higher levels of international skills in the arts and sciences as well as in business. The National Commission on the Role and Future of State Colleges and Universities has proposed a strong international dimension in general education that will provide, first, an international perspective that accurately reflects today's global, interdependent economy, as well as an understanding of values, viewpoints, and government structures of other nations; and second, skills in international communications and foreign languages that will enable students to think, behave, and create effectively in an interdependent world (American Association of State Colleges and Universities, 1986). Foreign language competency is now critical for successful competition in the world economy. For most Americans, foreign language means Spanish, French, or German. However, important languages of the future will be Chinese, Russian, Japanese, Portuguese, Arabic, Indonesian, and Swahili.

Schools and colleges of business and management must also examine their effectiveness in producing entrepreneurs and managers capable of competing in a world market. Faced with a loss of competitiveness brought on by foreign incursions into America's domestic and foreign markets, business schools need to include meaningful international training in their curricula. The globalization of the economy creates a need for improved knowledge and a heightened understanding of the cultures, markets, and languages of other countries. Managers and entrepreneurs must learn how to handle export trade, deal with foreign clients and foreign currency, and develop an understanding of economic developments abroad that affect a firm's capability to buy or sell in foreign markets. To compete effectively in foreign markets, American managers should study the capital structure, marketing strategies, governmental relationships, and management and personnel practices of their foreign competitors. According to Robert Ward, director of Stanford's International Studies Programs, however, most graduate schools of business notably fail to provide this sort of training. Of the seven leading business schools in the mid 1980s, only one included substantial international training in its curriculum; the rest offered only fragmentary training in a handful of elective courses. This has been the rule, not the exception, for America's business schools (R. Ward, 1986).

Learning how to learn is becoming a more important part of adult education. States that attempt to stimulate economic growth must stimulate the development of a state work force capable of competing in a global economy, a work force with access to the entrepreneurial and management skills required for developing and marketing new products in foreign markets. At the same time, the work force must be competent in learning how to learn, capable of growing and developing as the technology and the markets shift. The ability to learn and adapt is essential. The advances in science and technology are making it necessary for people to learn to do new things, as well as to learn to do old things in new ways. This creates a demand for constant retraining and updating of the local work force.

Retraining and Continuous Adult Learning. Basic education for entry-level positions may no longer be the central educational role of postsecondary educational institutions. The fastest-
growing segment of higher education is adult learners, and the
majority of students enrolled in the 1990s will be adults returning
part-time, not the traditional eighteen-year-old, full-time student.
From 75 to 80 percent of the people who will constitute the work
force in the year 2000 are already in the workplace today. The
graying of the baby-boom generation and the increasing number of
women in the work force indicate that new entrants into a
particular career or line of work are more likely to be mature adults.
Today, there is an unprecedented requirement for adult retraining
and continuous adult learning. The need for retraining will
continue to rise, increasing faster than total employment over the
next decade, for four reasons. First, job creation is occurring in
those telecommunication, knowledge, and service sectors that
typically require the most formal training and on-the-job training.
Second, growth in the work force is largest in the twenty-five-to-
forty-four-year-old population group, the age group that has
historically received the most training opportunities. Third, worker
displacement and dislocation are increasing dramatically as the
economy shifts from manufacturing to services; these displaced
workers need retraining for new careers and job opportunities.
Fourth, members of the baby-boom era are facing heavy competition for career advancement and are seeking increased training
opportunities to improve their chances for upward mobility
(Perelman, 1984). As the need for retraining expands, increased
attention by state and local governments must be focused on specific
retraining strategies, institutional roles, and relevant policies.

Retraining is most effective when it is targeted to specific
business enterprises. Recent research indicates that training
sponsored by the Job Training Partnership Act (JTPA) that
targeted a specific business closure or permanent layoff achieved
better results than projects not having such a focus (U.S. General
Accounting Office, 1987). Research in vocational education also
indicates that the retraining of displaced or soon-to-be displaced
employees is more effective and cost-effective when conducted in-
house (see, for example, Wilms, 1986). Another factor influencing

the success of worker retraining is that voluntary programs are consistently more successful and cost-effective than mandatory programs. This voluntary factor is often overlooked in the development of employee retraining efforts and is unfortunately seldom considered in evaluating public policy strategies. Effective retraining policies and programs should therefore include appropriate incentives that are targeted to a particular plant closure; they should be conducted in-house; and participation in them by the displaced worker should be voluntary.

The implications of these findings are significant for community colleges, four-year colleges, and universities. Business firms that do not provide retraining strategies ultimately place the responsibility for worker retraining on the shoulders of postsecondary educational institutions and corporate training programs. Large, mature companies may be able to institute internal retraining programs. However, firms that have recently relocated, or that are expanding from a small enterprise, or that are laying off employees are much less likely to establish internal retraining efforts. In these cases, the community or state needs to aggressively facilitate or broker employee retraining.

One example of brokering is the Technology Exchange Center, a nonprofit, community-based agency created in 1982 and based at a community college in California. The center identifies businesses in its region that have training or retraining needs that they cannot fill themselves and finds community colleges willing to set up flexible, custom-designed programs quickly. This center is only one of several around the United States that function as educational brokers to improve the match between community college programs and businesses' training needs (Fields, 1987).

New and expanding firms are finding that such brokers help identify ways to receive quality training at lower costs by contracting with colleges and universities. State and local governments can use various forms of educational brokering by creating quasi-public agencies with staffs that reach out to employers who need retraining for their employees. This strategy shifts the role of state and local governments from directly providing training and retraining to acting as catalysts or facilitators who link private firms with educational institutions. The Bay State Skills Corporation in

Massachusetts, a state-sponsored agency, has awarded several grants for employee retraining programs, lasting from twelve weeks to two years, designed to advance developing industries in the state, including fiber optics, artificial intelligence, robotics, telecommunications, photovoltaics, and marine science (Fields, 1987). The corporation arranges partnerships between educational institutions and business firms, helps negotiate contracts, and makes grants that are often matched by the private sector in money, equipment, facilities, or services.

In addition to modernizing production plants, research laboratories, and technology, economic development policy must focus on modernizing human capital through retraining and updating skills. Retraining programs are necessary as the pace of technological change quickens and economic dislocations brought on by international competition restructure people's jobs. Unfortunately, adult education is seen by many policymakers as something remedial or recreational or as something affecting only the disadvantaged, the poor, or the retired (Perelman, 1984). Continuous learning, however, is now a necessary part of any job, and it is a fundamental responsibility of colleges and universities to provide retraining opportunities in addition to basic education.

The major barrier to states, communities, and universities providing new and expanded retraining opportunities is the antiquated image of training activities. In the industrial era, training was seen as the programming of workers for the efficient performance of repetitive tasks. Skill requirements have obviously changed from manufacturing skills to information-processing skills. Vocational training programs, however, focus heavily on entry-level training and often neglect the current and future needs for advanced skilled-worker retraining. Additionally, public-sector training programs are typically structured toward helping the disadvantaged and entry-level workers and ignore the basic skill needs of functionally illiterate adults whose learning handicaps prevent them even from participating in job-specific training (Perelman, 1984). Retraining in the postindustrial economy may be required from two to four times in the course of a person's working life, making continuous learning a necessary part of any job. The scope of existing public policies toward retraining must now be expanded to focus on continued adult learning for the entire work force. Although long-term investments in human capital may take a decade to pay off, investment in public educational systems increase a region's ability to compete in national and international marketplaces (Weinstein and Gross, 1985).

Scientific Research and Technological Development

One aspect of the universities' role in economic development is the link between basic and applied research and business formation, expansion, and attraction. The educational system has traditionally been seen, for the most part, as the key supplier and producer of a competent work force. Not only is this human development role given serious attention today, but companies and business leaders have rediscovered the fundamental importance of universities in providing the technological foundations for new products.

First, the rapid, accelerating pace of technological changes in many industries requires that the time lag between basic research and commercial application become shorter. Universities are the primary producers of basic research, and industries perform by far the greatest portion of applied research and development (National Science Foundation, 1984). University faculty traditionally stressed basic research, while private enterprise looked for practical, and profitable, applications. The postindustrial economy, however, is blurring the traditional distinctions between basic research and applied research. As a result, research collaboration between universities and private corporations is steadily increasing. To hasten the movement of ideas and information from basic research to applied research and then to commercial development, industries are seeking cooperative projects with universities in such fields as microelectronics, biotechnology, health science, and computer hardware and software. Such collaboration produces new products and processes for commercial marketing. It can also enliven and refresh the knowledge base of the university and bring substantial new resources to campuses.

A second driving force for increased university-industry research linkages is that the boundaries between scientific disciplines have become blurred. Research that crosses traditional disciplinary boundaries has led to some of the most important recent advances, and many industries seek assistance from universities to stimulate these multidisciplinary developments. Industries are not only forging alliances with universities; they are also forming joint research efforts with other companies, even historical arch-competitors, collaboration that was nearly impossible in the 1970s. In the United States, corporations have formed more than forty research consortia to jointly apply their research effort to such common problems as television transmission and plastics recycling. Robert Price, chairman of Control Data Corporation, explains that "Technology is so complex and changing so rapidly that no one company can maintain all the necessary R&D resources" ("Now, R&D . . . ," 1986).

States are thus paying closer attention to their research universities and are increasing their support for research and development as one of several strategies to attract certain types of industries and to incubate new business enterprises. In 1980, for example, only four states had programs for the development of science- and technology-based enterprises; by 1985; thirty-three states had such programs, and at least five other states were making advanced research and development plans (Clarke, 1986). Although state programs differ, they are similar in three important respects: first, many states provide grants for research and development work by private firms as well as universities; second, they emphasize joint funding between the public and private sectors, for example, through "challenge grants"; and third, the funding to universities is most often directed to a research institute established for specified purposes rather than to a university's entire budget (Brawley, 1986).

Basic Research. Universities are the primary sources for developing new knowledge and providing basic research that have long-term payoffs. This role has increased in importance in the wake of rapid technological and scientific developments. Increasingly, this function is supported by state funds contingent on an industry match; this has resulted in new university research approaches and university-industry relationships. These efforts at stimulating basic research and increased technological development have met with the most resistance from university faculty. Concerns revolve around the politicization of basic research, potential conflicts of interest, and perceived threats to academic freedom. Two basic research strategies that have met with less resistance are centers of excellence and jointly funded research programs in targeted areas of statewide interest. Both focus on stimulating basic research at universities, not applied research or development.

Centers of excellence are a relatively new and unevaluated type of state initiative to attract world-class talent to produce high-quality research. Their purpose is to fund or stimulate development in a particular area of science or technology. Centers are identified and targeted either to existing university research strengths in which current expertise can be developed further or to a technological or scientific area that is a strategic need for the state as a whole and in which new expertise needs to be developed. New York has established centers at seven university campuses, each center reflecting the university's existing academic strength—optics at the University of Rochester, computers at Columbia, and agricultural biotechnology at Cornell, for example. These universities were also selected on the basis of the institution's propensity to collaborate with industry representatives. The University of Akron in Ohio built on the region's historical strength as the rubber industry capital of the United States to stimulate university research in newer areas. The university established the Edison Polymer Innovation Corporation to build new research capacity in polymers utilizing the special resources of the local rubber and chemical companies, and to cease being the "tire capital" and become "Polymer Valley" (SRI International, 1986a).

Joint government–private sector corporations are also being established to encourage research. Indiana, for example, set up a Corporation for Science and Technology in 1982 to stimulate basic and applied research. This nonprofit corporation is governed by a board of directors representing state and local government, private industry, and higher education. Two grants recently awarded by the corporation for biotechnology research illustrate its approach. Purdue was awarded a $4.5 million grant to conduct biotechnological research on new and improved crop strains and to create a knowledge base that can stimulate the growth of biotechnological firms in Indiana. A grant of $1.2 million went to Indiana University to produce specific antibodies for cellular research and to clone rare gene combinations for genetic research. The goal of both the centers of excellence and joint state-industry research efforts is to increase the amount of basic research occurring in universities by increasing investments targeted at specific fields and projects with high commercial potential, expanding the university's ability to produce new technologies that can be utilized by large industries and small business entrepreneurs.

Technology Transfer. Technology research and transfer programs are mechanisms for bringing scientific discoveries from the laboratory to the commercial marketplace. They attempt to facilitate the industrial commercialization of new scientific innovations and discoveries by stimulating the quick movement of a technological innovation through the several stages of research, development, adaptation, demonstration, and diffusion. However, the process of applying research findings and scientific insights to commercially viable ventures is not clearly understood. Much of the success in the United States has been due to government action, such as the encouragement of new techniques and technology by the government-funded agricultural extension services. Some is due to less direct incentives that have gradually evolved over the years through federal and state tax systems, security market regulations, and other financial factors, as well as unique social and cultural factors that have received scant attention (Diebold, 1986). The wide success of the more visible agricultural extension approach has provided a general model for technology transfer that has been adopted by many states.

Generally, the goal of technology transfer is to increase the accessibility of current research to business firms. This facilitates utilization and increases the speed with which business enterprises can utilize university discoveries in developing new products. Technology transfer activities are increasingly pursued by state governments to stimulate job creation and to increase the flow of new, targeted technologies from the university to the marketplace. One example is the University of Washington's Technology Center, which was established to carefully target specific university research programs in fields and technologies that may have significant commercial potential in the state of Washington. The center attempts to carry ideas developed by professors for new, potentially commercial technologies through the stage of experimental proof and then transfer the technologies to a business enterprise for further development. Its projects are general in nature in order to be of interest to more than one firm; it especially attempts to provide useful resources for smaller business enterprises that cannot afford in-house research and development capability (Zumeta and Stephens, 1986).

Pennsylvania's Ben Franklin Partnership and Ohio's Thomas Alva Edison Partnership programs are two of the best-developed examples of comprehensive state efforts to spur technology development and transfer. Both integrate state universities, state government, and private industry in collaborative efforts to stimulate the rapid commercialization of products and processes. The Ben Franklin Partnership, begun in 1982, is the largest state technology program in the country and aims its technology transfer at both mature industries and smaller, younger enterprises in Pennsylvania. Activity is focused at four Advanced Technology Centers in four different regions of the state. The center at Lehigh, for example, manages projects in the northeast, while Carnegie-Mellon and the University of Pittsburgh coordinate activities in the west. Each center has its own applied research thrust based on the particular strengths of the region's universities and industries. Both the Ben Franklin and Edison Partnership programs operate under a challenge grant system, in which centers must raise funds from industry that are then matched by the state. The Ben Franklin Partnership has been very successful in obtaining nonstate funding, and it is the most leveraged technology transfer program in the country. In fiscal year 1985–86, the state allocated it $21.3 million that was matched by $80.9 million in private-sector and federal funding (a 1:3.80 ratio of leveraging) (Brawley, 1986).

University-industry affiliate programs provide business firms near a university a means to exchange information and increase personal contacts, offering local firms easy access to a university's research minds. By paying annual dues or participation fees, affiliate members typically receive easy access to formal conferences and workshops, as well as previews of planned research activities. University-industry affiliate programs vary across the country. Two of the best-developed are at MIT, whose Industrial Liaison Program is one of the country's largest, with nearly 300 member firms, and at Stanford University, which has created a more decentralized approach in which twenty-one affiliate programs offer a spectrum of services and levels of membership under a flexible participation fee system (Doyle and Brisson, 1985).

Technical Assistance. University technical assistance is a third approach to stimulating scientific and technological development in industries and enterprises. It is less glamorous than technology transfer programs and centers of excellence and typically attracts fewer state and local government resources. Colleges and universities provide technical assistance to industry in a variety of ways. The two most common approaches are the industrial extension service (patterned directly on the agricultural extension services model) and the use of small business development centers. Both focus primarily on smaller business enterprises and fit well the recent findings in business formation, which indicate that small and medium-sized business firms need two kinds of extension services to survive and expand: technical assistance to help solve technological and production problems, and managerial assistance to help solve planning, financial, and human resource problems.

Although industrial extension programs have been around since the early 1960s, they have recently emerged as an important strategy for increasing higher education's contributions to state and local economies. Most technical assistance is in the form of small short-term projects that range from a one-hour counseling session to a ten-day project. They are free to business firms, making their services attractive to business owners. And they are conducted either by university faculty as a part of their applied research services or by staff experts, engineers, and management consultants hired specifically to provide this extension service.

Technical assistance extension programs can follow a passive approach or an aggressive approach in providing services. A passive program operates primarily as a clearinghouse of information and as a referral service to other agencies. Passive programs typically respond to client requests for assistance or information. One example is the Western Research Applications Center at the engineering school at the University of Southern California. The center was contacted by a company that was having recurrent problems with certain displays kept under water. The paint continually peeled away, and constant repainting had become expensive. The center, in response to the company's request, found a painting material that would last under water, thus reducing the cost of the displays by two-thirds (Turner, 1987).

An aggressive industrial extension program, on the other hand, targets specific industries that can benefit from direct assistance and exposure to new technologies. A very recent example is Michigan's Manufacturing Extension Service, which focuses on small manufacturing firms that can benefit by adopting innovative technological developments emerging from the state's universities. The service provides outreach assistance in solving production problems and targets industries such as auto supply firms that are an integral part of the state's base of small manufacturers.

A better-known industrial extension service, one that utilizes both aggressive and passive programs, is the Georgia Institute of Technology Industrial Extension Division, which targets small manufacturing firms and assists them by facilitating the dissemination of innovative technology and by sponsoring research. The service provides up to five person-days of free assistance to any Georgia firm. The extension works through a network of twelve field offices, each with one or two engineers. More than 600 companies per year turn to an extension office for help, ranging from a simple information request to week-long, on-site, technical assistance. Established in 1962, Georgia's extension service receives half of its funding from the state of Georgia and half from research contracts and consulting. Although the extension service is based at a university, many Georgia faculty find industrial extension unrewarding; as a result, the program utilizes its own full-time extension agents rather than students and faculty members (SRI International, 1986a; Doyle and Brisson, 1985).

Smaller businesses have managerial problems and needs that often require one-of-a-kind, individualized consultation, not the broad-brush educational programs provided by colleges and universities. Many states and communities are involved in providing this management assistance through university-based and community college–based small business development centers (SBDCs) and small business institutes (SBIs). SBIs provide short-term consulting services for small businesses that request help. They are typically based in university schools of business and involve a team of students monitored by a business professor. Teams of students are matched with companies from targeted areas that request assistance. The students meet with the business client, assess the managerial problem, and identify and recommend custom-designed solutions.

A more widespread approach to managerial outreach efforts are SBDCs, which provide the first line of advice, assistance, and training to small business owners and people interested in starting a new business enterprise. SBDCs involve a cooperative agreement between the SBA and a statewide network set up within a community college or university system. The SBA provides one-half of the annual funding, and the other half is arranged by the SBDC network and can be supplied by the state or the university. SBDCs were begun in 1976 in seven states. By 1985, thirty-five states had established statewide SBDC networks. The principal program of SBDCs is to provide individualized consulting and management analysis to small business enterprises that cannot afford private consulting and to facilitate business formation and growth. Although its goals are similar to those of SBIs, SBDCs' services are often more comprehensive and more accessible to small business owners. Furthermore, SBDCs can more effectively link a state's postsecondary educational system with small business enterprises.

SBDCs are organized within a state according to several SBA requirements. Each program must have a full-time state director, facilities should be located throughout the state, and each facility should be open forty hours per week. There must also be a lead agency or organization, designated by the state, that is responsible for securing matching funds, establishing the centers, operating the program, and being the SBA liaison. Although most SBDC lead agencies are universities, program flexibility allows other choices as lead agencies. The state of Illinois has designated its department of commerce as its lead agency. Pennsylvania's SBDC network, on the other hand, is coordinated through the Wharton School of Business at the University of Pennsylvania. Four Pennsylvania SBDCs are located at several universities that also house the state's Ben Franklin Partnership Advanced Technology Centers, thus providing a well-integrated approach to offering both technological assistance and managerial consulting. Another unique SBDC network is Oregon's, which is established and coordinated by the state's community college system. Oregon was the first to secure federal funding for community college–based centers. It chose the existing community college network for SBDCs because they were more locally based, closer for hands-on assistance to small businesses, and because the existing institutional system more easily facilitated coordination among the locally based centers. Community colleges in Arkansas, Florida, Georgia, Iowa, Kansas, New Jersey, and New York are also involved as partners or subcontractors to SBDCs.

Economic Analysis and Policy Development

The third role for higher education in state and local economic development is the provision of demographic and economic analyses and targeted capacity-building efforts to enhance economic policy-making. States and communities, in the rush to respond to economic dislocation, may establish public policies that are based on limited or inaccurate information and analyses. Economic policy-making requires sound information about critical economic variables, such as shifts in employment, business incorporation rates, demographic patterns, infrastructure capacities, and fiscal trade-offs involved in various development efforts. Although many relevant data are available in various government agencies, college and university faculty can be significant resources for collecting data from diverse sources and analyzing inherent trends. Short-term and long-term economic forecasts provided by federal agencies, for example, can be biased and often overoptimistic (Kamlet and others, 1987). More locally oriented information is necessary for public policy-making and can also be used by chambers of commerce, industrial development associations, port authorities, and others interested in guiding state and local economic policies.

Informing Public Policy. Effective economic policy requires accurate, up-to-date information and analyses. Universities have increasingly undertaken these analytical activities in recent years, either as ongoing analyses provided by a university research center or bureau or on a project-specific basis. An example is Cleveland State University's College of Urban Affairs, which has been providing economic information and analysis to assist local and regional economic development since 1977. It has provided assistance to city and neighborhood organizations, developed a data base on regional economic, labor market, and population trends, and analyzed local business retention and expansion efforts for their effectiveness (SRI International, 1986a).

A number of states have also sought from universities expert consultation, research, and analysis to inform state policy. Seeking a strong and objective analysis of the state's economy, Michigan's Council on Jobs and Economic Development utilized an academic task force of several economists and political scientists from the state's three major research universities. To ensure an analysis that would be relevant to government policymakers, the council selected scholars who had practical policy analysis experience. The scholars' time was donated by the universities, and the final report, *The Path to Prosperity,* cost less than $100,000. Other states have also used academic researchers in developing their strategic plans, while some have turned to private consultants for economic analysis. Indiana's *In Step with the Future* (1983) utilized the Arthur D. Little consulting firm, and Wisconsin enlisted Arthur Anderson and Company in its economic strategic planning efforts (National Association of State Development Agencies, 1987).

As an independent research unit, a university can produce findings and reveal trends that might be too political for a public manager to state publicly or too sensitive for a paid consultant to risk future research contracts. An economic analysis of Nebraska's economy in 1986, for example, revealed continuing large state investments in agriculture programs. The university report questioned the effectiveness of continued public investment in a sector of the state economy that had been declining for decades and for which agricultural trends indicated continuing decline in both the near and long term. The analysts identified prospective development targets that appeared more appropriate to the state's economic structure, such as insurance and telecommunications (Bare and others, 1986). This analysis was received with some hesitation; in prior years, this notion of reallocating Nebraska's public investments in agriculture had been taboo. An analysis of the regional economy surrounding Cleveland conducted by the College of Urban Affairs had similar political ramifications. This mid-1970s study revealed a shift in the regional economy from manufacturing to services; when published, it was criticized by industry leaders and public executives for being too negative. The analysis, however, accurately predicted a major loss of manufacturing jobs between 1979 and 1984 (more than 100,000 were eliminated) in the Cleveland metropolitan area (SRI International, 1986a).

The independent nature of most university economic analyses enables them to provide information that is useful, although not always well received initially. The differences between academic perspectives (typically longer-term and with minimal political consideration) and government or industry perspectives can often spark new and interesting policy dialogues and can offer information and insights that others may hesitate to provide publicly.

Capacity Building. Economic analyses provided by academics to assist in economic policy-making may not provide the appropriate intervention to stimulate serious policy discussions. This can be because states and communities lack the capacity to utilize the research. In smaller communities, sociological factors such as learned helplessness (Hibbard, 1985) or denial (see Chapter Two) may influence low capacity. In these situations, university attempts to provide appropriate economic analyses will be much less effective than efforts aimed at building capacity.

Capacity-building efforts focus less on factual data and more on processes of leadership development and preparedness for economic development. Here, academics must assume the role of facilitator-teacher rather than expert, and they must work directly with public- and private-sector leaders to help them define their own economic issues and problems and to facilitate the development of collaborative approaches to those problems. This demands a different style of interaction between academicians and community leaders. The capacity-building approach thus shifts the type of research needed from merely descriptive studies to more open-ended, change-oriented exploration of issues.

An example of a capacity-building approach used by universities is the community strategic investment process utilized by the Institute of Community and Area Development at the University of Georgia. Here, university faculty facilitate a two-day retreat for selected leaders in a particular community. The retreat utilizes a structured approach to facilitate the group in identifying strategic investment targets for community economic development. It is designed to maximize participants' involvement through discussion and consensus building. This capacity-building approach makes intensive use of group facilitators and recorders and therefore requires that university faculty possess group process skills. The approach also utilizes microcomputers and software packages to present information to the leadership group and to integrate and analyze investment choices suggested by the participants. This requires that the university faculty also be familiar with resource allocation modeling technology (Feldt and Whorton, 1987).

Emerging Roles for Higher Education

Higher educational institutes now play a central role in the postindustrial economy. Whether this role will continue into the 1990s depends on the ability of universities and colleges, state and local governments, and industries to form productive partnerships. It is clear, however, that to assist in state and local economic development, universities and colleges cannot merely provide more of the same. The restructured economy demands new efforts from higher education. Colleges and universities are rich resources for state and local governments in three areas: adult learning and human development, scientific research and technological development, and economic analysis and policy development. Within these three areas, ten broad categories of activities describe the spectrum of emerging university and college roles in economic development.

Human capital development roles include revising curricula and creating new educational programs to meet the intellectual needs of a work force in a postindustrial economy; offering remedial education for the estimated 20 million individuals who are functionally illiterate and who cannot effectively join the work force because of deficiencies in basic reading and writing skills; retraining and "reskilling" workers who are displaced by shifts from manufacturing and agriculture to services and knowledge-based sectors; renewing and updating professionals and managers in current and emerging technological advances; and developing entrepreneurial capacity in individuals, that is, educating people in strategies for making jobs as well as training people to take jobs.

Scientific research and technological development roles include doing basic and applied research to develop new knowledge, particularly to produce advances in science and technology that can eventually result in new products and services or improved forms of production; furthering the technology transfer of newly developed knowledge to industry, and assisting firms in utilizing state-of-the-art technology developed through university research; and offering technical assistance in applying existing knowledge to business enterprises, particularly by helping small firms learn to adopt or adapt effective managerial and engineering concepts through industrial extension services and small business development centers.

Economic analysis and policy development roles include performing economic analysis to provide independent, theoretically based information and analysis to government and corporate policymakers about a state's or community's economy, and building economic development capacity by assisting private, public, and nonprofit agencies to develop a capacity for local or regional strategic planning and policy development.

All educational institutions, from community colleges to large research universities, can offer more assistance in state and local economic development. Different roles need to be developed for different kinds of colleges and universities, roles based on a college or university's strengths as well as on the unique dynamics of the state and local economy. Higher educational institutions less well endowed than Stanford or MIT can still actively participate in state and local economic development in critical ways; appropriate roles vary by locality. Some universities and colleges develop a wide range of roles, while others target just one role.

Faculty and institutional resistance, however, may be the most difficult barrier to fully utilizing colleges and universities in state and local economic development. Universities are conservative institutions, slow to change their structures, values, and orientations. Academics warn that in capitalizing on the interest in competitiveness and economic growth, universities must maintain their autonomy and not become involved in the policies and economics of industry. The university's values need to be considered by local officials attempting to develop economic development partnerships; in particular, faculty will want to protect their ability to distribute research results freely and their freedom to pursue scientific questions of their choice. Other barriers to a university's increased involvement in economic development might be an unclear university mission, possible faculty conflicts of interest, lack of understanding of community and industry needs, lack of resources for economic development, administrative constraints, and lack of linkages to industry and community (SRI International, 1986a).

The development of and experimentation with various higher educational initiatives in economic development demonstrate that these are not insurmountable barriers. Whatever roles or activities are pursued by colleges and universities, they must be strategic in their approach. A planning process similar to the model discussed in Chapter Three can provide information and collaborative analysis for making such strategic university choices. The process should involve analyzing community and statewide business and industry needs, assessing university strengths and weaknesses, determining strategic targets where university involvement can make a significant impact, defining appropriate new roles for the university in stimulating economic growth, developing formal and informal organizations for these new roles, establishing and implementing new policies and institutional incentives, and evaluating successes and reiterating the planning process (SRI International, 1986a).

Conclusion

State and local governments should examine how higher education can stimulate economic growth and diversity. Three unique roles now exist for higher education: human development, technological development, and policy development. These three economic development roles fit well the traditional goals of higher education—research, education, and public service. Universities can be important resources for strategic economic development. In order to fully utilize universities and colleges as resources, however, policymakers must first overcome outmoded popular images of adult education and understand the critical role of colleges and universities in state and local economic development.

Although many innovative programs have been established throughout the country, rigorous evaluation is limited, since most of these efforts are relatively new. Elected officials who want to know what benefits will result from increased public spending cannot always be given specific answers; this makes it difficult to increase expenditures for higher education. One way of avoiding increased state expenditures involves budgetary reallocations to target certain activities for specific purposes. Industry funding, through challenge grants, for example, can provide another source of financing. Such targeting must at the very least be based on an assessment of institutional strengths and weaknesses. Other initiatives can be supported by policymakers that do not involve increases in direct expenditures. Giving strong support to basic education curricular reforms in state colleges and universities, for example, can be a positive strategy for fostering economic development.

Resistance exists in colleges and universities, a barrier that is not insurmountable but that must be recognized. In this context, state and local government managers can act as catalysts for engaging colleges and universities in pursuing economic development strategies. First, state and local government must establish clear development objectives that will guide the choice of the type of higher education partnership. Second, the establishment of formal and informal business-government-academic working groups and networks can generate important contacts for strategic efforts. Third, public managers can become familiar with the educational, policy research, and scientific resources available in the region's public colleges and universities. Fourth, public managers should seek university assistance in developing strategic economic development plans. Using academics to develop labor market analyses or demographic profiles can be an effective way to develop an ongoing working relationship. Finally, state and local governments should explore innovative programs that can only be established through joint efforts, such as training and retraining programs, technology transfer programs, and capacity-building efforts.

Part Three

Successful Leadership Strategies

Effective economic development strategies must be custom-designed to meet the unique strengths and opportunities of local and state economies. Chapter Nine focuses on the importance of community leadership strategies in tailoring plans; for example, capital financing, infrastructure improvements, regulatory relief, and improved public services can all be influenced by local leaders, using three main strategies. One strategy focuses a community's resources on particular stages of business life cycles; this might involve forming new entrepreneurial enterprises, expanding established enterprises, or retaining and assisting businesses in decline. A second strategic framework relies primarily on developing the community's existing "position" in the national economy—whether as a diversified service center, a specialized service center, or a production center. A third strategic approach is to focus a community's resources on one of three specific fiscal goals: increasing jobs, increasing average personal income, or improving the local government's tax base. The success of cities, counties, and regional councils of government (COGs) depends on their ability to mix and match strategic approaches and resources based on an accurate analysis of the state and local economy.

State government strategies are also expanding beyond the traditional efforts to attract industry and now include a wide variety of economic initiatives aimed at stimulating growth and diversification. Chapter Ten examines these initiatives and the four guidelines that provide direction for state efforts: First, economic development must be recognized as a set of interconnected policies and programs that relate and cut across many state agencies and functions. Second, development efforts must be viewed as policy experiments and should be innovative and tailored to the region or state. Third, efforts must be integrative, weaving together the combined efforts of cities, counties, and COGs as well as the different but related programs of the many state agencies. Finally, states' efforts can best be viewed as public investment strategies, with particular focus on four critical investment arenas: human resources within the state, public infrastructure, natural resources, and increasing entrepreneurial access to financial capital.

As a result of the growing economic interdependence, there has been a significant decline in state and local governments' capacities to unilaterally develop and implement economic development policies and programs. No one government department or individual public manager can effectively act single-handedly. This situation forces the invention of new collaborative mechanisms and collective development strategies.

Successful economic development strategies not only precipitate from an intergovernmental contest of cities, counties, COGs, and state and federal agencies, but also emerge from intersectoral collaboration between the public, private, and nonprofit sectors. Each sector depends on the vitality of the other.

In such an interconnected policy context, a new type of public leadership is required—catalytic leadership. Chapter Eleven examines this trend and shows how, unlike charismatic leadership, which rallies people around the leader's vision, catalytic leadership facilities cooperation among a group of leaders and stimulates the pursuit of a goal that is created collectively by the group. Catalytic leaders need interpersonal skills in collaborating, negotiating, and networking. They also need the conceptual skills to think strategically and to understand economic interdependencies, as well as knowledge of and expertise in development finance.

9

Community Leadership Strategies

Communities have a multitude of strategies they can consider for improving their local economies. These strategies focus on providing financing, regulatory relief, physical improvements, improved public services, and human capital. The key to implementing successful economic development efforts is for localities to match their existing and potential resources and tools to the strategies they have identified. This chapter will discuss how best to accomplish this. In particular, we will look at frameworks for developing specific strategies that are most likely to develop within local communities and the resources available to help implement those strategies.

Three Frameworks for Local Development Strategies

Previous chapters have proposed a number of ways to approach economic development. These approaches can be combined to develop an overall framework for implementing development strategies. One approach can be structured around the time frame or life cycle of a business. Another approach attempts to fit a strategy to a community's existing economic configuration. A third approach sets particular economic goals for improving a community's economic base.

Business Life Cycle. The needs of a business depend on its stage of development. Each step in its life cycle is linked to community strategies associated with efforts to create new businesses, attract new businesses, or retain and expand existing businesses. The resources necessary to assist businesses at different stages of development vary; the art of matching the two is the key to success in economic development efforts.

New businesses face problems of raising capital and often risk undercapitalization. Lenders may consider a loan too risky, and new businesses are likely to lack information about where capital might be located. This is especially true of new businesses located in declining areas (Richards, 1983). New businesses may also lack effective management skills that are necessary to move their products or services from a concept to reality.

Growing businesses, especially small businesses, face difficulties raising working capital. These businesses have growing demand but face substantial costs associated with expansion. Fewer private companies are selling shares in their corporation to the public. If a business decides to sell shares to raise equity capital, it would find it difficult to do so because of more conservative investment practices by institutional investors (such as pension funds), smaller numbers of individual investors, increased paperwork burdens, and a reduced number of small brokers willing to handle such securities.

Stable and declining businesses require assistance to modernize plant and equipment. They often require infusions of working capital to make up for a declining revenue base. These businesses may also have poor management practices and lack the internal strategic planning necessary to position themselves competitively in a changing private marketplace (Richards, 1983). Finally, they may find themselves located in a deteriorating area of the community, further compounding their problems.

The type and size of business to be assisted may also be considered in developing strategies. Different businesses may require different strategies that vary in cost and chances for success. Manufacturing businesses and retail or service businesses will need dramatically different skills in their labor force, physical space and equipment, inventory, management skills, marketing and promotion activities, and so forth. Further, each may hold differing opportunities for the community's economic health. Large firms will have a substantial, immediate impact on the local economy, but the chances of finding such a firm that will relocate or expand are increasingly slim. On the other hand, cities might find that the creation, expansion, and attraction of smaller firms are a better focus for their efforts, since small businesses created over 60 percent of all new jobs in the past decade (Mayer, 1987).

Community Position. Strategies at the community level must fit the existing position of the local economy. Noyelle (1984) classified the 128 largest metropolitan areas into three categories or positions reflecting the growth of the service sector (see Table 1). The first category, diversified service centers, represents those communities that, while facing major restructuring of their local economies, "are also doing considerable rebuilding through growth in corporate offices, producer service firms, wholesaling, transportation, communications, and, somewhat more selectively, universities, hospitals, and public sector services" (Noyelle, 1984, p. 14). These communities find themselves with strong competitive advantages in competing for increasing service employment.

Communities that are specialized service centers, the second category, have more difficulty adjusting to the structural changes in the economy because of their heavy dependence on manufacturing and traditional production employment. These cities have economies focused on engineering and regional headquarters, higher education, and some high-technology businesses. The final group of cities, production centers, have the most problems shifting to a service-sector orientation. This is the case not so much because they cannot attract such businesses, but because they have had difficulty retaining locally based firms. These communities are likely to have traditional assembly-line jobs that pay at lower rates and often require lower skill levels. Such communities are more vulnerable to competition from developing countries with cheaper labor costs and to rapid changes within the production industry itself.

Clearly, strategies for each group of cities vary. Attraction and expansion may be an important focus of diversified service centers and specialized service centers, while the production centers may see retention as a critical concern. This classification scheme focuses on service, but the same approach may be useful in evaluating local conditions for value-added manufacturing or trade.

Table 1. 128 Largest U.S. Metropolitan Areas Classified by Major Types, Subtypes, and Population Size.

Diversified Service Centers

National

1 New York	1
2 Los Angeles	1
3 Chicago	1
7 San Francisco	1

Regional

4 Philadelphia	1
6 Boston	1
10 Dallas	1
11 Houston	1
12 St. Louis	1
14 Baltimore	1
15 Minneapolis	1
17 Cleveland	1
18 Atlanta	2
21 Miami	2
22 Denver	2
23 Seattle	2
26 Cincinnati	2
28 Kansas City	2
30 Phoenix	2
32 Indianapolis	2
33 New Orleans	2
34 Portland	2
35 Columbus	2

Subregional

41 Memphis	3
45 Salt Lake City	3
46 Birmingham	3
52 Nashville	3
53 Oklahoma City	3
56 Jacksonville	3
58 Syracuse	3
65 Richmond	3
69 Omaha	3
91 Mobile	4
101 Little Rock	4
106 Shreveport	4
110 Des Moines	4
114 Spokane	4
120 Jackson, MS	4

Specialized Service Centers

Functional Nodal

5 Detroit	2
13 Pittsburgh	2
16 Newark, NJ	2
24 Milwaukee	2
31 San Jose	3
36 Hartford	3
38 Rochester	3
40 Louisville	3
44 Dayton	3
47 Bridgeport	3
50 Toledo	3
51 Greensboro	3
57 Akron	3
62 Allentown	3
63 Tulsa	3
67 New Brunswick	4
70 Jersey City	4
75 Wilmington	4
78 Paterson	4
86 Knoxville	4
96 Wichita	4
100 Fort Wayne	4
103 Peoria	4
137 Kalamazoo	4

Government and Education

8 Washington, D.C.	1
39 Sacramento	3
48 Albany	3
54 New Haven	3
64 Springfield, MA	3
77 Raleigh-Durham	4
81 Fresno	4
82 Austin	4
84 Lansing	4
85 Oxnard-Ventura	4
88 Harrisburg	4
89 Baton Rouge	4
90 Tacoma	4
99 Columbia, SC	4
111 Utica	4
112 Trenton	4
113 Madison	4
117 Stockton	4
130 South Bend	4
140 Ann Arbor	4

Production Centers

Manufacturing		
27	Buffalo	2
42	Providence	3
59	Worcester	3
60	Gary	3
61	N.E. Pennsylvania	3
71	Grand Rapids	3
72	Youngstown	3
73	Greenville	3
74	Flint	3
80	New Bedford	4
92	Canton	4
93	Johnson City	4
94	Chattanooga	4
98	Davenport	4
104	Beaumont	4
107	York	4
109	Lancaster	4
115	Binghamton	4
116	Reading	4
119	Huntington	4
124	Evansville	4
125	Appleton	4
131	Erie	4
134	Rockford	4
136	Lorain	4

Industrial-Military		
20	San Diego	2
37	San Antonio	3
49	Norfolk	3
87	El Paso	4
97	Charleston, SC	4
102	Newport News	4
121	Lexington	4

123	Huntsville	4
126	Augusta	4
127	Vallejo	4
128	Colorado Springs	4
132	Pensacola	4
133	Salinas	4

Mining-Industrial		
83	Tucson	4
105	Bakersfield	4
118	Corpus Christi	4
129	Lakeland	4
135	Johnstown, PA	4
138	Duluth	4
139	Charleston, WV	4

Note: Number preceding city indicates 1976 population rank. Number following city indicates population size bracket—size 1: 2 million and over; size 2: 1 to 2 million; size 3: one-half to 1 million; size 4: one-quarter to one-half million.

Source: Noyelle and Stanback, 1983.

A community strategic framework in which businesses are ranked by size (small or large) and type (retail, service, or manufacturing) may be useful in evaluating various approaches. Among the strategies that can be considered within such a framework are:

- Industrial recruitment and promotion—advertising, providing information, developing infrastructure and sites, and offering financial and tax incentives to attract new establishments of national concern into an area
- Expansion of existing industries—providing infrastructure financing, skills training, and marketing assistance to support the expansion of larger manufacturing already in an area
- New enterprise development—helping to identify feasible ventures, people to initiate them, and initial sources of financing
- Small business development—offering business counseling, business planning, and financing to expand local retail, service, and smaller manufacturing enterprises
- Transition to new ownership—a long-term strategy of finding viable, privately held businesses that do not have heirs, matching them with potential new owners, and structuring the acquisition financing needed to sustain the businesses as going concerns and to secure adequate compensation for the original owners
- Brokerage/financing services—assisting in sales and acquisitions by identifying and matching owners seeking to sell concerns with potential buyers, and securing financing from local investors and financial intermediaries in order to maintain employment levels in these businesses
- Technical assistance—defining and solving specific technical production or marketing problems to arrest the contraction of local concerns
- Management assistance—providing general advice and assistance to enhance the viability of stable local concerns (Malizia, 1985)

Each strategy has its own risks and rewards, as Figure 3 shows. Risks and rewards are measured in terms of jobs created or

Figure 3. Risk-Reward Framework.

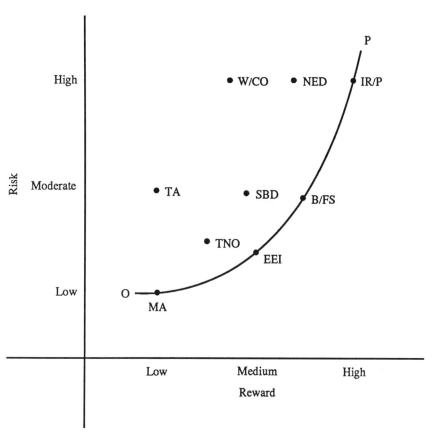

Business Development Strategies

OP	– Optimum portfolio of strategies
W/CO	– Worker/community ownership
NED	– New enterprise development
IR/P	– Industrial recruitment/promotion
TA	– Technical assistance
SBD	– Small business development
B/FS	– Brokerage/financing services
TNO	– Transition to new ownership
EEI	– Expansion of existing industries
MA	– Management assistance

retained in relation to dollars spent, and they vary, depending on the particular characteristics of the community (Malizia, 1985).

For example, in some regions industrial recruitment and promotion have the highest payoffs, but they also have the highest risks. The payoffs come in the form of higher value added to and income produced from a manufacturing industry as well as the primary and support services employment that will be created as a result of this business activity. The risks are associated with the limited number of manufacturing firms likely to relocate. Because 90 percent of business activity is created through expansion of exisiting firms or creation of new firms, very few business opportunities are created through the attraction of new firms from outside the city's boundaries. A state or locality must decide whether to place most of its resources into attracting a new employer, knowing that its chances of success might be low, or into an expansion strategy, where the payoffs are lower but the chances of success much greater. Some risks may be worth taking, depending on the economic position of the community. The key is to find that combination of strategies that will produce optimum results and acceptable risks. It is also important to understand that strategies will vary according to the particular characteristics of a community.

Economic Goals. A final strategy is structured around the fiscal goals of the community to improve its economic base in particular ways. Three interdependent goals most commonly cited are increasing employment or reducing underemployment, increasing personal income, and improving the fiscal tax base of the community (Borut, 1981). Each of these goals is related to the others. Improved fiscal conditions for communities are largely determined by an expanding tax base. The tax base expands as property tax value increases and as taxable sales increase. These increase in turn as the number of taxpayers increases, particularly those with higher incomes. Nevertheless, priorities can be developed within each category and strategies should attempt to achieve various improvements while focusing on the particular stage of the business life cycle that is most important.

Five variables are likely to influence employment, income, and tax base in any community: the migration of employees, the change in employment size of existing firms, the birth or death of firms, the location of private expenditures, and public expenditure patterns (Pulver, 1986). Migration of employees and businesses is largely a function of new branch offices of existing businesses rather than the relocation of corporation headquarters, although such relocations are more common today than five or ten years ago (Moore, 1987). Employment generation is largely the result of expanding firms already located within the community. Births of new firms represent a substantial number of new jobs and income, but these firms also represent a very high percentage of business closings as well. Jobs and income are stimulated by expenditures by both the private and public sectors. In the case of private firms, the economic impact is greatest for those who capture a larger share of the market outside their community, while local public agencies spend a higher percentage of their budgets in the locality itself.

Strategies should look toward increasing business activity that leads to a net export of goods or services or a reduction of imports into the community. While this effort can focus only on the flow of dollars into and out of the community, net benefits will be greater if it includes increasing exports and reducing imports at the state or national level. Failing this, conflicts over approaches may develop between the state and locality or among cities themselves. If, for example, one community improves its economic condition by luring shoppers away from a neighboring community, it will do little to improve the economic condition of the state because dollars are merely recirculating within its borders. Similarly, shifting economic activity among various states does little to improve the economic condition of the United States unless value is added to the stages of production of various goods and services. This helps explain the apparent lack of enthusiasm of many states in assisting localities to improve their central business districts—such improvements may do little to expand the state's economic base.

Strategic Resources

No matter which strategy or combination of strategies is considered, available resources must be matched effectively to achieve concrete results. Resources can be defined in a number of ways, but most fall within the categories described at the beginning of this chapter: financing, regulation, physical improvements, public services, and human capital.

Financing. Direct financial assistance in the form of grants and loans has historically been a major source of financing for local development efforts. While it has declined in absolute terms in recent years, the federal government still provides substantial dollars to spur subnational economic development efforts. State governments and private sources also serve as a source for grant dollars.

Federal dollars come in a myriad of forms and from a highly diverse group of agencies and departments. The Department of Housing and Urban Development (HUD) has two of the most extensive programs currently available for local development, the Community Development Block Grant (CDBG) and the Urban Development Action Grant (UDAG). Both have been substantially cut in recent years and, like other grant programs, face the possibility of elimination in the future. The CDBG program is operated by HUD for cities of more than 50,000 people and for urban counties; individual states operate the program for cities of fewer than 50,000 and for rural counties. CDBG funds can be used for a wide variety of economic development activities, including land acquisition, relocation, new construction, rehabilitation, public works projects, and business financing (land, construction, equipment, working capital, and equity/venture capital). Their major limitation is that funds are predominantly earmarked to benefit those who have low incomes. In other words, CDBG funds are directed at improving the economic condition of the poor in the community and should not be used for general economic development. Large communities and urban counties receive a formula-determined allocation of funds every year. Smaller cities and counties are allocated money by the individual states, usually on a competitive basis each year (Jennings and others, 1986).

The UDAG program is a competitive project grant that provides funding to both large and small cities strictly to stimulate private investment. UDAG funds can be used for a wide variety of purposes where the private sector requires a certain combination of public dollars to stimulate investment. The key restriction on UDAG funding is that the project must be one that would not occur but for the public dollars. The project must also amass as many private resources as possible for every dollar of public money that goes into the project. Furthermore, only communities with high levels of distress are eligible to apply. UDAGs have funded a wide range of projects, from hotels and convention facilities to neighborhood housing projects.

Several other HUD programs have been used to directly or indirectly stimulate private business investment. Assisted housing programs can be part of an economic development project. Cities can borrow against future block grant allocations to begin projects earlier. HUD has also been responsible for implementing specific economic development projects in the past (public works projects to stimulate the economy, for example), and should more money become available in the future, it may once again perform this function.

The Small Business Administration (SBA) uses three programs to assist small businesses, and states and localities use each program in conjunction with other resources to carry out their strategies. The SBA 503 program provides loans to small businesses to assist in increasing local investment. State or local nonprofit organizations create SBA-approved certified development companies that in turn act as conduits to provide loans to small businesses to cover the costs of purchasing fixed assets (buildings and equipment). The loans provided through a development company can be direct or indirect (such as loan guarantees). SBA provides a portion of the loan amount where the remainder is provided through a private lender or a combination of public and private lenders. Up to 90 percent of this loan is then guaranteed through the development company. The small business must secure at least 10 percent of the loan from its own resources (equity).

The SBA 7(a) program provides loans and loan guarantees for a firm's operating capital; to build, expand, or convert business facilities; and to buy buildings, equipment, and materials for venture creation and expansion. This program is aimed at independent, owner-operated small businesses that cannot find financing from other private sources.

Finally, SBA assists in funding the operation of Small Business Investment Companies (SBICs) and Minority Enterprise Small Business Investment Companies (MESBICs), whose purpose is to provide both equity and long-term debt financing to small businesses within particular geographical areas. These investment companies often operate in areas where disinvestment has occurred and where local efforts are required to stimulate new business activity. They can provide both working capital and fixed-asset financing and they can invest as equity partners with small businesses. This provides a great deal of flexibility to the community.

The Department of Labor's major economic development program is tied to job training. The Job Training Partnership Act (JTPA), passed by Congress in 1983, provides funding for job training of adults, youth, and dislocated workers. The program operates through state governments and their designated service delivery areas (SDAs). The SDAs develop a plan whereby the types of training that will be done are specified along with who is to receive the training and the goals and objectives that should be attained. JTPA dollars can be used in combination with other resources to increase business investment. Localities have used the guarantee of job training to attract expanded business investment where a skilled labor force is essential and where the business can reduce its operating costs by shifting the training outside. Greyhound Bus Lines expanded its reservation center into Omaha, Nebraska, in part because of the guarantee of such job training assistance.

The Economic Development Administration (EDA) within the Department of Commerce operates two programs that can be of assistance to local development efforts. Title II Business Development Loans provide loans and loan guarantees to private and nonprofit organizations for large commercial and industrial expansion projects. Loans can be for both fixed assets and working capital. The Title IX Special Economic Development and Adjustment Assistance program is directed at severe economic dislocation (such as plant closings) and long-term disinvestment (such as the decline of textile manufacturing in the Northeast). Its great advantage is its flexibility; its major drawback is higher competition for a diminishing pool of funds.

State resources directed at stimulating local economic development activities have expanded as federal dollars have declined. Many state programs have received at least partial support from the federal government. However, an increasing number of programs have been created at the state level in recent years to assist development. The most recent have been in the area of venture capital assistance, where states allocate dollars to provide equity financing for private ventures with high risk but with equally high chances for substantial business investment. States as different as Massachusetts and Wyoming have developed such programs and provide crucial financial resources for local economic development.

A rapidly growing area that offers opportunities for local governments is in federal procurement outreach programs, which help local firms capture a more competitive share of federal purchases. Three such programs in Buffalo, Cleveland, and New York City had by the mid 1980s obtained over 35 billion dollars in new contracts, created over 1,000 jobs, and assisted over 600 firms. These efforts have succeeded largely because of strong planning and design, strong marketing efforts, and persistent follow-through (Suss, 1982).

State and federal dollars provide indirect assistance by funding technical assistance efforts. HUD provides such assistance through Section 107 of the CDBG program. SBA assists by funding universities with dollars to provide small businesses with management assistance. EDA funds technical assistance projects throughout the country. States also provide a wide range of assistance through various state departments as well as through their funding of state colleges and universities.

Tax expenditures and allocations can provide a multitude of incentives for private investments, as discussed in Chapter Six. This is true not only for attraction and retention but for business formation and expansion strategies localities may consider. While existing firms that desire to expand may need assistance in reducing existing or future tax burdens, new firms just forming may be more interested in tax credits and deferrals that can help increase their initial cash flow at a time when it is most crucial. Small firms may see the local property tax as a major concern, while larger corporations may focus on the costs associated with a state or local income tax. Local firms interested in exporting products and foreign investors interested in local business opportunities may require a different set of tax incentives.

Tax expenditures refer to reductions in potential tax earnings because of a change in tax policy. By reducing the tax base, additional revenue that would have been raised through the tax code is kept by the persons and businesses affected. Exemptions on certain kinds of property, such as stocks and bonds, are an example of a tax expenditure, as are the exemptions on certain kinds of sales (such as services) and particular kinds of income (such as health care benefits). Tax expenditures are attractive to business investors because they reduce their overall costs of operation and are therefore likely to increase profits. There are substantial costs associated with such expenditures, however, because they reduce the flow of dollars into government by reducing the tax base; therefore, government must either do less or increase tax rates and the tax burdens of others. This creates a difficult policy tension: high-quality government services supported by taxes are considered an important resource to spur investment, yet reducing taxes and thus reducing government services provides tax advantages to private investors.

Tax allocations refer to the use of earmarked tax revenues for business investment. These are common at the state and local level. Tax increment financing, discussed in Chapter Six, is an example of such an allocation. Funds raised by the property tax are earmarked to retire bonds that finance improvements directly related to a business investment. Business improvement districts are another form of tax allocation. In this case, the state or locality approves the use of increases in property tax rates to fund business district improvements in order to make the area more attractive for investment and to spur business development and business traffic for retail trade.

Local tax dollars can be earmarked for stimulating business investment where state constitutional provisions allow it. Such resources can be particularly useful where gaps exist in state or federal funding. Another increasing source of both state and local dollars for development is public pension funds. In the city of

Cleveland, for example, a venture capital fund operated by a number of chief executive officers has received capital from public pension funds to help earn a competitive return on investment while creating new jobs and expanding the tax base in Ohio (National Association of State Development Agencies, 1985).

Private dollars are often raised for particular projects and activities that implement local strategies. For-project development corporations, discussed in Chapter Four, sell stock to raise funding for such activities. Privately sponsored venture capital clubs are being created to raise dollars to provide equity capital for new firms. These often work in conjunction with state-sponsored venture capital pools. Local foundations can help provide funding for these activities. The time is past when localities could look to others to pay for their economic development initiatives. They must begin looking toward local dollars to support these efforts. The smaller the jurisdiction, the more difficult this may be, but it is not impossible. In fact, the effort reflects the real commitment to the strategies that have been developed.

Regulatory Control. Perhaps one of the most powerful tools available to local governments is the use of regulation. Many businesses believe that local government power over business investment really centers on government's ability to kill projects and investment opportunity through regulation rather than stimulate investment through financial incentives. Local government regulation centers on health and safety concerns. It also focuses on a concern with planned development of both residential and commercial activity. There is often an immediate trade-off between the protection of the common good and increased costs to business. Whether regulations focus on traditional zoning and subdivision development or the use of particular building materials and sprinkler systems, all cost money and can reduce business profits.

Localities must attempt to meet the needs of the public while doing what they can to reduce the burdens associated with regulation. One area that has become the focus of much effort is the business delay caused by regulatory requirements. One-stop permits, business ombudsmen, and "fast-track" development are all concepts associated with this concern. In Lincoln, Nebraska, the development of a major hotel/retail complex was predicated on the ability of city government to clear all regulatory roadblocks by a certain date. If this had not been accomplished, the development would not have occurred. Time is money, particularly for private investors concerned with obtaining financing and completing projects on a schedule. Regulatory delays can be expensive, and for marginal investment activities they may be sufficient to kill a project altogether.

A more difficult decision facing local governments is the revision or elimination of regulatory requirements that appear to be impeding business investment. Changing building codes or zoning ordinances, for example, may reduce business costs but increase public costs. Zoning ordinances restricting cottage industries are a clear example. Research literature indicates that a rapidly growing sector of the economy is made of small firms producing products and services with the potential of expanding substantially in the future. These firms often start at home or where space costs are very low. New businesses, often described as cottage industries, may be operating in violation of local zoning ordinances that restrict the use of residential property for commercial enterprises. These regulations were created for a good reason—to eliminate the possibility of incompatible land use and reduced property values as a result of that use. What is a locality to do in this case? To eliminate the prohibition against such cottage industries raises the specter of the lawn mower repair shop in a single-family residential neighborhood. To keep such restrictions may prohibit the birth of new firms and delay the expansion of venture activities within the community.

The creation of business incubator facilities is one possible alternative. These incubators assist small businesses, usually those just starting, by providing many support services (office space, clerical help, management assistance, and so forth) in order to reduce the financial and management burdens often associated with such firms (see Chapter Five). One such incubator was created in Girard, Pennsylvania, through a combination of federal and local funds to provide management and business services to eighteen small businesses. These businesses ranged from light manufacturing to engineering services. Rents charged these firms were kept low and the incubator facility provided assistance in such areas as loan packaging, product development, and marketing assistance.

Physical Assets and Public Services. Perhaps the most fundamental resource available to communities is their physical assets and the services they provide. Physical assets include land, buildings, utilities, and so forth. In Los Angeles, for example, a coordinated asset management program has allowed the county to generate considerable revenues while stimulating economic development. In one project, a lease of public land was developed for a commercial venture in Long Beach and Signal Hill that resulted in over $43 million for the two cities and approximately $1.3 billion for the county (Grgas, 1985). Utilities at reasonable cost can be attractive to firms that are expanding or thinking of relocating elsewhere. The availability of incubator facilities can be a positive resource to those wishing to test new products and services. Retail firms are concerned about the quality and attractiveness of their locations, since they depend heavily on customer access and satisfaction. Many efforts by communities to improve the access to commercial areas (streets, lighting, parking facilities, and so forth) play an important role in this regard. Local governments should never underestimate the importance of these facilities to those who make investment decisions.

Similarly, public services and those associated with the public can be a key to overall economic development. Quality of life is the term most often associated with such services. A report of the Joint Economic Committee of the U.S. Congress states: "A city's quality of life is more important than business related factors. . . . The results of a survey suggest that individual programs and policies which respond to a particular business need will probably be of limited success in encouraging firms to expand or attract new firms if they are not part of a comprehensive effort to upgrade the quality of life in the city. One of the primary policy conclusions to be drawn is that improving the city quality of life where it is poor can have a significant impact on decisions firms make regarding location and workforce changes" (Penne, 1985, p. 12). Examples of quality-of-life improvements can be seen in developments such as

Baltimore's Harborplace, Pittsburgh's Gateway Center, and Dallas's Arts District (Penne, 1985). Still, quality of life is more than neighborhood or downtown commercial renovation. Police and fire protection, the quality of the local educational system, health and social service delivery, cultural facilities, and the responsiveness of public officials all fit in this category. As with public facilities, services set the tone for the quality of a community and its attractiveness as a place to live and work. Quality of life is also the area with which local government is most comfortable and for which it has a clear mandate. Attempts to implement exotic business investment strategies at the price of lower-quality public facilities and services may be short-sighted at best and disastrous at worst.

As mentioned earlier, conflicts arise between the desire to improve the business climate by reducing tax burdens and the need to maintain quality public facilities and services. It is not clear that states and localities with low tax burdens invariably receive increased business investment. For every example where this may be the case, an example exists to counter it.

Nebraska, for example, faced a major policy issue recently when a major employer considered moving from Omaha to Knoxville because the total tax costs for both the corporation and its employees were considerably less in Tennessee than in Nebraska. Much of the policy debate centered on Nebraska's comparative tax structure and overall tax burden relative to other states. Little attention was paid to the facilities and services associated with that tax burden. It could be argued, for example, that the difference in taxes between the two states was associated with the tax support of public schools. There is no easy solution to this dilemma, except that a balance must be struck between tax burdens on individuals and businesses and the corresponding quality of services that such taxes provide.

Human Capital. Perhaps the most vital resource for implementing any community economic development strategy is human capital. This resource is more intangible and invisible than the others discussed but it is no less critical to success. Not only is a community's work force a critical element of human capital (see

Chapter Eight), but leadership resources must be available. Leadership and vision are necessary elements of community strategic planning efforts. Leadership must be supported by an effective delivery system of people willing to commit their time and effort to see that those strategies are carried out. This includes not only paid executives working for the city, the local chamber of commerce, and the development corporation, but a wide variety of volunteers as well (Reed, 1977).

The people who search out and administer economic development grants and loans and the people who oversee the day-to-day efforts to implement strategies are critical to a successful development program. The communities with a critical mass of such people are the ones that will be most competitive. Ask several state officials responsible for economic development to name communities that reflect this kind of leadership and can-do capability and you will usually end up with similar lists. Leaders attract quality personnel to work for them. Such leaders quickly gain the respect and trust of those interested in business investment. Businesses are attracted to localities that are stable and reflect competent administration. Stable governments are often associated with stable business climates. Success is much easier to achieve where quality people are involved.

Conclusion

Numerous frameworks exist to guide community strategies in economic development. Among the most useful are those that consider the stages of business development, varying approaches to improving community economic activity, and the size and sector characteristics of the businesses themselves. No matter which framework or combination of frameworks is most appropriate, the community must tie the strategies it develops to the basic economic realities it faces.

Various strategies for attraction, creation, expansion, and retention can be successfully matched with the needs, resources, and capabilities of a community. Resources and capabilities are crucial. All communities have resource strengths and weaknesses. Some may be more important than others. Financing, regulatory control, community services, and human capital all play a role.

Success will depend on the ability to mix and match strategies and resources. This can best be accomplished by understanding the characteristics of the community and the businesses that are the focus of those strategies and resources.

10

State Leadership Strategies

In 1936, Mississippi introduced into the economic development vocabulary the notion of industrial recruitment. This approach—using tax incentives, industrial development bonds, and promotional advertising—emerged as the central strategy to revitalize state economies. As noted earlier, the effectiveness of this strategy in a postindustrial economy has declined; in order to meet the challenge of revitalizing state economies in the 1980s, new thinking and new strategies are being attempted. From 1981 to 1983, the Indiana legislature enacted a three-phase, $120 million economic development program based on the adoption of fifty-three bills relating to small business assistance, job training, research development, infrastructure improvements, and investment capital. In 1986, the state of Kansas enacted a nine-bill package that reorganized the state's economic department, established a venture capital agency called Kansas Venture Capital, Inc., granted tax credits for venture capital firms, provided tax credit for research and development, created the Kansas Technology Enterprise Corporation to facilitate the transfer of research from universities to the private sector, and proposed several constitutional amendments to empower state and local governments to join more actively in private-sector partnerships (Pilcher, 1986).

State economic development efforts have begun to extend beyond attracting industry to include policies aimed at promoting the formation of new businesses, utilizing the states' indigenous assets; encouraging the expansion of existing businesses; and ensuring that those businesses that are declining do so with minimal disruption to local communities (Council of State Policy and

Planning Agencies, 1986). In addition, many states are carefully reexamining the significance of various types of risk capital, the role of infrastructure and telecommunications investments, the necessity of a well-educated, skilled, and adaptable labor force, and the effects of state regulation of financial institutions on economic growth. At least fourteen states have attempted to incorporate a comprehensive approach to economic development.

This chapter will examine the strategic activities being spearheaded by state governments throughout the country. It will discuss the most recent attempt to assess state business climates by utilizing indicators of economic capacity. Finally, this chapter will provide a strategic framework that suggests a policy guide for potential economic development interventions at the state level.

Determining the State's Economic Condition

States have little power to control the migration of people and employment across their borders. As a result, the state's role in stimulating job creation has often been described as minor and efforts to become competitive have often been viewed as useless or even counterproductive. On the other hand, many policymakers— driven by economic distress and declining real wages—have argued for active and immediate state interventions in the economy. Given this divergence of perspective, clarifying the appropriate governmental role is the first step in state economic development strategic planning. This is inherently both a philosophical and a political question, one that can be illuminated by an analysis of available powers for state intervention and by existing evidence, empirical and anecdotal, of what actually works.

While local economic development strategies and interventions are best directed at specific local opportunities, state interventions can be more appropriately aimed at general economic conditions and at stimulating a productive entrepreneurial environment statewide, as well as at targeting public investments to specific regions and strategic sectors of the state economy. States have powers not available to local governments that directly affect economic growth, including the provision of state public services fundamental to the private sector (such as highways and postsecondary education), regulatory and adjudicatory powers, taxing and spending powers that can affect statewide economic activity, the ability to respond to conditions that vary by region, the ability to stimulate the formation of partnerships by matching key economic players, and the opportunity to experiment on a regional basis (Committee for Economic Development, 1986).

On the basis of an analysis of available state powers, the Commission on Kentucky's Future, for example, identified the role of its state government as ensuring a fertile business and entrepreneurial environment. This role was to be fulfilled by establishing programs linking entrepreneurs with those providing technical assistance, removing unnecessary barriers in higher education that impede research and the transfer of new ideas to the marketplace, supporting the expansion of existing business enterprises, creating a tax structure that encourages innovation and risk taking, and providing assistance in identifying and developing sources of capital (Kentucky Tomorrow Commission, 1986).

Utilizing empirical research to further refine an appropriate state role is a more difficult task, since many of the new approaches and strategies for managing state economic development are too recent to have been systematically evaluated. Existing empirical evidence (Carlino and Mills, 1987), however, indicates that state policies focusing on financial incentives (such as industrial revenue bonds and tax reductions) have little effect on stimulating employment growth, and that targeting state funding to physical infrastructure and education is likely to have a greater effect.

In addition, some preliminary evidence indicates that a state's general business climate can be enhanced by state policies that affect the availability of financial capital. It is clear from existing data that effective state policy must focus first on what it does best: education and human resource development, transportation and infrastructure development, protecting the state's natural resources, and enhancing the state's business environment. Development of strategies in these four policy areas, however, must also be guided by diagnosis of the state's economy, active experimentation, and ongoing evaluations.

Managing economic development strategically requires an accurate diagnosis of the state's economy and policies and programs that span several state agencies. A recent study by the Council of State Policy and Planning Agencies persuasively argues that diagnosing the state's economy requires more than the traditional "newspaper analysis" of economic trends, such as the unemployment rate and productivity growth, that are only partial indicators of a state's economic performance and "do not distinguish between a slowing in the rate of growth and an acceleration in the rate of change" (Vaughan and others, 1984, p. 45). A diagnosis of the state's economy must be based on a wider set of indicators and an expanded definition of economic development.

In any diagnosis of a state's economy, it is important first to ascertain what constitutes a healthy business climate for economic growth. There are methodological problems in measuring what is meant by a good business climate (Erickson, 1987), and there have been mounting criticisms of the most prominent analysis done on this subject, conducted by GrantThorton (formerly Alexander Grant) since 1979. The GrantThorton study's ranking of general manufacturing climates focused on the variables of state and local taxes, state fiscal policies, union strength, wages, energy costs, and worker's compensation and unemployment benefits. The focus on these measurable variables inevitably led to the conclusion that to improve its business climate, a state should initiate policies to lower its taxes, worker's compensation, and welfare benefits and should have a low percentage of unionized workers. Not surprisingly, in GrantThorton's 1986 analysis it was South Dakota that ranked first as the state possessing the best manufacturing business climate. The New England, Middle Atlantic, and Great Lakes states ranked near the bottom of the list.

The 1986 *Inc.* study, on the other hand, ranked states according to three measures of business health: the rate of new business formation, the number of new companies, and the percentage of growth in employment (Kahn, 1986). The *Inc.* rating system, while acknowledging the importance of taxation levels, stressed more heavily the availability of capital, direct state aid to business, labor cost and quality, and business activity (Skoro, 1987). The difference between *Inc.*'s and GrantThorton's studies is that low taxes do not by themselves encourage a good business climate; rather, the availability of capital for small business growth and the active role of governmental policies to stimulate future business formation are critical in promoting a healthy business environment.

Two recent studies on what constitutes a productive business climate have directly challenged the validity of GrantThorton's premises. The first study, published in 1986 by SRI International/ AmeriTrust and entitled *Indicators of Economic Capacity,* emphasized what it referred to as the forces of economic change. Previous analysis of what constitutes an attractive business climate had assumed slow technological change, limited foreign competition, and the prevalence of large corporations. In the 1980s, this assumption is incorrect. In short, the GrantThorton analysis may have some validity for certain firms with a relatively stable market, but it is inappropriate for a new economy that is rapidly changing both technologically and internationally. Economic competitiveness is now measured in terms of the adaptability of state economies to this economic transformation. New factors need to be considered, such as the availability of venture capital, the quality of universities and colleges, and industry outlays for research and development. Other related factors are state spending on education and the number of academic degrees in science and engineering. Given the importance of these factors, the focus of public managers and policymakers should not be exclusively on current business activity, but rather on how to increase the economic capacity of their state economies.

With this new approach, the SRI/AmeriTrust analysis concluded that New York and Michigan—states traditionally viewed as discouraging business retention and growth because of their high taxes—actually offer a favorable business climate. Although Michigan was rated rather low in the 1986 GrantThorton study, it has some of the best science and engineering faculty in the country. Furthermore, it has a supportive regulatory environment and strong programs dealing with venture capital funds and state loan guarantees. Although Michigan's present economic situation is mixed, as made evident by its low rating on both R&D expenditures and the number of sixteen-to-twenty-four-year-olds attending four-year colleges, it has tried to create an entrepreneurial environment conducive to a new economy. New York has been considered unattractive to businesses because of its high state taxes and high energy costs. Yet in New York, expenditures per pupil for education are among the highest in the nation. Like Michigan, its engineering and science faculty are ranked high nationally, and it produces many more science Ph.D.'s per capita than the national average. New York has strong state venture capital funds and state loan guarantees as well as business incubators. Overall, this study concluded that the Pacific, New England, Middle Atlantic, and Great Lakes states are in a strong position to take advantage of a new emerging economy.

Similarly, a study conducted by the Corporation for Enterprise Development (CfED), entitled *Making the Grade: The Development Report Card for the States* (1987), analyzed seventy-eight factors that it contends have a direct bearing on future economic growth. These factors were grouped into the following categories (Kasouf, 1987, p. 12): economic performance, including employment growth, income per capita, equity, job quality, and quality of life; business vitality, including competitiveness of existing businesses and ability to spawn new ones; economic capacity, including human and capital resources, infrastructure capacity, and amenities to attract and retain talent; and policy strength, including the effectiveness of governance and regulation, tax policy, commitment to enabling capital mobilization, improved education and research, and help for distressed communities.

The CfED analysis, written specifically as a diagnostic tool for self-examination by state governments, concluded that the Northeast and the Middle Atlantic regions possessed the most potential for future economic growth. The region that showed the least potential for economic growth was the Southeast. The regions facing deleterious trends are those heavily dependent on forestry and agriculture. Three states that are ranked in the top ten in Grant-Thorton's index because of low taxes and low wages (North Carolina, Mississippi, and South Dakota) rank in the bottom ten of the CfED report. The CfED report challenges the premise that lower taxes and costs alone are helpful to state economies and in fact claims that they can divert attention from other resources, such as human capital, crucial to future economic growth.

From an empirical perspective, it is highly questionable whether a business climate can be measured accurately (Skoro,

1987). While each of the studies mentioned has serious methodological flaws, the SRI/AmeriTrust and CfED analyses legitimately raise the issue that the emphasis should no longer be on business climate but on what constitutes economic capacity for state economies. In this sense, economic development becomes more than the creation of new jobs. *State economic development involves the creation of wealth, a process that increases the capacity of individuals and organizations to create and sustain wealth.*

A major focus of the state's diagnosis must therefore be its economic capacity. Unfortunately, there is no single indicator that provides an unambiguous measure of the capacities of state economies. Instead, each state must develop a set of indicators that best fit its particular economic structure and program needs. One indicator that can be used to measure aspects of the state economy is overall economic performance: the rate of long-term (more than twelve weeks) unemployment, growth in per capita income, and traditional indicators such as housing starts, vehicle registrations, and tax revenues. Another is entrepreneurial climate: the rate of new business formation and failure, venture capital placements in-state, R&D activity at universities, over-the-counter stock issues, and the growth rate of the number of self-employed people. A third is long-term growth prospects: the rate of diversification of the economy during the past ten years, measures of the performance of primary and secondary schools, reductions in the illiteracy rate during the past five years, and the average educational attainment of the work force. A fourth includes other aspects of a state's wealth: changes in air quality in major cities, changes in water quality, the poverty rate (after allowing for government transfers and in-kind benefits), and the crime rate (Vaughan and others, 1984).

Four Guidelines for Revitalizing State Economies

During the 1980s, many states initiated bold new experiments that constitute a shift away from traditional development approaches. These experiments primarily address entrepreneurial development, largely because they are designed to cultivate indigenous businesses. More important, certain states are beginning to understand that finding the economic development suited to their particular needs implies a systematic rethinking of the development process along four broad categories: interdependent policy strategies, innovative and inventive efforts, integrated strategies involving local, state, and federal involvement, and investment approaches.

Interdependence. Economic development is best viewed as a set of interconnected programs and policies that relate to education, job retraining, international markets, physical infrastructure, natural resources, public and private relationships, intersectoral management, and political leadership. Policy interdependence is a new, pivotal factor in strategically planning an economic development program. An example of policy interdependence is illustrated by the Massachusetts Machine Trades Action Project (MMTAP). This project, partially supported by the state's JTPA funds, links educational policies for retraining the work force in the western part of the state with a "bottom-up" program for marketing the area to stimulate, expand, and attract new national and international firms that are compatible with the region's economic base. Another example of policy interdependence worth noting is Maine's TOPS program. This program uses a venture capital pool that invests in certain firms only if they agree to hire a set percentage of welfare recipients. This illustrates the importance of the interconnectedness between economic development and social policy.

Fostering state economic development goals, as these brief examples demonstrate, inherently requires a multifaceted approach. Managing these interdependencies is the greatest challenge for state officials in formulating new policy strategies.

Innovation. Many states are presently initiating a range of innovative policies that are not merely more of the same but rather are innovative, custom-designed policies focused on long-term investments in the state's future economic prosperity and wealth. Some of the most innovative approaches recently utilized by state governments are programs concerning venture capital. Twenty-eight states now have venture capital programs. The oldest of the venture capital programs is the Connecticut Product Development Corporation (CPDC), which provides state businesses with seed capital to develop new and innovative products. The CPDC is eventually repaid through a royalty agreement of 5 percent of the sales of the product (Pilcher, 1986). Presently, the CPDC has invested nearly $15 million in innovative products. Another example is the Massachusetts Technology Development Corporation (MTDC), created in 1978 to develop the technology potential of small firms. The MTDC provides risk capital to new technology firms in distressed areas of the state. This risk capital, in the form of subordinated debt, is provided below market interest rates. So far, the MTDC has invested nearly $5 million, with private investment nearly double that amount. Minnesota has recently started the Minnesota Seed Capital Fund (MSCF) to help small businesses' need for critical start-up money. This capital fund—capitalized at $10 million in 1981—is filling a common financing gap between seed capital and debt financing by providing "mezzanine" financing. Investments by the MSCF usually range from $50,000 to $250,000. What makes these examples noteworthy is that there was a deliberate attempt by policymakers to design venture capital programs compatible with the state government's economic development aims.

These strategies show that innovations and experimentation are taking root at the state level and that state governments are becoming the laboratories for economic experimentation. In many respects, states are now designing the outline for a strategic national economic policy for the 1990s.

Integration. A strategic economic plan not only attempts to stimulate an entrepreneurial environment for business formation, expansion, attraction, and retention; it is also a tool for fostering the capacities of state agencies to integrate local, state, and federal resources more effectively. As the federal presence dwindles, state agencies are taking on more of the burden of managing economic development. This requires careful coordination and integration of the activities of various state government agencies.

Connecting the established state institutions to respond to the needs of the new economy more effectively becomes the primary challenge of state government. For this reason, thirty-seven states have each formed an independent line agency for economic development activities (Clarke, 1986). One of the most ambitious efforts was initiated by Illinois, which, in 1979, combined three state agencies into a newly created agency called the Department of Commerce and Community Affairs (DCCA). This agency, with a budget of half a billion dollars, not only provides traditional assistance of management support, exporting, and procurements but also coordinates activities related to job training, marketing its localities, overseas state tourism, and assistance to local governments (Clarke, 1986). Moreover, it administers several federal grants, such as the JTPA, the CDBG program, and the EDA Title IX Grant and Community Services Block Grant (CSBG) Program. The DCCA is noteworthy because it integrates both employment and training within one agency as well as coordinating all statewide local, state, and federal economic development activities. This approach is at present a rarity among states. Only three other states (Delaware, Rhode Island, and Utah) have followed the example of Illinois, but many others are examining this approach to integrating state efforts.

One of Minnesota's recent development policies also warrants attention. Minnesota has stipulated that education and training provided for the structurally unemployed must be specifically coordinated with federal job training legislation in order to encourage businesses to hire and train the economically disadvantaged. As a strategic program, Indiana's Economic Development Council (EDC) was created in 1985 to serve as an umbrella development agency to coordinate and evaluate all economic development policies. The EDC, much like the California Economic Development Corporation, is a publicly chartered but privately incorporated corporation. Although it includes key actors in the state legislature, it is independent of the state government. This approach was used because it could further integrate public and private involvement and, more important, be free of political pressures to evaluate the efficacy of the numerous strategic efforts.

The importance of an integrative approach is that it coordinates economic activities in order to overcome the obstacles presented by institutional barriers. Training and retraining of workers, for example, typically involves from four to six state agencies as well as federal training programs. Some integrative approaches to managing economic development include the following:

- *A Joint State Employment and Training Economic Development Board.* This structure encourages cooperation among state agencies, local governments and school districts, vocational schools, community colleges, and private training and placement services. The board brings together critical pieces of state policies—economic development, postsecondary education, and employment services.
- *Integrated Employment and Development Finance Programs.* Too often, training and business finance programs operate in a vacuum. One is training workers and the other, ideally, is creating new jobs, but without linkages there is no guarantee that the newly trained workers will be hired. States can require that all development finance programs have an employment policy linkage. Such a link could range from merely ensuring that all aided businesses advertise job openings at local Private Industry Councils (PICs) and Job Service offices to requiring that firms work with area training efforts to help the disadvantaged.
- *Community Economic Adjustment Teams.* Plant closings and mass layoffs take a heavy toll—financial, physical, and psychological—on workers and their families, employers, communities, cities, and states. State governments using funds from the Job Training Partnership Act in combination with other resources can establish an Economic Adjustment Team that will provide a structure and framework for launching a state-sponsored strategy, maintain an inventory and serve as a broker of existing public and private monies and expertise, determine the magnitude and nature of the economic dislocation program, design new training, social service, and business retention initiatives and an early warning system, and evaluate program results. Such an economic adjustment strategy is not simply a training policy or a means of reacting to plant shutdowns. Rather, it is also a fundamental tool for increasing the capacity of communities to forge their economic futures, to integrate state and federal resources, and to mesh employment with

economic development efforts (Friedman and Schweke, 1986, pp. 32–35).

Investment. As traditional recruitment and attraction strategies decline in potency, the conventional efforts to develop an economic strategy lose their influence. With the increased importance of business formation, expansion, and retention, a state's efforts must shift to investment strategies. Public expenditures in economic development are most effective when viewed as investments that can be targeted or tailored to areas that enhance the state's economic capacity to grow.

Where is public investment most likely to stimulate statewide economic growth? The SRI/AmeriTrust study (SRI International, 1986b), for example, has identified three general areas for state investments: increasing accessible technology, providing a skilled and adaptable work force, and making capital available. These key investment areas suggest that closer attention must be paid to factors that are pertinent for advanced technology, high-innovation firms. According to this study, state investments are needed for these highly innovative firms, which require not only a highly skilled and adaptable work force, but a strong educational and infrastructural system as well.

The problem facing states is not to develop a strategy competitive with that of other states; rather, it is to target resources strategically toward enhancing the state's own economic capacity. Indicators of the state's economic condition in the areas of accessible technology, a skilled and adaptable work force, and capital availability will guide states in targeting their investments.

Advanced technology and innovative firms are in need of institutions that can conduct relevant research in furthering technological capacity. The quality of these institutions, therefore, is an essential part of fostering a state's economic growth. Some key indicators utilized by SRI/AmeriTrust to measure capacity in this area include total R&D in universities per capita, state and local government R&D in universities per capita, industry R&D per capita, and university-industry initiatives.

The quality of the work force is one of the most salient elements in strategically managing economic development. States with a poorly educated populace are especially vulnerable to stiff competition from countries that have an abundance of low-cost labor. Indicators to assess the quality of the work force include some of the following factors: total education expenditures per capita, expenditures per capita on K–12 education, percentage of population over twenty-five with a college degree, and percentage of sixteen-to-twenty-four-year-olds attending four-year or two-year colleges.

While the availability of capital is crucial for firms of all sizes, it is particularly critical for new and young business enterprises. More important, capital allocation to businesses in distressed communities is essential for generating jobs and future economic wealth. However, there are major barriers to obtaining capital for new and existing businesses, such as a lack of competition among financial institutions, governmental regulations, and the cost of information (Advisory Commission on Intergovernmental Relations, 1985). Given these obstacles, the SRI/AmeriTrust indicators of economic capacity in this case highlight the following factors: total equity capital per capita, venture capital per capita, state initiatives for capital formation, and state regulation of capital markets.

The value of these indicators is that they draw attention to the kind of state investments needed for long-term economic growth. Moreover, they focus attention on economic output as it is related to the inputs of human resources, technology, capital, and government policy. The state's capacity for future economic wealth depends on how these elements can be linked in a strategic program.

A Strategic Guide

Given the importance of strategic planning, what specific guidelines should states follow? First and foremost, states must design policies tailor-made to their economies. A state with an agriculture-based economy and minimal venture capital must proceed differently from a state that is highly urbanized and possesses substantial venture capital resources. Second, state policymakers must assess the strengths and weaknesses of the state economy. Third, each state must determine the appropriate organizational strategy to best coordinate and integrate economic development programs. Finally, an examination must be made of the financial, managerial, and legal constraints of potential alternatives for revitalizing a state economy. Generally speaking, these four guidelines include, at least implicitly, the variables of investment, innovation, integration, and interdependency. With these variables in mind, a strategic framework for public investment can be identified that focuses on four investment areas:

- *capital availability*—creating and increasing access to debt and equity capital and seed capital for business start-ups and expansions, as well as for retention and attraction;
- *human resources*—investing in education and training to improve the skills, knowledge, and flexibility of the state's work force;
- *infrastructure*—improving the transportation and telecommunications infrastructure of the state; and
- *natural resources*—investing in the state's renewable resources and promoting a healthy environment.

Capital Availability. Three policy strategies can be undertaken by states to improve the accessibility of investment capital for business formation, expansion, attraction, and retention. First, states can remove barriers to the efficient flow of capital in the private financial market. State governments typically establish the guidelines that regulate private financial markets. Generally, states should develop policies that encourage competition among financial institutions.

Banks can create and destroy capital through the control of money and credit. Although banks are usually privately owned, profit-oriented businesses, their role in directing state investment is significant and often invisible. Since banking is a heavily regulated industry, the regulatory power of state governments must be considered a separate element in public policy and one of the first areas where effective economic development policy must be examined. States should review finance industry regulations and tax policy (that is, how the earnings of investors are taxed). Policies should be considered that develop ways to encourage investments and loans in targeted industries without jeopardizing the financial integrity of the institutions and without creating equity problems. There are several ways that banks can provide more capital for new, small business enterprises without excessively interfering with the market flow of capital.

First, state regulators can permit banks to designate moderate-risk, high-reward loan portfolios for which they would charge slightly higher rates for loans to offset the possibility of additional losses. This would yield net income to the banks equal to or better than current risk-adverse lending. Second, states can enact a state loan loss reserve program wherein individual banks would create reserve funds, financed equally by borrowers, lenders, and the state, to back a riskier portfolio. Third, states can exempt equity kicker payments from state usury ceilings. With an equity kicker, a bank lends at a low interest rate but receives, in addition to interest, payments related to the success of a venture. Exempting such payments from usury ceilings would increase the availability of capital for new enterprises. Fourth, states can make quid-pro-quo deals with banks as part of financial deregulation incentives. For example, states can give banks new business privileges, in exchange for which banks will create bank CDCs, invest in minority banks, and set aside assets for an in-state capital pool (Corporation for Enterprise Development, 1984).

State taxation policies have a more limited effect on the availability of capital than state regulatory policies. Business taxation is not a significant issue for smaller and younger enterprises, since they seldom pay taxes during their first few years. Business taxes thus have little effect on capital availability for business formation. As a business matures and becomes more profitable, business taxes begin to increase and corporate concerns emerge, often in the form of increased lobbying to reduce taxes. By the time an enterprise has acquired a noticeable tax burden, it has developed much greater accessibility to the capital market, and corporate taxes have only a minor effect on capital accessibility. Taxes on personal investments can influence individual investment decisions, since most seed capital for new businesses comes from personal savings (see Chapter Five). Federal income taxes, however, encourage real estate investments over business investments, and state income tax policy may have difficulties in stimulating personal investments in business enterprises.

A second strategy to increase capital availability is the development of new financial institutions that provide venture capital, debt financing, and loans. These venture capital programs involve five basic approaches (Marlin and Vieux, 1986): creating a public-sector fund (a fund capitalized with state or federal money and administered by a state economic development department; six states use this type of program); operating a fund through a quasi-public entity (these funds are restricted to investment in high-technology firms and administered by independent agencies created by state government; fifteen states use this approach); creating a singular state-initiated private fund (a fund in which the state can be an investor in the capital pool but the majority of investments are created by giving tax credits to private investors for capitalization of the fund; six states have initiated this type of program); encouraging public pension funds to make capital investments (pension funds invested in venture programs vary from 1 to 5 percent and usually involve limited partnerships with other capital funds; eight states use this approach); and providing tax incentives encouraging investment in venture capital programs (the state provides tax incentives for private investors to invest funds in state-certified capital funds; eight states use this incentive).

Because these different approaches have only recently been implemented, it is difficult to determine their efficacy in raising capital. Nonetheless, venture capital programs have a better chance of succeeding when the state government has first developed a consensus regarding economic development objectives and how such programs fit into achieving those objectives (Marlin and Vieux, 1986).

Thirty states, moreover, have created development banks for targeting investment. States should be careful, however, when considering setting up new public financial institutions to stimulate the flow of investment capital. Successful financial institutions require a high level of private investment expertise, considerable local information, and diversified portfolios; public agencies are bound by public laws and have difficulty in obtaining these. Moreover, they can rarely pay salaries high enough to retain the best personnel, and they are often too small to diversify effectively. Many are very conservative, and they face the political necessity of showing quick results and the pressure to assist enterprises associated with elected officials. Because of these pressures, few state or local lending or equity investing agencies have proved successful (Vaughan and others, 1984). New financial institutions must therefore be tied closely to the private sector, limiting the public sector's role to that of partner or catalyst. The state of Indiana, for example, established the Corporation for Science and Technology, a nonprofit corporation that makes direct investments in applied research and product development ventures by private firms.

A third strategy for making capital available involves direct investments in target industries or enterprises by state governments through two funding sources: federal grants (for example, CDBG) that can be used to provide debt or equity financing and state pension funds. Some states are establishing pension fund investment units that search out and recommend new investments. Pennsylvania, for example, has been experimenting with various mechanisms for moving state pension fund money into venture capital and business enterprise investment. By 1987, at least twelve states had taken up pension fund venture capital investing. Pension managers in the 1980s have diversified their portfolios, expanding into overseas investments, futures options, and leveraged buyouts; venture investments are increasing but, because of their high risk, are typically kept to a small fraction of a portfolio (Pierce, 1987).

State-operated finance agencies, another mechanism for direct investment, may not be a cost-effective approach to providing investment capital. A successful public development agency can probably serve only a few firms and is likely to have much less effect than regulatory changes or tax reforms. States should therefore first consider the following initiatives:

- Repealing usury ceilings to exclude bank lending
- Reforming state capital-gains taxes to treat gains on "collectibles" (such as gold and antiques) as ordinary income
- Initiating tax credits for new venture capital programs

- Changing regulations to allow more investment by insurance companies and pension funds in new and small firms
- Encouraging pooled loan programs to minimize risk in investing in new businesses, especially in their need for services and infrastructure (Shapero, 1985)
- Encouraging employee stock ownership programs (ESOPs) that can provide critical funds for business continuation
- Developing a computerized information exchange that expands communication channels between small businesses and informal risk-capital investors (Daniels, 1985)
- Consider the deferral of capital gains taxes on businesses, particularly if the gains are reinvested within one year in targeted industries or enterprises

Human Resources. Economic development depends on human resources, and the postindustrial economy requires a work force that is increasingly technologically literate, adaptable to rapid market changes, capable of continuous relearning and retraining, and internationally oriented. Some states are far ahead of others in reacting to changing circumstances. Economic development depends mainly on people: engineers, scientists, and inventors; entrepreneurs and skillful state business managers; and skillful employees. The inventiveness, entrepreneurial talent, adaptability, technical and analytical skill, and motivation of the state's population are essential ingredients for economic growth and development. Human capital has become a key requirement of successful state economic development. State governments have a very important role in building a statewide human capital infrastructure and can significantly influence the human resource development process. States help finance most primary, secondary, and postsecondary education; they administer job and employment services for the unemployed; and they regulate many aspects of the workplace, from safety and health to wages (Vaughan and others, 1984).

States have only begun to wrestle with ways to make the investments in human resources required in a modern economy, and many are confronting the economic implications of neglecting programs in human resource development. Because a sound economy now requires a well-educated and trained work force in order to pursue entrepreneurial opportunities, new policies are needed that substantially invest in the citizenry. By calculating educational investments, rather than weighing costs, state policymakers can play a more dynamic role in stimulating economic development.

States have significant influence over elementary and secondary education as well as authority over a wide variety of social service programs that affect the development of children and youth. A relatively untapped strategic area of concern for state government activity is the growing proportion of uneducated and unskilled youth moving toward adulthood. There are a number of indications of the seriousness of this national decline in younger human resources:

- The United States is tied for the worst rate of infant mortality among all the industrial nations.
- Nearly 60 percent of today's four-year-olds will live in a single-parent household before they turn eighteen.
- The United States has one of the highest rates of malnutrition of all the industrial countries.
- Delinquency rates among children aged ten to seventeen have increased 130 percent since 1960.
- Dropout rates from public schools, particularly among Hispanics, are high.
- Rates of adult illiteracy are high.
- The United States has the highest rate of teenage pregnancy among the industrial countries, twice the rate of any other Western country (Bundy and Hallet, 1987).

Child-centered strategies are necessary for investment in the emerging pool of human resources, and strategic economic development must include activities aimed at developing well-nourished and well-educated children. Child-centered strategies should focus first on improving the quality of primary and secondary education for all children, not just those at risk. Other state strategies can focus on the following problems: adolescent malnutrition, abuse and neglect of children, and quality before- and after-school care for school-age children.

Postsecondary education contributes greatly to a state's economic vitality and growth. Learning is the principal capital formation process in the postindustrial economy (Perelman, 1984). Basic adult-centered educational strategies must focus on educating a technologically literate population and developing a work force that is able to adapt to the changing circumstances inherent in an information-based, global economy. Specific strategies for adult-centered human resource development, discussed in Chapter Eight, include:

- Revised educational programs that better meet the intellectual needs of a work force in a postindustrial economy, including international education, telecommunications and related technical training, improved instruction in science, mathematics, and foreign languages, and skills in learning how to learn
- Remedial education for the estimated 20 million individuals who are functionally illiterate and who cannot effectively join the work force because they lack basic skills in reading and writing
- Retraining workers who are displaced by the shifts from manufacturing and agricultural sectors to services and knowledge-based sectors
- Renewing and updating professionals and managers, such as engineers and medical scientists, in current and emerging technological advances
- Entrepreneurial instruction that educates people in strategies for generating jobs and teaches people to take an idea, scrutinize it, identify market potential, and implement appropriate entrepreneurial strategies

Child-centered strategies are crucial and have been the subject of many critical evaluations and reform proposals. Since the bulk of the future work force, however, is already past secondary school, significant state attention must also be paid to adult-centered strategies. Key reform efforts have been made in basic educational curricula in colleges and universities. States, however, have the unique responsibility of integrating employee training programs with higher education. There have been experiments, for example, that have tried to integrate customized job training programs with local colleges to provide quality jobs. The challenge is to make innovative, interdependent investments in education and training.

Massachusetts, for example, established the Bay State Skills Corporation (BSSC). The BSSC attempts to retrain workers for the state's high-growth industries. This is achieved by giving grants to educational institutions, which must also get matching grants from the private sector. The program primarily focuses on the educational and training needs of workers who lost their jobs in plant closings, unemployed youth, and welfare recipients. A unique aspect of this program is that "a firm that participates in a training program targeted to one of these groups must match only 20 percent of the BSSC grant, compared to 100 percent for an untargeted program" (Advisory Commission on Intergovernmental Relations, 1985, p. 99).

Another innovative approach to enhance the state investment in human capital is to create a trust fund for low-interest loans to workers. As proposed by the Corporation for Enterprise Development (1984), workers who borrow money from this trust fund could repay it on a schedule determined by their gross income after they have become employed.

Infrastructure. The state's infrastructure is the physical public-works framework that supports and sustains virtually all economic activity. Definitions of infrastructure typically include transportation facilities (such as interstate highways, roads, and bridges), water resources, and waste treatment systems; increasingly, they also include energy distribution systems (electrical utilities, for example) and telecommunications facilities, both of which are becoming more important for economic growth in an information-based, global economy.

Infrastructure investments affect not only local uses but the overall level of economic activity in a region or state (Eberts, 1987). For instance, expanded transportation, water supply, and waste systems are needed to accommodate growth; specific infrastructure improvements may be required in order for particular projects to proceed. Inadequate maintenance of existing systems can interrupt economic activity or increase its costs. Underutilized capacity offers opportunities for economic growth at low additional cost but creates high operating costs for present users. The costs of infrastructure expansion, maintenance, and operation constitute an important cost of doing business (Committee for Economic Development, 1986). However, economists have been unable to measure precisely the economic development stimulus provided by infrastructure development. This difficulty is partly due to the unique nature of public works, which are typically characterized by high fixed costs, long service life, interconnection with other physical facilities, and public ownership. The public-works infrastructure can provide a significant inducement to economic development and is essential to a state's quality of life, economic health, and international competitiveness. The supply of paved roads and the number of miles of interstate highway within a region are strongly correlated with employment growth (Carlino and Mills, 1987). Infrastructure investments, however, tend merely to move economic activity around, rather than stimulate new productive capacity. Infrastructure expenditures are therefore necessary investments, but alone they are not sufficient to generate new economic development (National Council on Public Works Improvement, 1986).

State governments are now recognizing the growing importance of financing public works, particularly those involving capital construction as well as operations and maintenance. Two major issues confront state governments in meeting this responsibility. First, investment in public infrastructure nationally has not kept pace with expanding needs, and the repair and rehabilitation of serviceable older facilities have been neglected. Public-works investments have been neglected by many states that are constrained by tight budgets. The growth rate of public infrastructure investment has slowed significantly since the 1960s, compared with the growth rate of private capital formation (National Council on Public Works Improvement, 1986). The share of GNP invested in public works declined from 5 percent in 1965 to only 2 percent in 1985. Seventeen percent of the nation's bridges are in critical or intolerable condition. Some major cities lose nearly half their water through water-main leaks. Not only have states cut spending, but they have not developed planning and budgeting procedures to ensure that public investments are integrated into strategic economic targets. State and local governments are now paying for more than half of public-works capital outlays and will probably finance even larger shares in the future (National Council on Public Works Improvement, 1986). Given that fiscal constraints will continue in the future, state governments must develop new financial strategies in targeting investments, financing, and policy to prevent the further deterioration of the public infrastructure.

With revenues stable or declining, states must target their infrastructure investments toward critical and strategic needs. Needs studies completed in the 1970s were the earliest attempts to define and categorize infrastructure needs and to assess the relative size of the public-works needs gap for state legislatures to fill. However, needs studies are changing, partly as a result of the increasing awareness of the links between infrastructure and economic development. The focus of state infrastructure studies is now on determining investment priorities (National Council on Public Works Improvement, 1986). Such investment studies help determine whether there is a funding shortfall in small rural or large urban systems, for example. They also serve to alert policymakers to large investment backlogs while steering them away from areas where investment is not yet required (Peterson and others, 1984). Establishing an investment analysis that better informs public policy-making entails estimating the costs of upgrading facilities to certain standards, clarifying the implications of failing to reach these standards, and providing policy choices among alternative capital spending and maintenance strategies, tied to the specific investments (Peterson and others, 1984).

As state and local governments confront increasing responsibility for financing infrastructure construction and maintenance, earmarking or dedicating revenues for investments must be considered (National Council on Public Works Improvement, 1986). Historically, governments have obtained financing in one or more of the following ways: by receiving aid (direct and indirect) from another unit of government; by issuing tax-exempt debt where the principal raised is repaid over time, with interest, from future tax and fee revenues; and through current taxes and fees. Revenue earmarking or dedication should include: direct user fees and charges (such as highway tolls, water and sewage fees, and transit fares); dedicated revenues (such as motor fuel taxes for roadways, lottery revenues, and a portion of broad-based levies such as sales taxes); impact and developer fees extracted from private developers as a condition for issuing building permits, occupancy certificates, or zoning changes; and tax increment financing techniques associated with the real property tax.

Targeting financing toward strategic needs requires creative integration of traditionally separate infrastructure policy areas into statewide economic development strategies. A central aspect of a state's infrastructure, for example, is its highway improvement programs. Presently, thirty-six states incorporate highway activities into economic development plans. However, fifteen of these states merely mention the relationship to economic development without providing any funds for the purpose of enhancing development activities (Forkenbrock and Plazak, 1986). Florida has been especially aggressive in linking its highway improvement plans to economic development. In 1981, it started the Economic Development Transportation Fund. Appropriations since 1981 have ranged from $7 million to $11 million. The Florida Department of Commerce has estimated that capital investment in highway improvement has directly created about 63,000 new jobs. In 1985, Iowa started the Revitalize Iowa's Sound Economy program (RISE). This program is funded by a two-cents-per-gallon motor fuel tax that is expected to raise about $30 million annually. This approach was designed to both strengthen and diversify Iowa's economy. According to Forkenbrock and Plazak (1986, p. 157), the program involves two types of projects: "One is intended to facilitate development negotiations with private sector investors. And the other seeks to improve local communities' potential to attract economic development." While there is a lack of empirical data to judge RISE's effectiveness, the program represents a significant step in the direction of improving investment opportunities in the state.

While states have recognized to a certain degree the validity of linking highway improvements to economic development, overall only fifteen states incorporate infrastructure development into economic development policies (Clarke, 1986). This means that the infrastructure of transportation, water supply and sewage, communications, energy, housing, and waste management are, for the most part, treated by states as policy issues separate from an economic development plan. An exception to this practice is the Mississippi Business Investment Program, which gives low-interest loans to its localities, matched by funds from the private sector, for infrastructural investments to generate business formation. Other strategic combinations for infrastructural investment might include:

• Establishing a program or coordinating council that integrates manpower/human resource training, investment capital policies and regulations, and infrastructure investment policies.
• Creating an infrastructure trust fund that makes loans to local governments in order to repair the existing infrastructure. As in the case of Washington's Public Works Trust Fund, the localities would be required to impose an excise tax for capital improvements and institute a long-range capital financing plan (Committee for Economic Development, 1986).
• Creating trust funds for specific infrastructural activities (such as sewage) that can be capitalized by state bonds and thus enable states to issue revenue bonds in support of loans to improve a particular facility (Committee for Economic Development, 1986).
• Targeting investments to areas identified as "corridors of statewide significance," and funding these investments with a state lottery or state trust fund financed through gas taxes and vehicle registration fees.
• Requiring private-sector involvement by requiring investors to reach an agreement prior to construction or improvement of a facility. For example, a 30 percent matching fund from private firms or local government might be mandatory. Two key factors ensure project viability: cost-effectiveness (a specification of state funding per job created or retained that should not exceed, say, $3,000 to $4,000) and capital leveraging (the ratio of

nonstate funding of total capital investment to state funding should be at least 5:1) (Forkenbrock and Plazak, 1986).

- Improving capital planning and budgeting by analyzing social and economic factors that could increase demand for public facilities. This would include estimating the depreciation rate of infrastructure as well as the effect of new projects on future operating budgets (Dyer and Pollard, 1986).

Natural Resources. Natural resources are for many states their most important heritage, and investment in natural resources directly influences economic growth. In the 1970s, environmental controls were seen as deterrents to economic growth. Recent research, however, indicates the increasing importance of natural resources in attracting business firms (especially advanced technology firms) and people through their effect on the quality of life and tourism. As a result of inadequate investments in natural resources, many of these resources are deteriorating or in increasingly short supply (Northdurft, 1986). Investments in natural resources focus on preserving and enhancing nonrenewable resources (such as beaches) and developing renewable resources for their commodity value (such as forests).

States with tourism as a major sector of their economy rely heavily on their natural resources. Tourism depends greatly on the preservation of coastal areas, scenic vistas, clean air and water, abundant fish and wildlife, and other natural assets. Similarly, a state's natural amenities attract and retain skilled employees over competitive locations elsewhere. One analysis found that Oregon's environmental protection and land-use regulations, which balance conservation with development, attract non-resource-based firms (such as services) and advanced technology firms (such as electronics) to the state (Simmons, 1985). Research by MIT (Birch, 1987b) and the U.S. Office of Technology Assessment (1984) clearly shows that attractive natural resources attract firms and investment opportunities.

Renewable resources, such as forests, fisheries, and agricultural land, are fundamental industries in most states and provide natural resource targets for state investment. States must develop policies that sustain the productivity of their natural resources and encourage investment in the renewable resource base of soils, water, fisheries, and forests. Dependence on a particular resource-based industry, however, leaves a state vulnerable to declines in markets. States that fail to diversify their economic base and continue to rely on a few resource-based industries will seriously endanger their long-term economic interest as the global market expands.

In formulating strategic goals targeted to resource-based development, the following factors should be considered (Northdurft, 1984, pp. 167–168): maximizing sustainable resource yield (ensuring that natural resources are managed to enhance their long-term productivity), increasing reliance on renewable sources (designing policies to insulate the state from the effects of declining supplies of nonrenewable factors of production), enhancing environmental quality (enhancing the environment to retain business activity and to ensure health and safety), increasing stability and self-reliance (providing protection from external fluctuations in the supply and price of resources critical to economic activity), reducing economic waste (removing regulations or tax subsidies that make resources inexpensive and distort their true production cost), and improving value added (guaranteeing that maximum economic value is received within the state from the use of the state's natural resource assets).

In achieving these goals, state governments, unlike the federal government, can play a pivotal role with the private sector in developing a set of natural resource policies. According to a recent empirical study, chief executive officers (CEOs) of major companies nationwide reveal support for nonfederal approaches to natural resource problems (Bowman and Davis, 1987). In view of the interest among CEOs in working with state governments, policymakers should consider creating a council of public and private leaders to examine the impact of natural resources on economic development. Along these lines, the state government can work with the private sector by encouraging the growth of enterprises that are involved in renewable resources. For example, the state of Maine has created a Natural Resource Financing and Marketing Authority that utilizes private investment for agricultural and fishing enterprises. California, on the other hand, has started a fund to assist small businesses that are involved in energy-conserving systems. While resource-based development can be improved by preferential tax policies to protect valuable resources (for example, wildlife, land, and coastal areas), it can also be enhanced by fostering venture capital programs that promote job generation by targeting monies to resource enterprises. An obvious risk is involved in implementing this strategy, but state government participation is warranted in fostering the expansion of industries dependent on indigenous renewable resources (Northdurft, 1986).

State Assistance for Local Governments

State government is in the best position to take the leading role and responsibility for targeting public investment statewide in financial capital, human resources, infrastructure, and natural resources. In addition, states have four responsibilities to substate and local economies. First, states must assume responsibility or, at the very least, participate as a partner in specific development projects of statewide significance. Major retention projects, such as preventing a large enterprise from closing or relocating in another state, require a level of effort often beyond what communities can provide. Some states, such as California, assist by holding predevelopment conferences with companies intending to locate in the state. At these conferences, all state and local governments involved in permit-granting and land-use approval for the project meet with the company's representatives and the governor's representatives for the purpose of accelerating the governmental permit process.

Second, states should be involved in development projects targeted to areas experiencing economic shock and severely depressed areas. Regions of a state that are hard hit by major shifts in the national and international economy require state assistance. Helping rural and urban areas with extremely high unemployment is often beyond the capacity of many local governments alone. One approach is for states to offer strategic investment block grants, targeting state investment to specific regions of the state.

Third, states can assist industrial prospects by matching an industry's needs with the right location in the state. State executives can act as catalysts or matchmakers in bringing one or more companies within an industry together with state universities to cooperate in joint ventures. Potential matchings include medical schools and biological science departments with biotechnology enterprises and pharmaceutical companies.

Fourth, states should empower city and county governments and regional councils of governments to plan strategically for economic growth and to establish innovative development programs. State statutes provide the legal framework within which local government economic development operates. In addition to providing direct financial assistance, states are also sources for local capacity building through technical assistance and training for local government managers. Helping local governments build their own management capacities to stimulate job creation and providing appropriate enabling legislation might go far in generating more jobs for those presently unemployed. State government can be less involved in making decisions for communities and more active in helping communities design their own strategies, thus encouraging intelligent local decision making in light of local strengths and weaknesses.

Conclusion

The shift in state economies and the increasing responsibility felt by state governments to stimulate economic development have induced state leaders to formulate strategic economic development plans to help target their efforts. State governments are aggressively experimenting with economic development strategies, most of which are too new to evaluate empirically at this time. Ongoing evaluations of these new state interventions can identify what works in certain economies.

The state's activities in economic development—investment capital, human resources, infrastructure, and natural resources— provide a strategic framework for future efforts. Policymakers are now realizing that public expenditures in these four areas are investments of statewide significance that only government can adequately provide. In addition, states play an important role in local development by targeting severely depressed areas, matchmaking, and empowering local governments.

Emphasizing economic development activities in these areas does not require abandoning existing programs and their constituents. Rather, it entails involving numerous actors in a learning process that stresses the elements of policy innovation, integration, investment, and interdependency. Moreover, it involves a continuous process of identifying the problem, assessing the proper organizational implementation structure, evaluating and monitoring the effect of economic policies, and utilizing the information learned to further clarify specific statewide policy needs. In this way, a strategic process is part and parcel of providing the proper policy guidelines to initiate state action.

11

Catalytic Leadership:
The Key to Successful
Economic Development

Stimulating state and local economic development efforts may be the most difficult problem and the most important challenge confronting public managers. Economic development has become a top priority for states and communities, and job creation has emerged as an important responsibility for public officials. Federal involvement in state and local economic development has declined sharply; federal grants and subsidies to states and localities have been dramatically reduced, forcing state and local governments to fend for themselves in an increasingly interdependent, global economy. Because of this new context, public managers must learn new skills and must look outside more and inside less, focusing on the external environment rather than internal administrative mechanisms.

The Global Economy and the Shrinking World

In the last two decades, technology has lessened geographical and social distances and rendered the world smaller and smaller, making the interaction of international, national, and local systems more pervasive, visible, and routine. Technology is knitting together corporations, governments, and individuals on a global level never before imagined. Small business enterprises and local governments, for example, are now busy transcending state and national boundaries in order to stimulate local business expansion into the global marketplace. Many of the technological developments that have been catalysts for this transformation are merely a decade old and result from the very recent interweaving of three public infrastructures: transportation systems, energy grids, and communications networks (Bell, 1979). Transportation systems are the oldest of these. For centuries, trade and commerce relied on trails, roads, rivers, and canals. Later development of energy grids (for example, such utilities as electricity and telephone service) and their overlay with transportation systems propelled the spread of industries and towns. While advances in transportation technology shrank geographical distance, very recent advances in communications networks have further reduced social and political distances. These advances in global communications were not even envisioned a hundred years ago, yet they have now encircled the planet beyond any possibility of retreat into the past. The communications network is the new, central infrastructure tying together the globe. With satellite teleconferencing, microcircuit electronics, and cable television, every part of the world is immediately accessible and potentially visible to every other part. The era of remoteness has passed (Cleveland, 1985a); state and local governments are now, and perhaps forever, inextricably connected to global events.

Communication is the new environmental glue, and the communications infrastructure expands the economic development policy arena, drawing in new participants and multiplying the number of potentially influential stakeholders at all levels of public policy-making and corporate decision making. Fundamentally new managerial skills and perspectives are now required. Today's economic context bears little resemblance to the contexts that existed during the last 200 years of American history; nothing so interdependent has existed. Historically, notions of independence, self-sufficiency, and economic insulation guided economic policies. However, to continue along with these assumptions will ultimately lead to ineffective development policies, policy inertia, or policy paralysis of state and local government agencies.

Economic interdependence limits governments' capacity to pursue economic development in old, conventional ways. The interconnected environment increases national and international competition and severely hampers industrial recruitment strategies, and it defies traditional assumptions of what is required to stimulate private investment in a state or community. The experience and working knowledge of the seasoned economic development manager are increasingly ineffective and, in many cases, even detrimental when applied to the new interconnected economic context. Competing with other cities for scarce industrial prospects creates adversarial, competitive relationships that can actually hinder future economic development. New collaborative strategies are required for several reasons. One is the expanding and crowded economic development policy arena, in which economic growth depends directly and indirectly on most other policy decisions (transportation and higher education, for example) and policy-making responsibility is dispersed and shared by a multiplicity of elected and appointed public officials. Another is a significantly reduced capacity for any one government agency or individual manager to effectively act unilaterally. A third is the slowness of policy formulation and implementation (except on those occasions when they are stimulated by a major economic crisis), which leads to an increase in slow-acting remedies for job creation. A fourth is the inevitable increase in vulnerability and openness to outside economic forces, with cities and states increasingly influenced by corporate investment decisions made in other cities on the globe. Economic development is now set in an intergovernmental and intersectoral web of pulling and pushing, and governments can seldom deal with economic problems independently.

From the corporate perspective, the rapid crystallization of interdependence is having an equally profound impact. Globalization—the shift from national to international competition—is creating problems for business survival in the world economy. More significant, the expanding network of interdependence is forcing business leaders to shift their attention from a known number of shareholders or stockholders to unknown numbers of stakeholders. Corporate executives are finding an expanding network of policy actors who partially share power and responsibility or in some way influence the directions of the firm, resulting in a changing view of "managerial capitalism" (Evan and Freeman, 1988). The old view, in which managers have a fiduciary responsibility to a fairly stable number of stockholders, is being replaced by a situation in which the corporate manager bears a fiduciary relationship to an expanding network of stakeholders—individuals, organized groups, professions, communities, and governmental institutions—who increasingly influence the behavior of a business enterprise. Unilateral action is increasingly difficult in the private sector, since decisions of any significance can be blocked, thwarted, or checked by the expanding network of stakeholders.

There is also a growing recognition of the interdependence between a community's economic vitality and the investment decisions of private business. The distinction between the public and private sectors is blurring; the connection between generating new jobs and maintaining a healthy local tax base is becoming more evident. No longer can the public and private sectors make highly independent decisions and operate in isolation from each other. Government action not only precipitates from an intergovernmental context, it emerges from the intersectoral dynamics of public-private interaction. Each sector depends on the vitality of the other.

Catalytic Leadership

The skills required for managing local economic development have changed over the last ten years. As industrial attraction and development strategies receive less support from the federal government and become more expensive to pursue, new strategies are being developed that focus on commercial and service activities, many involving formation and expansion of new, indigenous businesses. This policy shift requires a concomitant shift in managerial skills at the state and local levels. Close, active collaboration with the private sector is required, reducing the adversarial role some governments have historically played with developers, business entrepreneurs, and multinational corporations.

Managing economic development strategically in an interconnected web of community stakeholders, business managers, nonprofit agencies, government departments, and multinational corporations requires catalytic leadership skills. The relevant skills are primarily interpersonal and cognitive and secondarily technical in nature. They involve the ability to be a facilitator for planning and a catalyst for action. They involve the capacity to pull together crucial stakeholders in a common effort; the ability to assess correctly differences and similarities among key policy actors in goals, values, perspectives, and stakes; and the conceptual skill to see the subtle interdependencies among these individuals. Generally, such catalytic leadership requires identifying where the relevant policy actors and stakeholders exist, including those that are subtle and nearly invisible, as well as the more obvious; assessing who among these policy actors may resist collaborative efforts, how strongly, and why; and developing working relationships with these individuals or agencies to facilitate the analysis, negotiation, or experimentation required to stimulate action toward economic development.

What is essentially required for strategic economic development is a leader who can stimulate collective action toward a particular goal or vision. A *charismatic leader* at the state or community level, with his or her own individual vision, is seldom able to move the web of government and corporate actors in a particular policy direction. What is required in an interconnected context is a *catalytic leader* who engages in strategic thinking and who facilitates the development of a collaborative vision or collaborative goal. Unlike a charismatic leader, who gets people to follow his or her vision, a catalytic leader is able to facilitate the development of a critical mass of diverse policy actors, motivated by a goal or vision that is created collectively among themselves. A catalytic leader brings forth individual talent and collective action from the state or community. The kinds of catalytic leadership skills needed to manage economic development strategically fall into three specific categories:

1. *Human Skills.* These generally include an ability to interact with groups and policy actors outside an organization and to manage organizational interfaces—a skill requiring the capacity to negotiate in situations where core values may conflict, to build coalitions, and to collaborate in situations

where it is necessary to agree on general goals and strategies for job creation.

2. *Conceptual Skills.* These include an ability to think strategically—to recognize how changes in one part of the economy will affect other parts, and how a community's attitudes as well as the international economy influence the local economy.

3. *Technical Skills.* These include skills that are relevant to stimulating business investment within a community's jurisdiction, particularly development finance skills.

Human Skills: Collaborating, Negotiating, and Networking. Economic development is a unique type of policy area and has several characteristics that distinguish it from other policy areas. Economic development is not the property of any one organization. No single agency is responsible for the local economy, especially as local economies link into the emerging global economic network. Economic development thus requires the participation of multiple interest groups through collaborative strategies. State and local governments cannot effectively pursue economic development unilaterally; the policy arena is shared, interconnected, and often crowded, requiring collective strategies of related policy actors.

Managing economic development strategically requires the use of coalitions, because no single person has the information or the leverage to generate new jobs. Successful economic development efforts must therefore link loosely coupled interorganizational policy actors, linking public agencies at the state and local levels with interdependent economic actors of local and international businesses and financial institutions. The policy-making process that links these public and private organizations involves collaboration and negotiation, not hierarchical authority, and is characterized by shared power, not unilateral power.

First, state and community leaders seeking to manage economic development strategically must learn how to facilitate cooperative and collaborative efforts among the public, private, and nonprofit sectors as well as among the local, regional, state, and federal levels of government. Economic development strategy formulation and implementation are interorganizational, multilateral, and collective. The public manager as facilitator must manage a process where diverse groups and individuals can come together to discuss, thrash out, and find common ground. Interdependence provides opportunities for highly creative and innovative strategies if managers can facilitate. Diversity and interdependence can generate and nurture creative and original policies if pursued synergistically and not adversarily.

In order to facilitate the development of a common vision and sense of direction, managers must develop and refine their skills in collaboration, networking, bargaining, and negotiation. These skills are not new, but they are now fundamental for developing the necessary joint task orientation and collective strategies increasingly required in interconnected policy systems.

As interdependencies in the environment increase, there is an increase in requisite levels of coordination and increased potential for conflict. Incentives for collaborative action already exist in the economic policy arena owing to the shared stake people may have in generating new jobs; however, the successful manager must have the skills to further stimulate, nurture, and maintain adequate levels of collaboration outside his or her organizational boundaries.

Historically, few public officials have understood how private investment decisions were made, placing them at a severe disadvantage. It was often difficult to determine what public resources were necessary to make an investment occur; many officials would therefore provide either too few or too many. This led to a lack of respect by many private-sector representatives, who complained that public officials had no grasp of their needs and concerns.

This pattern began to change in the mid and late 1970s for several reasons. No one event, however, may have had greater impact on this increasing understanding and sophistication than the creation of the Urban Development Action Grant (UDAG) program. For the first time, a grant program required extensive negotiation between public and private participants. It also required a great deal of sophistication on the part of public participants about how investments were made and what resources were necessary for projects or activities to occur. Localities seeking UDAG grants had to learn how to negotiate with private developers and investors; they had to understand investment decisions as well as those wishing to make the investment. This led to a rapid increase in the knowledge and sophistication of public executives and, in many areas, an increasing level of respect from private investors.

As a result of these experiences, several elements of successful public-private negotiation efforts have been identified. First, each side must understand the goals and objectives of the other. The private investor brings an idea for a product or a service and hopes to turn that product or service into a profit-making enterprise. The public sector brings an interest in seeing that the public interest is served through a stronger state and local economy and a correspondingly stronger tax base. Second, there should be a clear understanding of the strengths and weaknesses associated with each participant's negotiating position. Each side should have a clear understanding of the commitment and motivation of the other. Third, each participant must understand the obstacles the other faces to achieving what he or she wants. This places both parties in the position of understanding the needs of the other. Fourth, each party should have a clearly defined strategy of what it wants to achieve and how it wishes to go about achieving it. Fifth, public managers must understand the limits of their authority. A side should not promise what it cannot deliver or else should certainly make such promises conditional on approval by others. Sixth, public managers must negotiate in good faith and not become involved in a process where agreement is unlikely or impossible.

Seventh, both sides should have participants who are knowledgeable about the specific project. If they do not understand some aspects of the project or activity, they should find someone who does. There is no more dangerous position to negotiate from than ignorance. Eighth, participants should identify as many issues as possible early in the negotiation process. New topics or requirements should not be thrown in at the eleventh hour, because they will be treated as bad-faith negotiations. Ninth, negotiators should always keep in mind what they are trying to accomplish. It is easy to get bogged down in detail and fail to meet the original objectives. While compromise is a key to negotiation, it should not deter participants from their objectives. Tenth, information provided during negotiations should be verified, where possible.

This is a particular concern for public officials where financial assumptions and business costs cannot be accepted unless they are double-checked. Comparable ventures should be reviewed to develop some frame of reference for costs and potential revenues. Expertise from other professionals should be called on where appropriate to substantiate private business assertions. This is not an inappropriate action when public dollars are being committed to a private investment. The public should expect no less. Finally, participants should be innovative and never leave the negotiation table in anger. Differences in philosophies and interests will clearly exist, and these differences can cause strain at times. Successful negotiation requires public managers to pursue their goals without resorting to deception, bullying, threats, or coercion; these tactics seldom work in an interdependent policy context and can actually cause more harm than good.

No economic development policy can be formulated and implemented by one actor, because no one actor controls all the essential elements of successful job generation. Cooperation in an interconnected policy area, however, is likely to be less than total; bargaining and compromise also are required. Difficulties in collaboration and negotiation emerge from three sources: interorganizational conflict, community resistance to mobilization, and group dependence on a policy leader.

Interorganizational conflicts emerge naturally in interconnected environments, where power and influence exerted by organizations are much stronger than in less interdependent environments (Milward, 1982). As a result, conflict will virtually always be present in economic development projects, particularly those that involve land development decisions (Kirlin and Kirlin, 1982). Individual stakeholders who perceive themselves to be the weaker in the policy formation process will more eagerly join in collaborative efforts. Individual agencies that have strong stakes in traditional approaches and are in positions of institutional power (a state department of economic development, for example) may resist efforts at joining hands and may see this collaboration as a weakening of power (Gray and Hay, 1986).

At the local level, mistrust and misunderstanding have historically existed between government and private enterprise.

Two primary barriers to establishing a collaborative climate exist in communities. The first is an attitudinal barrier; local government officials may see their role as being as an adversary to private business interests. Similarly, business entrepreneurs too frequently consider local government regulations to be major barriers to their pursuit of profits. A second barrier is educational in nature. Local business entrepreneurs often misunderstand the role, policy parameters, and legal constraints of local government in stimulating private investment. Similarly, local government officials seldom understand the operating constraints of commercial businesses. Key factors in the economic development policy arena must develop realistic expectations of one another's situations very early in the process. This approach now requires stretching a manager's responsibility from intergovernmental management to include intersectoral management. A local government administrator, for example, needs to:

- Utilize chamber of commerce officials, banking and financial managers, and other community leaders as resources for possible business formation and expansion and other economic development projects, because they usually have a considerable knowledge of their own business communities.
- Utilize local government resources to stimulate and nurture small businesses and commercial revitalization by coventuring with local firms in equity partnerships, removing administrative and regulatory barriers to business formation and expansion, and generally developing an attractive business climate and improving the quality of community life.
- Generally serve as the center for diffusion of ideas and provide intellectual stimuli to other policy actors.

Community resistance to mobilization is another obstacle to catalytic leadership. Creating a critical mass of leaders, an economic development network, becomes a crucial skill, especially in an intersectoral network where a public manager has little legitimate authority over key stakeholders. Effective economic development has multiple pilots guiding separate efforts toward common goals. This can be most difficult at the local level, where some communities are less willing to mobilize their leaders into a coalition, creating significant barriers for even the most skillful of public managers. Small rural communities driven by an ethic of self-sufficiency, self-reliance, and individualism are particularly resistant to coalition building (Hibbard, 1986). Mobilizing a community's leaders to assess, plan for, and implement economic development programs is difficult because it implies that "I couldn't do it myself." Small-town culture often reinforces the notion that individual problems of unemployment can best be solved by the unemployed person, not the community. The stages of economic death and dying (see Chapter Two) also create significant attitudinal barriers to developing a critical mass of local leaders.

Dependence on a single leader for his or her vision and strength is a third difficulty that can emerge after a policy group or coalition has been formed. Traditional perspectives on leadership define a leader as one who has a vision for the group and who utilizes his or her authority to move the group in its direction. In groups where there is no hierarchical authority and power is shared, many persons may seek this traditional leadership role, resulting in a group that has many "committees of one." The challenge becomes one of getting everybody to pull in the same direction at the same time without shifting the entire responsibility for developing solutions to one leader. This tendency toward leadership dependence has a considerable history and can be traced back to the days of the prophet Samuel, when people demanded a "King to fight our battles" (Rigoglioso, 1986).

In today's economic development context, however, the single leader cannot provide all the answers and now requires a coalition or network to take more responsibility in diagnosing issues, articulating a collective sense of direction or vision, and ensuring implementation. The public manager's role as leader changes from problem solver to catalyst. It requires the skills to orchestrate a process in which individual group members can digest new information at a tolerable rate and can be helped to discover strategic opportunities. The public manager can be the key figure here, alternating between catalyst and facilitator, and must have interpersonal flexibility to be both a leader and a follower as a situation demands.

Conceptual Skills: Strategic Thinking. The crying need in managing economic development strategically is for expanded conceptual skills—the ability to see the local and state economy as a part of the national and global economy, to understand how the various sectors and geographical areas depend on one another, and to understand the evolving shifts in the international economy. The tendency is to think in terms of industrial attraction or downtown revitalization or tourism or high-tech, rather than to consider all parts in relation to one another. Successful economic development requires the difficult task of "wrapping one's mind around the world."

Some knowledge of urban economics and land use planning is necessary but no longer sufficient. The major difference between conceptual skills, defined here, and traditional planning skills, historically prescribed, is the emphasis of conceptual skills on developing workable interdependent strategies that take advantage of the shifts in the state and local economy.

In an interconnected policy environment, managers and policymakers have difficulties in achieving the outcomes they want and may even have trouble avoiding the outcomes they do not intend. Strategic thinking (see Table 2) becomes the premium conceptual skill for job creation. It involves analyzing which interventions into the economic system lead to the desired objectives. Developing a workable strategy requires an ability to conceptualize the long-term effect on the economy of a specific strategy, such as the loss of tax revenue over ten years resulting from the provision of various tax incentives. Whether a community considers its most pressing need to be industrial retention, expansion of existing small businesses, or investment in a central business district, its leaders must be able to visualize how such strategies will achieve the overall objectives of increased job opportunities and a larger tax base.

Not only is the conceptual capacity for strategic thinking required, a dramatic expansion in perspective is needed. Managing economic development strategically requires an international

Table 2. Strategic Thinking in Economic Development.

- Understanding the broad relationships between the historically separate and distinct policy areas of transportation, commerce, land use planning, and postsecondary education
- Anticipating how policy decisions in any one policy area directly or indirectly influence economic development policy
- Anticipating how government policies, programs, and activities influence the image of an area
- Asking what kind of information is needed to assist in the development of a particular economic development strategy
- Considering a broad set of stakeholders in economic policy-making, including local entrepreneurs, multinational corporation executives, nonprofit community organizations, and labor unions, for example
- Considering a "web" of economic development strategies that can be continually updated, altered, and refined
- Considering unintended outcomes and secondary consequences of economic development strategies

perspective and the capacity for seeing global and regional trends that influence the process of development. This perspective is required for the smaller rural towns struggling with infrastructure decay, population emigration, and decline as well as for the metropolitan areas struggling with unemployment and underemployment. The national and global interdependencies of the local and state economy must be understood. Unintended consequences and ripple effects naturally occur when the economy is manipulated. Whether these consequences are the closing of a grocery store owing to development of a regional mall or the layoffs following a corporation's moving its labor-intensive industry to a Third World country, understanding subtle and direct interconnections requires a heightened sensitivity to larger system dynamics. The Oregon Commission on Futures Research (1987, p. 4) succinctly stated: "State policy makers must have a broad understanding of these interrelations. They also must improve their ability to foresee the future consequences of present decisions. This will require development of the organizational and programmatic tools necessary to discharge their growing responsibilities in the interconnected web of policies and problems facing the state."

Extremely crucial is an ability to use state and local economic data bases and market analyses. In order to analyze business and geographical opportunities, public managers must consider such questions as what businesses would be appropriate for the area, what businesses have the strength or potential to expand into national and international markets, and what the economic base can hold. These questions must be answered in order to develop a custom-designed strategic plan. At the local level, three variables should be initially analyzed and sorted out: the local labor market, locational factors, and the quality of public services and the local economic base (see Chapter Nine). At the state level, there is no single indicator for assessing the performance of state economies (Vaughan and others, 1984). A state must develop a set of indicators that best fits its unique economic structure and should include, at the least, trends in overall economic performance, the entrepreneurial climate, long-term growth prospects, and other aspects of a state's wealth (see Chapter Ten).

Technical Skills: Understanding Available Public Financing Tools and Development Finance. Specific technical skills related to economic development make up the third major area of skill development and are primarily related to development finance. They generally require an understanding of the economic realities of a growth strategy or development project and the ability to put together the necessary public and private investment to implement a development strategy. Technical skill requisites revolve around two specific roles inherent in state and local economic development. The first is that of leverager, in which a public manager uses available public money to leverage private investment in economic development. The second is that of packager, in which officials arrange land assembly or financing (tax incentives, loan guarantees, or tax increment financing, for example) to implement specific economic development projects.

Managers must understand the available menu of federal and state financing and tax incentive programs aimed at encouraging private investment, including direct financial incentives available from federal, state, and local agencies and tax incentives (credits, deductions, and exemptions). One example is the Small Business Investment Company (SBIC) approved and licensed by the SBA and often nurtured by local governments. SBICs provide financing packages to business entrepreneurs in the form of subordinated debt with equity kickers, convertible debt financing, and pure equity. Such loan packaging can appear complex to the brightest of public managers uninitiated in private development finance.

In addition to knowledge of available public finance tools, public managers are increasingly forced to understand the details of commercial finance. Cities nationwide are providing debt and equity financing for developers and business entrepreneurs, but such techniques as credit analysis require local officials to understand the details of the proposed business venture. Providing loan packaging for local businesses to start up or expand requires similar technical expertise in analyzing private-sector balance sheets, profit and loss statements, quality indicators, and cash flow. Even in communities that employ an economic development specialist, public managers coordinate the implementation of the overall development finance strategy and require at least a general understanding of development finance and credit analysis. These skills are relatively new to public management and may be the most serious area for skill development and training. Although these skills are highly technical, it is possible to gain a broad understanding of business through national training programs provided by various agencies such as the National Development Council (NDC), the National Community Development Association (NCDA), and the Council for Urban Economic Development (CUED).

Conclusion

State and local economic development will be a key issue for public managers into the 1990s. New and innovative policy strategies are being experimented with at the state and local levels to stimulate job generation. State and local government managers need the perspective, knowledge, skills, and collaborative decision-making environment to create new economic development strategies. Key elements are collaboration and negotiation rather than blueprints and operational plans. Interventions in the state and local economy do require sound planning, but this now must emerge from collaborative analysis and joint identification of economic targets of opportunity and learning from experience.

Since the more innovative approaches to stimulating economic development are relatively new, few have been systematically evaluated for their effectiveness. Furthermore, what works in one state or community may not work in another. As a result, managing economic development strategically requires a learning approach inherent in the strategic planning model (see Chapter Three). This model, when reiterated successively over a period of several years, produces new ideas and information as a consequence of strategic action. New, more targeted strategies can thus emerge after an information base has been developed from experience. This explicit, targeted problem-solving strategy—identifying and ranking strategic issues to be tackled through collective effort—is the essence of state and local economic development.

The role of the chief elected official and the public manager can best be characterized as catalytic, neither charismatic nor passive. Catalytic leadership requires a blend of interpersonal, conceptual, and technical skills. A catalytic leader must be capable of stimulating cooperation and collaboration in bringing together diverse policy actors and stakeholders; overcoming differences between the public and private sectors, through effective communication, consensus building, and negotiation; gaining agreement and support for strategic goals from corporate and government executives; understanding the economic realities of development projects; and packaging or leveraging public investment while containing or avoiding excessive expenditures.

Public-sector leaders are in the best position to bring together the myriad key actors needed for successful economic development: business executives, labor leaders, academicians, media representatives, community and political leaders, and leaders of nonprofit organizations. Leadership approaches and economic development strategies will invariably differ from one state to another, and from one community to another. Yet public executives can provide a catalyst to initiate a policymaking process that develops a strategic long-term view.

References

Academy for State and Local Government. *Where Will the Money Come From? Finding Reliable Revenue for State and Local Governments in a Changing Economy.* Washington, D.C.: Academy for State and Local Government, 1986.

Adell, P. "Philadelphia: We Set Up a Separate Corporation." *Planning*, 1983, *49* (9), 18-19.

Advisory Commission on Intergovernmental Relations. *The States and Distressed Communities: The Final Report.* Washington, D.C.: Advisory Commission on Intergovernmental Relations, 1985.

American Association of State Colleges and Universities. *To Secure the Blessings of Liberty: A Report by the National Commission on the Role and Future of State Colleges and Universities.* Washington, D.C.: American Association of State Colleges and Universities, 1986.

Ansoff, H. I. *Implanting Strategic Management.* Englewood Cliffs, N.J.: Prentice-Hall, 1985.

Armington, C., and Odle, M. "Sources of Job Growth: A New Look at the Small Business Role." *Economic Development Commentary*, Fall 1982, pp. 3-7.

Atkinson, R. "Small Business Incubators." *Small Town*, Mar.-Apr. 1986, pp. 22-26.

Augustine, N., and Elfine, D. *NASDA Enterprise Zone Roundup.* Washington, D.C.: National Association of State Development Agencies, Dec. 1986.

Bare, C., and others. "Nebraska's Economic Structure." In J. Luke and V. Webb (eds.), *Nebraska Policy Choices*. Omaha: Center for Applied Urban Research, University of Nebraska, 1986.

Beaumont, E. F., and Hovey, H. A. "State, Local and Federal Development Policies: New Federal Patterns, Chaos, or What?" *Public Administration Review*, 1985, *45*, 327-332.

Bell, D. "Communications Technology: For Better or for Worse." *Harvard Business Review*, May-June 1979, p. 18.

Bellah, R. N., and others. *Habits of the Heart*. Berkeley: University of California Press, 1985.

Bellus, J. J. "St. Paul: We Kept It in City Government." *Planning*, 1983, *49* (9), 16-17.

Benest, F. "Removing the Barriers to the New Entrepreneurship in City Government." *Western City*, 1985, *61* (2), 13-14.

Bergman, E. M. *Local Economies in Transition*. Durham, N.C.: Duke University Press, 1986.

Birch, D. "Job Generation in Seattle." Seattle, Wash.: King County Economic Development Council, 1985. (Mimeographed.)

Birch, D. L. *The Job Generation Process*. Research report prepared for the Economic Development Administration, U.S. Department of Commerce. Cambridge: Massachusetts Institute of Technology Program on Neighborhood and Regional Change, 1979.

Birch, D. L. "The Changing Rules of the Game: Finding a Niche in the Thoughtware Economy." *Commentary*, Winter 1984, pp. 12-16.

Birch, D. L. "The New Economy: No Respect." *Inc.*, 1987a, *9* (5), 22-24.

Birch, D. L. "The Q Factor." *Inc.*, 1987b, *9* (4), 53-54.

Bluestone, B., and Harrison, B. *The Deindustrialization of America*. New York: Basic Books, 1982.

Borrus, M. Unpublished study, Berkeley Roundtable on the International Economy. Institute of International Studies, University of California, Berkeley, 1985.

Borut, A. *Creating a Framework for Economic Development Decision-Making: A Guidebook for Economic Development Practitioners*. Washington, D.C.: National League of Cities, 1981.

Bowman, J. S., and Davis, C. "Change in the Attitudes of Industry

Executives Toward Environmental Issues, 1976 to 1986: Implications for Regulatory Reform." Unpublished paper, Department of Public Administration, Florida State University, 1987.

Boyle, R. "An Economic Development Strategy for the Greater Omaha Metropolitan Area." 1986a. (Mimeographed.)

Boyle, R. "Refining the Target Industry Study for Today's and Tomorrow's Economy." *Economic Development Review,* Winter 1986b, pp. 18–21.

Brawley, P. *Keeping California Competitive in Research and Development.* Briefing paper prepared for the Assembly Committee on Economic Development and New Technologies, Sacramento, Calif., 1986.

Brockhaus, R. H. "Risk Taking Propensity of Entrepreneurs." *Academy of Management,* Sept. 1980, pp. 509–520.

Brody, H. "The High-Tech Sweepstakes: States Vie for a Slice of the Pie." *High Technology,* 1985, *5,* 16–28.

Bruno, A. V., and Tyebjee, T. T. "The Environment for Entrepreneurship." In C. A. Kent, D. L. Sexton, and K. H. Vesper (eds.), *Encyclopedia of Entrepreneurship.* Englewood Cliffs, N.J.: Prentice-Hall, 1982.

Bryson, J. M., and Roering, W. D. "Applying Private-Sector Strategic Planning in the Public Sector." *American Planning Association Journal,* 1987, *53* (1), 9–22.

Bundy, E., and Hallet, S. "Foundations, Human Capacities and Economic Opportunities." Paper presented to the Pacific Northwest Grantmakers Forum, Seattle, March 1987.

Business–Higher Education Forum. *America's Competitive Challenge: The Need for a National Response.* Washington, D.C.: American Council on Education, 1983.

California and the Pacific Rim: A Policy Agenda. The Pacific Rim Task Force report. Sacramento: California Economic Development Corporation, May 1986.

California and the 21st Century: Foundations for a Competitive Society. Report of the Senate Select Committee on Long Range Policy Planning, Sacramento, Calif., January 1986.

California World Trade Commission. *Newsletter,* Winter 1986 (entire issue).

Carlino, G., and Mills, E. "The Determinants of County Growth." *Journal of Regional Science,* 1987, *27* (1), 39–54.

Churchill, N. C., and Lewis, V. L. "Bank Lending to New and Growing Enterprises." *Journal of Business Venturing,* 1986, *1,* 193–206.

Clarke, M. K. *Revitalizing State Economies: A Review of State Economic Development Policies and Programs.* Washington, D.C.: National Governors Association, 1986.

Cleveland, H. *The Knowledge Executive: Leadership in an Information Society.* New York: E. P. Dutton, 1985a.

Cleveland, H. "The Twilight of Hierarchy: Speculations on the Global Information Society." *Public Administration Review,* Jan.-Feb. 1985b, pp. 185–195.

Cohen, S. S., and Zysman, J. *Manufacturing Matters.* New York: Basic Books, 1987a.

Cohen, S. S., and Zysman, J. "The Myth of a Post-Industrial Economy." *New York Times,* Business Section, May 17, 1987b, p. 2.

Commission on the Future of the South. The Southern Growth Policies Board. *Halfway Home and a Long Way to Go.* Research Triangle Park, N.C.: Southern Growth Policies Board, 1986.

Committee for Economic Development. Research and Policy Committee. *Leadership for Dynamic State Economies.* New York: Committee for Economic Development, 1986.

Cooper, A. C., and Dunkelberg, W. C. "A New Look at Business Entry: Experiences of 1,805 Entrepreneurs." In K. H. Vesper (ed.), *Frontiers of Entrepreneurship Research.* Wellesley, Mass.: Babson College, 1981.

Corporation for Enterprise Development. *Entrepreneurial Economy.* Washington, D.C.: Corporation for Enterprise Development, 1984.

Corporation for Enterprise Development. *Making the Grade: The Development Report Card for the States.* Washington, D.C.: Corporation for Enterprise Development, 1987.

Cortwright, J. "Small Is Bountiful: Manufacturing, Small Business, and Oregon's Economy." Staff report to the Joint Legislative Committee on Trade and Economic Development. Salem, Oreg.:

Joint Legislative Committee on Trade and Economic Development, 1988.

Coughlin, C. C., and Cartwright, P. A. "An Examination of State Foreign Exports and Manufacturing Employment." *Economic Development Quarterly*, 1987, *1* (3), 257-267.

Council for Economic Development in Oregon. *One State, One Voice*. Portland: Council for Economic Development in Oregon, 1987.

Council for Urban Economic Development. *Small City Economic Development Training Manual*. Washington, D.C.: Council for Urban Economic Development, 1983.

Council for Urban Economic Development. *Competitive Advantage: Framing a Strategy to Support High Growth Firms*. Washington, D.C.: Council for Urban Economic Development, July 1984.

Council of State Policy and Planning Agencies. "About the Council of State Policy and Planning Agencies." Newsletter published by Council of State Policy and Planning Agencies, 1986.

Crowley, W. *Seattle's International Agenda Conference Report*. Report sponsored by the Municipal League of Seattle and King County, World Affairs Council, City of Seattle, Department of Community Development, Seattle Urban League, July 24, 1984.

Dandridge, T., and Dennis, W. J. *NFIB Report on Small Business in America's Cities*. Washington, D.C.: National Federation of Independent Business, Nov. 1981.

Daneke, G. "Small Business Policy Amid State Level Economic Development Planning." *Policy Studies Journal*, June 1985, *13* (4), 722-729.

Daneke, G. "Revitalizing U.S. Technology?" *Public Administration Review*, Nov.-Dec. 1986, *46* (6), 668-673.

Daniels, B. "Oregon Small Business Finance: Recommendations for Legislative Initiatives." Report submitted to Oregon Joint Legislative Committee on Trade and Economic Development, Cambridge, Mass., 1985.

Diebold, J. "A National Research Strategy: Commentaries." *Issues in Science and Technology*, Spring 1986.

Dillman, D. "The Information Age." *Urban Resources*, Spring 1986, *3* (3), 42-47.

Doyle, P., and Brisson, C. *Partners in Growth*. Washington, D.C.: Northeast-Midwest Institute, 1985.

Drucker, P. F. *Innovation and Entrepreneurship*. New York: Harper & Row, 1985.

Drucker, P. F. "The Changed World Economy." *Foreign Affairs*, Spring 1986, *64* (4), 768-791.

Duchacek, I. D. "The International Dimension of Subnational Self-Government." *Publius*, 1984, *14*, 5-31.

Dyer, B., and Pollard, R. "Investing in Public Works." In D. R. Jones (ed.), *Building the New Economy: States in the Lead*. Washington, D.C.: Corporation for Enterprise Development, 1986.

Eadie, D. C., and Steinbacher, R. "Strategic Agenda Management: A Marriage of Organizational Development and Strategic Planning." *Public Administration Review*, 1985, *45*, 424-430.

Eberts, R. W. "Estimating the Contribution of Urban Public Infrastructure to Regional Growth." Federal Reserve Bank of Cleveland, Working Paper no. 8610. *Review of Economics and Statistics*, Feb. 1987.

Edmunds, S. "Barriers to the Growth of Small Business." *Public Affairs Report*. Berkeley: Institute for Governmental Studies, University of California, Dec. 1980, *21* (6), 1-4.

Elder, A. H., and Lind, H. S. "The Implications of Uncertainty in Economic Development: The Case of Diamond Star Motors." *Economic Development Quarterly*, 1987, *1* (1), 30-40.

Erickson, R. A. "Business Climate Studies: A Critical Evaluation." *Economic Development Review*, 1987, *1*, 62-71.

Eugene, City of. Department of Development and Department of Planning. "Survey of Economic Development in Twelve Cities." Eugene, Oreg., 1987. (Mimeographed.)

Evan, W., and Freeman, E. "Managerial Capitalism in a Context of Shared Power." In R. Einsweiller and J. Bryson (eds.), *Shared Power*. Lanham, Md.: University Press of America, 1988.

Evans, E., and others. *Small Business Incubators: A Tool for Local Economic Development*. Eugene: Community Workshop, University of Oregon, 1985.

Feldt, J. A., and Whorton, J. W. "Beyond Aspirations: Getting to Specifics Through Decision Conferencing in the Strategic

Planning Process in Smaller Cities: A Process/Content Model for Planned Change." Paper presented at National Conference of the American Society for Public Administration, Boston, Mar. 30, 1987.

Fields, C. "Education Brokers Are Helping 2-Year Colleges Train Workers to Fill Needs of Local Businesses." *Chronicle of Higher Education,* Mar. 11, 1987, p. 30.

Forkenbrock, D. J., and Plazak, D. J. "Economic Development and Street-Level Transportation Policy." *Transportation Quarterly,* 1986, *40,* 143–157.

Friedman, R. E., and Schweke, W. "Investing in People." In D. R. Jones (ed.), *Building the New Economy: States in the Lead.* Washington, D.C.: Corporation for Enterprise Development, 1986.

Gardner, N. "The Law of the Other Guy's Thing." In J. Uvegas, Jr. (ed.), *Cases in Public Administration.* Boston: Holbrook Press, 1982.

Gartner, W. B. "A Conceptual Framework for Describing the Phenomenon of New Venture Creation." *Academy of Management Review,* 1985, *10,* 696–706.

Gellman Research Associates, Inc. *Indicators of International Trends in Technological Innovation.* Report prepared for the National Science Foundation. Washington, D.C.: Gellman Research Associates, Inc., 1976.

Gellman Research Associates, Inc. *The Relationship Between Industrial Concentration, Firm Size, and Technological Innovation.* Research report prepared for the U.S. Small Business Administration. Washington, D.C.: Gellman Research Associates, Inc., 1982.

Grady, D. "State Economic Development Incentives: Why Do States Compete?" *State and Local Government Review,* Fall 1987, *19* (3), 86–94.

GrantThorton International. *Annual Study of General Manufacturing Climates in Forty-Eight Contiguous States of America.* Chicago: GrantThorton International, 1979, 1986.

Gray, B., and Hay, T. M. "Political Limits to Interorganizational Consensus and Change." *Journal of Applied Behavioral Science,* 1986, *22* (2), 95–112.

Green, R. E., and Brintnall, M. *State Enterprise Zone Programs: Variations in Structure and Coverage.* Paper presented at annual meeting of the American Society for Public Administration, Anaheim, Calif., 1986.

Gregerman, A. S. "Competitive Advantage: Framing a Strategy to Support High-Growth Firms." *Economic Development Commentary,* 1984a, *8* (2), 18-23.

Gregerman, A. S. "Federal, State, and Local Economic Development Initiatives." *Urban Land,* 1984b, *43,* 21-25.

Grgas, V. "L.A. Asset Management Program Boosts Revenue, Development." *Economic Developments,* Dec. 15, 1985, *10* (22), 1.

Hartman, C. "Who's Running America's Fastest Growing Companies?" *Inc.,* 1983, *5* (8), 41-47.

Heller, S. "A New Wave of Curricular Reform." *Chronicle of Higher Education,* Sept. 2, 1987, p. 2.

Henry, M., and others. "Rural Growth Slows Down." *Rural Development Perspectives,* 1987, *3* (3), 25-30.

Hibbard, M. "Social Reproduction and Learned Helplessness in a Dying Community." *Journal of Sociology and Social Welfare,* Mar. 1985, *12* (1), 23-40.

Hibbard, M. "Community Beliefs and the Failure of Community Economic Development." *Social Service Review,* 1986, pp. 183-200.

"The Hollow Corporation." *Business Week,* Mar. 3, 1986, pp. 57-85.

Hubbird, J. *Absentee, Local and Employee Ownership: Impacts on Community Stability.* Eugene: Department of Planning, Public Policy and Management, University of Oregon, 1987. (Mimeographed.)

"Illinois Export Authority Completes One Year of Successful Operations." *Business America,* Aug. 3, 1987, *10,* 14-19.

Jacobs, J. *Cities and the Wealth of Nations.* New York: Random House, 1984.

Jacobs, S. "Once Ignored, Small Business Now Influences State Policies." *Wall Street Journal,* May 13, 1985, p. 21.

Jennings, E., and others. *From Nations to States: The Small Cities*

Community Development Block Grant Program. Albany: State University of New York Press, 1986.

Joint Economic Committee. U.S. Congress. *Location of High Technology Firms and Regional Economic Development.* Washington, D.C.: U.S. Government Printing Office, June 1, 1982.

Kahn, J. P. "Report on the States." *Inc.,* 1986, *8,* 57–66.

"Kalamazoo May Be Home to GM's Saturn Plant." *National Journal,* 1985, *17* (29), 1663.

Kamer, P. "Economic Growth and Development on Long Island." Hofstra Business Research Institute, Hofstra University, 1985. (Mimeographed.)

Kamlet, M. S., and others. "Whom Do You Trust? An Analysis of Executive and Congressional Economic Forecasts." *Journal of Policy Analysis and Management,* 1987, *6* (3), 365–384.

Kasouf, D. "State Economic Index Adds Fuel to Debate." *Public Administration Times,* 1987, *10* (1), 1, 12.

Kelley, R. *The Gold-Collar Worker: Harnessing the Brainpower of the New Workforce.* Reading, Mass.: Addison-Wesley, 1985.

Kentucky Tomorrow Commission. *Meeting the Challenges: An Agenda Today for Kentucky's Tomorrow.* Frankfort: Kentucky Tomorrow Project, 1986.

Kieschnik, M. *Venture Capital and Urban Development.* Washington, D.C.: Council of State Planning Agencies, 1980.

Kincaid, J. "The American Governors in International Affairs." *Publius,* 1984, *14,* 95–114.

Kirchhoff, B. A. "Analyzing the Cost of Debt for Small Business." *Policy Studies Journal,* 1985, *13,* 735–746.

Kirchhoff, B. A. "Small Business and Economic Development for Nebraska." In J. Luke and V. Webb (eds.), *Nebraska Policy Choices.* Omaha: Center for Applied Urban Research, University of Nebraska, 1986.

Kirlin, J., and Kirlin, A. *Public Choices—Private Resources.* Sacramento: California Tax Foundation, 1982.

Klauser, A. E. "State Roles in Foreign Trade." *Business America,* 1985, *8,* 12–17.

Kline, J. M. *State Government Influence in U.S. International Economic Policy.* Lexington, Mass.: Lexington Books, 1983.

Kline, J. M. "The International Economies of U.S. States." *Publius*, 1984, *14*, 81–94.

Kubler-Ross, E. *The Final Stage of Growth*. Englewood Cliffs, N.J.: Prentice-Hall, 1985.

Kysiak, R. C. "City Entrepreneurship: Institutionalizing the Process." *Economic Development Commentary*, 1983, 7 (3), 20–23.

Lawrence, R. Z. *Can America Compete?* Washington, D.C.: Brookings Institution, 1984.

Levine, P. J. "Export Development Program: Local Roles and Options." *Public Management*, 1986, *68*, 9–10.

Levinson, M. "Small Business: Myth and Reality." *Dun's Business Month*, Sept. 1985, pp. 30–34.

Lind, N., and Elder, A. H. "Who Pays? Who Benefits? The Case of the Incentive Package Offered to the Diamond Star Automotive Plant." *Government Finance Review*, Dec. 1986, *2* (6), 19–23.

Liner, C. D. "State Economic Development Policies: A Review of Four Reports." *Popular Government*, Spring 1987, *52* (4), 61–63.

Luther, V., and Wall, M. *The Entrepreneurial Community: A Strategic Planning Approach to Community Survival*. Lincoln, Nebr.: Heartland Center for Leadership Development, 1986.

McClelland, D. C., and Winter, D. G. *Motivating Economic Achievement*. New York: Free Press, 1969.

Madlin, N. "The Venture Survey." *Venture*, Oct. 1985, p. 24.

Malizia, E. *Local Economic Development: A Guide to Practice*. New York: Praeger, 1985.

Manning, B. "The Congress, the Executive, and the Intermestic Affairs: Three Proposals." *Foreign Affairs*, 1977, *55*, 306–324.

Marchak, P. *Green Gold: The Forest Industry in British Columbia*. Vancouver: University of British Columbia Press, 1983.

Margolis, N. "Report on the States." *Inc.*, Oct. 1985, pp. 90–93.

Marlin, T., and Vieux, D. "State Venture Capital Financing Programs." Report published by Kansas Department of Economic Development, Policy Analysis, and Research Unit, 1986.

Mayer, V. "Small Business Termed Basis for Long-Term Health of Localities." *Nation's Cities Weekly*, Aug. 24, 1987, *10* (34), 1.

Mentor International. *Report on Feasibility of Overseas Offices for the State of California.* San Francisco: Mentor International, May 31, 1985.

Mikesell, J. L. *Reforming the State Tax System.* Washington, D.C.: National Conference of State Legislatures, 1986.

Miller, T. "Small Business Role in Downtown Revitalization." Washington, D.C.: Urban Institute, 1977.

Milward, B. H. "Interorganizational Policy Systems and Research in Public Organizations." *Administration and Society,* 1982, *13* (4), 605-622.

Moore, J. W. "Corporate Kidnapping." *National Journal,* June 13, 1987, *19* (24), 1518-1521.

Moore, T. S., and Squires, G. D. "Industrial Revenue Bonds in Wisconsin: Public Costs and Private Benefits." *Research and Opinion.* Milwaukee: Urban Research Center, University of Wisconsin, Milwaukee, 1985, *2* (3), 1-6.

Nathanson, J. *Early Warning Information Systems for Business Retention.* Washington, D.C.: Public Technology, Inc., Sept. 1980.

National Association of Regional Councils. "The Future of Regionalism in the United States: Special Report 128." Washington, D.C.: National Association of Regional Councils, Mar. 20, 1987.

National Association of State Development Agencies. *The NASDA Letter,* Apr. 8, 1985 (entire issue).

National Association of State Development Agencies. *The NASDA Letter,* Jan. 21, 1987 (entire issue).

National Commission on Excellence in Education. *A Nation at Risk: The Imperative for Educational Reform.* Washington, D.C., Apr. 1983.

National Council on Public Works Improvement. *The Nation's Public Works: Defining the Issues.* Washington, D.C.: National Council on Public Works Improvement, 1986.

National Governors Association. *Jobs, Growth and Competitiveness.* Washington, D.C.: National Governors Association, 1987.

National League of Cities, International Economic Development Task Force. *Making Sense Out of Dollars: Economic Analysis for Local Government.* Washington, D.C.: National League of Cities, 1979.

National League of Cities, International Economic Development Task Force. *International Trade: A New City Economic Development Strategy.* Washington, D.C.: National League of Cities, 1984.

National Science Board. *Science Indicators, 1976: Report of the National Science Board.* Washington, D.C.: U.S. Government Printing Office, 1977.

National Science Foundation. *Science and Technology Resources.* Washington, D.C.: National Science Foundation, 1984.

Nebraska Department of Economic Development. *Building Prosperity: Nebraska Economic Development Strategy.* Lincoln: Nebraska Department of Economic Development, 1987.

North Carolina Economic Development Board. *North Carolina's Blueprint for Economic Development.* Raleigh: North Carolina Economic Development Board, 1986.

Northdurft, W. E. *Renewing America.* Washington, D.C.: Council of State Planning Agencies, 1984.

Northdurft, W. E. "Investing in Natural Resources." In D. R. Jones (ed.), *Building the New Economy: States in the Lead.* Washington, D.C.: Corporation for Enterprise Development, 1986.

Norton, R. D. "Industrial Policy and American Renewal." *Journal of Economic Literature,* 1986, *24,* 1-40.

"Now, R&D Is Corporate America's Answer to Japan, Inc." *Business Week,* June 23, 1986, pp. 134-138.

Noyelle, T. J. "The Service Era: Focusing Public Policy on People and Places." *Economic Development Commentary,* Summer 1984, *8* (2), 12-17.

Noyelle, T., and Stanback, T. *The Economic Transformation of American Cities.* Totowa, N.J.: Rowman & Allanheld, 1983.

Office of Technology Assessment. U.S. Congress. *Technology, Innovation, and Regional Economic Development.* Washington, D.C.: U.S. Government Printing Office, July 1984.

Office of Technology Assessment. U.S. Congress. "Common High Technology Initiatives and State Government Initiatives." In B. Weiss (ed.), *Public-Private Partnerships: Financing a Common Wealth.* Washington, D.C.: Government Finance Officers Association, 1985.

Oregon Commission on Futures Research. *Emerging Issues for Oregon.* Salem: Oregon Commission on Futures Research, 1987.

Oregon Joint Legislative Committee on Trade and Economic Development. "Staff Report for the 1987 Legislative Session." Salem: Oregon Joint Legislative Committee on Trade and Economic Development, 1986.

Paulsen, D. F., and Reed, B. J. "Nebraska Small Towns and Their Capacity for Economic Development." In R. L. Smith (ed.), *Nebraska Policy Choices.* Omaha: Center for Applied Urban Research, University of Nebraska, 1987.

Penne, L. R. "Urban Amenities." *Economic Development Commentary,* Summer 1985, *9* (2), 12–17.

Perelman, L. J. *The Learning Enterprise: Adult Learning, Human Capital and Economic Development.* Washington, D.C.: Council of State Planning Agencies, 1984.

Petersen, G. E., and others. *Guide to Benchmarks of Urban Capital Condition.* Washington, D.C.: The Urban Institute, 1984.

Pierce, N. "Pension Systems Wise Up, Get Lucky." *Public Administration Times,* June 1, 1987, p. 2.

Pilcher, D. "Economic Development: Old Term Has New Meaning." *State Legislatures,* 1986, *12* (7), 18–21.

Posner, A. R. *State Government Export Promotion: An Exporter's Guide.* Westport, Conn.: Quorum Books, 1984.

President's Commission for a National Agenda for the Eighties. *A National Agenda for the Eighties.* Washington, D.C.: U.S. Government Printing Office, 1980.

President's Commission on Industrial Competitiveness. *Global Competition: The New Reality.* Washington, D.C.: U.S. Government Printing Office, Jan. 1985.

Pulver, G. C. *Community Economic Development Strategies.* Madison: University of Wisconsin Extension, Sept. 1986.

Raab, J. *Energy and Economic Development: A Qualitative and Quantitative Analysis.* Eugene: Bureau of Governmental Research and Service, University of Oregon, 1987.

Reed, B. J. *The Policies of Urban Planning in Twenty Small and Medium Sized Communities in Missouri.* Unpublished Ph.D. dissertation, Department of Political Science, University of Missouri-Columbia, 1977.

Reed, C. M., Reed, B. J., and Luke, J. S. "Assessing Readiness for Economic Development Strategic Planning: A Community Case Study." *American Planning Association Journal*, 1987, *53* (4), 521–530.

Regional Planning Council. *RPC's 1985–86 Annual Report.* Baltimore, Md.: Regional Planning Council, 1986.

Reich, R. B. *The Next American Frontier.* New York: Times Books, 1983.

"Report of the North Carolina Commission on Jobs and Economic Growth." Raleigh, N.C.: Office of the Lieutenant Governor, Nov. 12, 1986.

Rhode Island Strategic Development Commission. *The Greenhouse Compact.* Providence: Rhode Island Strategic Development Commission, 1984.

Richards, J. W. *Fundamentals of Development Finance: A Practitioner's Guide.* New York: Praeger, 1983.

Rigoglioso, M. "A Change in Leadership." *Leadership,* Fall/Winter 1986, pp. 6–7.

Ross, A. L. "Tax Collectors Target Services." *Washington Post,* Section H, May 3, 1987, p. 3.

Rubin, B. M., and Zorn, K. C. "Sensible State and Local Economic Development." *Public Administration Review,* 1985, *45,* 333–340.

Schultz, T. W. *Investment in Human Capital: The Role of Education and Research.* New York: Free Press, 1971.

Schultze, C. L. "Industrial Policy: A Dissent." *Brookings Review,* 1983, *2,* 3–12.

Schumpeter, J. A. *The Theory of Economic Development.* (R. Opie, trans.) Cambridge, Mass.: Harvard University Press, 1934.

Schumpeter, J. A. *Capitalism, Socialism and Democracy.* New York: Harper & Row, 1976. (Originally published 1942.)

Schweke, W. "Why Local Governments Need an Entrepreneurial Policy." *Public Management,* Dec. 1985, *67* (12), 3.

Shapero, A. "Entrepreneurship: Self-Renewing Economies." In E. E. Malizia (ed.), *Local Economic Development.* New York: Praeger, 1985.

Shatten, R. "Public Forum: Starting New Companies in Cleveland." *REI Review,* 1985, *2* (2), 3–9.

Shelp, R. K. "A Novel Strategy for Economic Revitalization." *Economic Development Review*, 1985, *3*, 24-31.

Shelp, R. K. "Giving the Service Economy a Bum Rap." *New York Times*, Business Section, May 17, 1987, p. 2.

"The Shrinking of Middle Management." *Business Week*, Apr. 25, 1983, pp. 54-80.

Simmons, B. "Environmental Protections Help Attract Business to Oregon." *California Journal*, Jan. 1985, *16* (1), 10-12.

Skoro, C. L. "Rankings of State Business Climates: An Evaluation of Their Usefulness in Forecasting." Paper prepared for the Pacific Northwest Economic Conference, Seattle, April 1987.

Smith, A. *The Wealth of Nations.* (E. Cannan, ed.) New York: Modern Library, 1937.

Sorkin, D. L., and others. *Strategies for Cities and Counties: A Strategic Planning Guide.* Washington, D.C.: Public Technology, 1984.

Sower, J. and Vitarello, J. "CDCs—Little Known or Understood Development Tool." *Nation's Cities Weekly*, 1987, *10* (19), 12.

SRI International. *The Higher Education–Economic Development Connection.* Washington, D.C.: American Association of State Colleges and Universities, 1986a.

SRI International. *Indicators of Economic Capacity.* First Report. Cleveland, Ohio: AmeriTrust Corporation, Dec. 1986b.

Stenberg, C. W. "States Under the Spotlight: An Intergovernmental View." *Public Administration Review*, 1985, *45*, 319-326.

Suss, W. "Tapping the Federal Market." *Economic Development Commentary*, Winter 1982, *6* (4), 19-23.

Temali, M., and Campbell, C. *Business Incubator Profiles: A National Survey.* Minneapolis: Hubert H. Humphrey Institute of Public Affairs, July 1984.

Tigan, M. "The Eight Phases of Export Transaction." *Public Management*, 1986, *68*, 15-17.

Tocqueville, A. de. *Democracy in America.* 2 vols. New York: Vintage Books, 1945. (Originally published 1835 and 1840.)

Tolchin, M. "Foreign Investment in U.S. Mutes Trade Debate." *New York Times*, Feb. 8, 1987, p. 30.

Touche Ross & Company. *Survey of the Nation's Mayors on Small Business.* New York: Touche Ross, 1985. (Mimeographed.)

Tucker, M. "State Economic Development and Education: A Framework for Policy Development." Paper prepared for the National Conference of Lieutenant Governors Task Force on Education and Economic Development, June 1985, p. 11.

Turner, J. "Little-Known Extension Services Enable Universities to Help Industry." *Chronicle of Higher Education,* Jan. 7, 1987, p. 13.

U.S. Bureau of the Census. "The Big Chill (Revisited)." *American Demographics,* Sept. 1985, pp. 23–29.

U.S. Extension Service. *Revitalizing Rural America.* Washington, D.C.: U.S. Department of Agriculture, 1987.

U.S. General Accounting Office. "Dislocated Workers: Exemplary Local Projects Under the Job Training Partnership Act." Washington, D.C.: U.S. Government Printing Office, 1987.

U.S. Small Business Administration. *The State and Small Business: Issues, Initiatives and Innovations.* Conference Report. Washington, D.C.: Office of Advocacy, Oct. 1983.

U.S. Small Business Administration. *The State of Small Business.* Washington, D.C.: U.S. Government Printing Office, 1984–1986.

Van de Ven, A. H., Hudson, R., and Schroeder, D. M. "Designing New Business Startups: Entrepreneurial, Organizational, and Ecological Considerations." *Journal of Management,* 1984, *10* (1), 87–107.

Vaughan, R. J. *Local Business and Employment Retention Strategies.* Washington, D.C.: Public Technology, Sept. 1980.

Vaughan, R. J., and others. *The Wealth of States.* Washington, D.C.: Council of State Planning Agencies, 1984.

Ventriss, C. "American Federal Deficit and Its International Economic Effects." *International Journal of Public Administration,* 1986, *8,* 103–123.

Vesper, K. H. "Commentary." In D. E. Schendel and C. W. Hofer (eds.), *Strategic Management.* Boston: Little, Brown, 1979.

Vesper, K. H. *New Venture Strategies.* Englewood Cliffs, N.J.: Prentice-Hall, 1980.

Vesper, K. H. "Expanding Entrepreneurship Research." In K. H. Vesper (ed.), *Frontiers of Entrepreneurship Research.* Wellesley, Mass.: Babson College, 1981a.

Vesper, K. H. "Scanning the Frontier of Entrepreneurship Research." In K. H. Vesper (ed.), *Frontiers of Entrepreneurship Research.* Wellesley, Mass.: Babson College, 1981b.

Vincent, P. "Encouraging Economic Growth." In J. Kirlin and D. Winkler (eds.), *California Policy Choices.* Vol. 2. Sacramento: Sacramento Public Affairs Center, University of Southern California, 1985.

Walzer, N., and Chicoine, D. L. *Financing Economic Development in the 1980s: Issues and Trends.* New York: Praeger, 1986.

Ward, R. "The Future of America: A Perspective on International Studies." Keynote speech for the 40th anniversary of the University of Oregon International Studies Program, Eugene, Nov. 1986.

Ward, T. E. "Today the Region; Tomorrow the World." *Public Management,* 1986, *68,* 4–7.

Washington State Economic Development Board. *Washington's Challenges and Opportunities in the Global Economy.* Olympia: Washington State Economic Development Board, Jan. 1987.

Wechsler, B., and Backoff, R. W. "Policy Making and Administration in State Agencies: Strategic Management Approaches." *Public Administration Review,* 1986, *46,* 321–327.

Weinberg, M. L. "Business Incubators Give New Firms in Rural Areas a Head Start." *Rural Development Perspectives,* Feb. 1987, *3* (2), 6–10.

Weinstein, B., and Gross, H. *Regional Growth and Decline in the United States.* New York: Praeger, 1985.

Weiss, B. (ed.). *Financing a Common Wealth.* Washington, D.C.: Government Finance Officers Association, 1985.

White House Conference on Small Business. *The State of Small Business: A Report of the President.* Washington, D.C.: U.S. Government Printing Office, 1985.

Whitelaw, E. "The Once and Future Northwest." *Pacific Northwest Executive,* July 1986, pp. 2–4.

Whyte, W. F. *The Organization Man.* New York: Simon & Schuster, 1956.

Widner, R. R. "The Philadelphia Experiment: Unifying Economic Development." *Economic Development Commentary,* Winter 1983, 7 (3), 16–19.

Wilms, W. W. *Reshaping Job Training for Economic Productivity.*

Research Report No. 86-1. Berkeley: Institute of Governmental Studies, University of California, 1986.

Wishard, W.V.D. "The 21st Century Economy." *Futurist,* May-June 1987, pp. 23-28.

Wolf, V. L. "Business Retention and Expansion Programs." *Minnesota Cities,* 1986, *18* (9), 45.

Zumeta, W., and Stephens, D. *Increasing Higher Education's Contributions to Economic Development in Washington.* Olympia: Washington State Institute for Public Policy, 1986.

Index